The Transnational History
of a Chinese Family

The Transnational History of a Chinese Family

IMMIGRANT LETTERS, FAMILY BUSINESS, AND REVERSE MIGRATION

HAIMING LIU

Rutgers University Press
New Brunswick, New Jersey, and London

Library of Congress Cataloging-in-Publication Data

Liu, Haiming, 1953–
    The transnational history of a Chinese family : immigrant letters, family business, and reverse migration / Haiming Liu.
        p. cm.
    Includes bibliographical references and index.
    ISBN 0-8135-3596-4 (hardcover : alk. paper) — ISBN 0-8135-3597-2 (pbk. : alk. paper)
    1. Chang family. 2. Chinese Americans—California—Biography. 3. California—Emigration and immigration—History. 4. China—Emigration and immigration—History. I. Title.

    F870.C5L58 2005
    304.8'73051'0922—dc22

                                                                2004023483

A British Cataloging-in-Publication record for this book is available from the British Library.

Manufactured in the United States of America

To my own family

CONTENTS

ACKNOWLEDGMENTS

I am deeply grateful to many people and organizations that provided assistance, advice, and encouragement during this research project. Suellen Cheng introduced me to the collection of Sam Chang's letters and other family papers years ago, when I worked as a research assistant for the Chinese American Museum in Los Angeles. I greatly appreciate her assistance and comments on my early research on Chinese family life; she is a true friend. The Chinese Historical Society of Southern California has always been kind and generous in giving me access to the Chang family papers, and to copies of interviews of Sam Chang and his relatives available at the Historical Society. The Society is truly dedicated to procuring and preserving archival material that promotes greater understanding of the Chinese experience in the United States; the Sam Chang letters are just one part of its growing collection of documents, artifacts, and information. Gilbert Hom of the Association helped me reproduce some photographs of the Chang family and scheduled my visit to Lillian and Marie, daughters of Yitang Chung.

This book is partially based on my dissertation; as my dissertation advisor, John M. Liu of the University of California, Irvine, guided me throughout the writing process. His mentorship is instrumental to my development as an Asian American scholar; although we are unrelated, I always regard him as an elder brother. I am also indebted to my other U.C. Irvine faculty mentors, including (though not limited to) Dickran Tashjian, Raul Fernandez, Kenneth Chew, and Gordon Chang (currently at Stanford), who either served in my dissertation committee or read the entirety or a portion of my dissertation. Dickran hosted me in his house when I first arrived in America, with two suitcases, as a graduate student.

My special thanks also go to the Asian American Studies Center of the University of California, Los Angeles, which offered me a prestigious

Rockefeller Foundation Fellowship in 1990 to further my research on Sam Chang's letters. Both Russell Leong and the late Yuji Ichioka of the Center shared their perceptive thoughts on my research and their interest in trans-Pacific Chinese family history, and assisted me in publishing an article on Chinese trans-Pacific family experience in the *Amerasia Journal*. I have fond memories also of life as a graduate fellow at the University of California Humanities Research Institute, which provided me with a precious Minority Discourse Fellowship in 1991–92. This fellowship was crucial to my development as a research scholar and enabled me to seek advice and share and exchange thoughts with faculty fellows, including distinguished scholars from various U.C. campuses. Faculty fellows, especially Abdul JanMohamed, Clara Sue Kidwell, and Sterling Stuckey, kindly read and commented on my research on Chinese herbalists in America, research later sent to *Journal of Asian American Studies (JAAS)* for publication. John Liu, Gary Okihiro, and two anonymous JAAS readers offered insightful suggestions for revision. Paul Chase, a very knowledgeable scholar on Chinese Americans, also provided important comments. I am particularly grateful to these persons because herbal medicine is so important a topic in this book.

I also wish to express deep gratitude to California State Polytechnic University, Pomona, my academic home, which provided one summer stipend, a two-quarter sabbatical leave, and one course release for this project. Dean Joan S. Bissell has offered me genuine encouragement. With such support, I was able to revise my manuscript substantially.

I want to express sincere thanks to the relatives of Sam Chang, including (though not limited to) Lillian and David Wong, Marie Louie, the late Estelle Wang, Joyce Koe, and Karen Koe in America and Tang Wensheng in China, who shared generous time, valuable recollections, and family photos of their and Sam Chang's life experience. Their transnational family life in many ways mirrors my own. It is their story that inspired me to write this book. I am fortunate to know Him Mark Lai, who generously shared information and thoughts about Sam Chang and his family. A selfless scholar, Lai has repeatedly provided comments and feedback on my research. Xiao-huang Yin, a genuine scholar and true friend, discussed transnationalism in Asian American studies with me at length, greatly impacting my writing. Two anonymous readers have provided insightful comments, meaningful suggestions, and sincere criticism. I also thank Xiaojian Zhao, whose thoughtful and detailed comments on the manuscript have pushed me to expand the scope of my research focus and sharpened my thoughts on transnational Chinese family history; she is a true friend. Young Chen is also a great friend whose support and encouragement are indispensable. Other friends who offered genuine encouragement and inspired me in my writing on the transnational experience of the Chinese include Wei Li, Zong Li, Huping Ling, Jinqi Ling, Yuan Shu, Fenggang Yang, Philip Yang, Da Zheng, and Min Zhou. I also thank the National Archives and its staff specialists. Archivist Lisa B. Gezelter of the National Archives and Records Administration at Laguna Niguel, California, gave indispensable support and assistance when I researched immigration files of the Chang family. She helped me locate all the Chang family files there available. Other staff also helped me in my research, and reproduced photos of the Chang family immigration files. William Greene of the National Archives and Records Administration at San Bruno, California, also selflessly researched immigration files of the Chang family; I have included several photos provided by him in the book. Selia Tan, a scholar researching the Guangdong watchtowers in China, kindly provided me a recent photo of the Chang family reading house in their home village.

I express my deepest appreciation to the Rutgers University Press for its interest in this project. Melanie Halkias expressed her confidence in the manuscript when we began to communicate with each other on how to revise it. She was also professionally understanding to my responses to readers' comments and suggestions, and remained supportive and patient when I was revising the manuscript while a scholar with a heavy teaching load. I am truly grateful to Paula Friedman for her meticulous copyediting and kind words on my writing. Assistance from Marilyn Campbell has been invaluable.

Members of my family have long supported me in my academic pursuit. My wife and son became transnational family members themselves when, years ago, I came to study in the United States. My parents took care of my son after my wife sacrificed her own promising career in China to join me in America. We did not see our son for a few years, until my parents brought him over. Although we missed him dearly, we knew we might not be able to come back to the United States on our student visas if we returned to visit him. Deep in our hearts, we still regret this separation. My family members have always understood and tolerated my interest in and sometimes frustration over the messy, handwritten letters of Sam Chang. In the early period of my research, they even helped organize those letters. My wife helped me discern many words and phrases that were difficult to recognize. My son also assisted me to design the Chang family lineage chart and the book cover. Sam Chang is a familiar name to my wife and son. Without their support and love, this book would not have been possible.

NOTE ON ROMANIZATION

This book uses pinyin to Romanize Chinese names and terms from Chinese-language sources. The Wade-Gile spellings of *Canton* and *Toisan*, for example, are rendered as *Guangzhou* and *Taishan* in pinyin. For a few popular names such as *Cantonese*, *Hong Kong*, or *Sun Yat-sen*, if the pinyin system is used, the spelling based on the Wade-Gile system is in parentheses. The last name of the Chang family is, however, not given the pinyin spelling *Zhang,* as the family papers and immigration files have used *Chang* or *Chung* and it thus makes more sense to refer to the family as the *Chang* family.

The Transnational History
of a Chinese Family

Introduction

*F*amily and home are one word, *jia,* in the Chinese language. Family can be apart, home relocated, but *jia* remains intact, as it signifies a system of mutual obligations and a set of cultural values. Deeply rooted in members' emotional affinity, ethical beliefs, and lifelong obligation to one another as family, many Chinese immigrant families had the viability and adaptability to survive long physical separation, expand economic activities beyond a national boundary, and accommodate continuities and discontinuities in the process of social mobility. Based on analysis of over three thousand family letters and other family documents, and of hundreds of recently released immigration files at the National Archives and Records Administration (former Immigration and Naturalization Service) offices at Laguna Niguel and at San Bruno in California, this book presents a composite picture of one immigrant/herbalist/farming Chinese family and its transnational history from the late nineteenth century to the 1970s. For three generations, Chang family members inhabited a space both geographically and culturally transnational. When social instability in China and a hostile racial environment in the United States prevented them from being rooted on either side of the Pacific, transnational family life became a focal point of their social existence.

Family as a Network

The Chang family's immigration history unfolds with the arrival of Yitang Chung (Yick Hong Chung) in the United States in 1900 as an herbalist.[1] He came from Kaiping County, one of the Four Districts (*Siyi*) in Guangdong Province, which sent numerous Chinese immigrants to the United States. Yitang established an herbal medicine business in Los Angeles and remitted money to China to support his wife and three children. When his wife died of illness in 1908, he married Nellie Yee, an American-born Chinese woman, who bore him another four children. In 1915, his eldest son, Sam, arrived in California as a visiting government official. Yitang asked his son to stay and manage an asparagus farm in which Yitang had recently invested. Although racist immigration laws restricted Chinese laboring immigrants during this period, the United States still permitted the entry of merchants and their family members, as well as of American-born Chinese and their descendants.

The transnational voyage of the Chang family was not an individual adventure but a collective action, with family and kinship relationship forming a central organizing unit. "Family" here, it is important to note, refers to parents, spouse, and children in a nuclear family, while "kinship" includes siblings, uncles and aunts, cousins, nephews and nieces, and other extended family members. Following a chain migration pattern, pioneer male immigrants of the family arrived in the United States, gained a foothold, and then sent for other family members. With their herbal store and farming business, Yitang and Sam managed to sponsor over forty family members and relatives to the United States.

For most Chinese immigrants, migration to the United States was not an exotic adventure but a rational choice based on aspirations for social advancement. The immigrants saw migration abroad as a way to explore new opportunities and improve their economic status. The Chang family history illustrates how kin networks became the basis of a chain migration, a process in which socially related individuals or households move from one place to another through a mutual help system. Within this system, immigrants exchange information and experience, with each in turn providing initial accommodation and assistance. Once human migration is set into motion, ties among family, kin, and friends form the social networks to sustain momentum regardless of legal restrictions. Family letters are instrumental in chain migration, providing a crucial link in the immigrant social network.

When family relations and kin networks were transplanted into America, they expanded and created new possibilities. Yitang and Sam, for example, while self-employed, often hired their cousins or nephews to work in their herbal or asparagus farming business, after having sponsored them to come to America. Family members and relatives hired as laborers pulled together, working long hours and sharing common risks to sustain a small business. Some relatives would send for their own families and set up their own businesses when they became more familiar with American society and accumulated a modest capital. With relatives supporting one another and bonds between parents and children remaining strong, Chinese merchant immigrants and their families survived a hostile racial environment.

Chinese migration is essentially a socially embedded, group-oriented, and family-supported movement. Kin and other social networks play important roles in this chain migration process. An individual immigrant's success is supposed to benefit not only his or her nuclear family but the extended family as well. Thus an obvious divergence of Chinese family history from the assimilationist model is the strengthening, rather than weakening, of family and kinship ties in the migration process.

Life between Two Worlds

After Yitang and Sam settled in America, their life became a combination of two worlds. While adapting to the socioeconomic reality of American society, they maintained their personal and cultural ties to China. Yitang's herbalist career represented something unique in Chinese American experience. As a transplanted culture, herbal medicine had to remain distinctively Chinese for effectiveness. Since herbal teas were made from hundreds of indigenous herbs gathered on the mountains and in the valleys of China, the supply of medicines relied on constant importation of herbs from China. Herbal medicine was thus an illuminating example of trans-Pacific flow of people, medical skill, and ethnic goods.

Clients of Yitang and other herbalists were mainly white Americans. When the Chinese population began to shrink under the shadow of Chinese exclusion laws, professional herbalists served more and more white American patients. They advertised their services in mainstream newspapers, hired white interpreters and receptionists, and set up offices outside Chinatowns. They had also to bypass unfair legal restrictions by presenting themselves as merchants selling herbs rather than as medical practitioners. The practice of herbal medicine is a rare instance of a profession that allowed Chinese immigrants to make a living for a prolonged period of time using a truly ethnic skill. Crossing ethnic boundaries, Chinese herbalists expanded their market from Chinatowns into mainstream American society.

The herbalists' success also involved their continuous resistance against racial prejudice and unfair competition. Like a Chinese restaurant, herbal medical practice served the needs of both Chinese and non-Chinese. Unlike Chinese cuisine, herbal medicine could not change its ingredients, flavor, or dispensation to suit the taste of mainstream America; rather, it had to remain distinctively Chinese to be effective. Herbal medicine was also a risky skill, as it dealt with human health; any failure or problems in the treatment could result in a harsh response from the dominant society. In fact, racist attacks on Chinese herbalists were persistent and sometimes rampant, though such attacks actually came from orthodox medical associations rather than from patients. Rejecting distortions and stereotypes against their profession, the herbalists published books and pamphlets to explain and actively promote herbal medicine in the United States.

The herbalists' history reveals a little-known aspect of cultural relations between mainstream America and Asian Americans. Chinese herbalists did not become less Chinese in developing roots in America, but white Americans adapted themselves to an Asian therapy. The interaction thus became an interesting instance of reverse assimilation.

Even while Yitang and Sam worked hard in their herbalist and asparagus businesses, they sent money home, read newspaper articles about their hometown, wrote letters to family members and friends in China, and sponsored their immigration to the United States. More important, the family's transnational networks and attachment to China also provided a significant option for their children's education and career orientation, during a period when many Chinese American youth could not find jobs in the United States that matched their college educations.[2] For example, Yitang's third son Elbert (Weiying) arrived in the United States when he was twelve years old. After graduating from Georgetown University Medical School, he could not find a job in the United States, but received an offer to become an intern in the prestigious Beijing (Peking) Union Medical College established by the Rockefeller Foundation. Arthur (Weixun), the fourth son, was born in America but went to Nankai University in Tianjin, and Yanjing (Yenching) University in Beijing, for his college education, and then to the National Medical College of Shanghai for his medical degree. He worked as an established physician in China until he returned to America in 1975. Yitang's American-born daughter Lillian (Qiaoixin) went to work in China after she graduated from the University of Southern California in 1933. His third daughter, Marian, also American-born, married a medical student from China in New York, then settled in China in 1949.

Among Sam's children, his son Tennyson (Tingxun) stayed in China by himself and attended high school in Tianjin, a city in the north, before arriving in the United States to earn a B.A. degree from the University of Southern California, a master's degree from Columbia University, and a Ph.D. degree from Georgetown University. As a son of Chinese immigrants, however, his first job was as a diplomat at the Chinese embassy in Nicaragua. Sam's daughter Constance (Yuhua) was born in China and arrived in the United States in 1923. However, she returned to China four years later for her high school and college education. She did not return to America until 1937. Sam's third daughter, Estelle, went to China when only eight years old and stayed there five years.

From 1900, when Yitang left China, to the 1950s, when most of the family members eventually settled down in the United States, the Chang family lived between the two worlds. While Yitang and Sam worked hard in the United States to support the family, their children maintained both English and Chinese language abilities, and pursued their education and careers on both sides of the Pacific. Transnationalism was deeply rooted in the Chang family history.

Sojourning and Migration

During the exclusion period (1882–1943), U.S. immigration laws barred Chinese laborers and their family members. Many working-class Chinese immigrants could not send for their wives and children, and suffered from long family separation. However, immigration laws still allowed merchants or American-born Chinese, and their family members, to travel back and forth between China and America. Separation between parents and children in the Chang family history shows how some Chinese took advantage of such loopholes in the immigration policy and, for example, pursued professional jobs in China when they found it difficult to get such careers in the United States. Such family separation was more voluntary than compulsory, though it reflects the hostile racial environment.

The transnational life of Chang family members also represents a sojourning tradition among Chinese in search of opportunities. In traditional Chinese society, talented young men often spent their formative years in prestigious academic institutions away from home. And once scholars passed the civil service exams and became government officials, the imperial government could place them anywhere but their home district until they retired. To be accessible to commodities, markets, and transportation networks, merchants dwelled for months in *huiguan,* or native-place meeting halls, in metropolitan centers away from home. Sailors and international trade businessmen traveled abroad for years to support distant parents, wives, and children. Hunger, natural disasters, or population pressures could push many people from their native villages, with success elsewhere bringing the displaced back. Thus in Chinese society, sojourning has been a common strategy for social mobility.

No doubt, some people might eventually settle in a region away from home, but sojourning was the first step in any such relocation. Susan Mann defines the family system, the civil service examination system, and patterns of male sojourning as three grand social structures that impacted human actions in traditional Chinese society.[3] In their quest for a new and better life, ambitious Chinese often expected to lead a sojourning life away from home while maintaining economic and cultural attachment to their native places. Following this sojourning tradition, Yitang and many other Chinese migrated to America and did not hesitate to send their American-born children back to China when U.S. racial stratification blocked their children's career mobility. Sojourning tradition not only concerns immigrants' attachment to their homeland but also reveals human aspirations for a better life and new opportunities. As Madeline Hsu points out, "experiences of sojourning within China provided the foundations for the expectations and goals of Chinese who traveled abroad as well as their strategies for economic and social adaptation overseas."[4]

However, the Chinese sojourning tradition should not be misunderstood by the "sojourner" and "settler" concepts created and used in some scholarly writings to distinguish Chinese from European immigrants.[5] Such writings labeled the Chinese as "sojourners" incapable of settling down in America because of their attachment to home. The label implies that Chinese immigrants came from a traditional and inward-looking society, incompatible with European culture. Deeply embedded in nationalistic discourse, these two concepts define migration as a rigid and predetermined one-way trip, and suggest that immigrants are people from one nation state moving to another. The mission of migration must be either to claim other people's land as one's own or to become citizens of a new country. Chinese immigrants did not refer to themselves as "settlers" or "sojourners." When Yitang visited his home village in 1929, he was one of the *jinshanke* or "Gold Mountain guests," which means they had been away long enough to become guests in their own home village but were still treated as part of it when they returned for a visit or retirement.

Although the sojourning tradition has long existed in Chinese society, the purpose of migration in general is not to look for another place to reside but to explore opportunities away from home. In the process of immigration, returning home is normal. Many immigrants, after years of hard work, accumulated sufficient savings or capital to return to their home country. The United States was not necessarily assumed as the immigrant's ultimate destination. During their stay in America, immigrants or their descendents might move again when opportunities became available elsewhere (including in their home country) or when they were disappointed by their American experience. Immigrants were not passive victims of powerful social forces that had uprooted them from their old life, but people who continuously explored opportunities with deliberate moves. "Settler" and "sojourner" are crude concepts with little theoretical depth, as human migration is never a simple, two-step, unidirectional movement in which people are mechanically "pushed out" of homelands and then "pulled" into another country.

Push and Pull Factors in Reverse Migration

Reverse migration of Yitang and Sam's children to China reflects a dilemma that confronted many Chinese American youth during the Chinese Exclusion period. Many second-generation Chinese discovered that college education could not help them achieve social mobility in American society. When they applied for skilled professions, an employer would base the decision on racial criteria rather than on individual merit; professional jobs were closed to them by racial prejudice. It is ironic that Elbert returned to China for a physician position after obtaining an American medical college degree while, in the 1920s, Yitang's herbal store received hundreds of Caucasian patients. Carey McWilliams has recorded that the color barrier was the main stumbling block in the lives of American-born Chinese. He has pointed out that, though many were well educated and had professional training, the Chinese were often trapped in low-skilled ethnic service labor markets. According to the 1938 report by the Oriental Division of the U.S. Employment Service in San Francisco, ninety percent of Chinese youth in the area were service workers. Although the defense industry was in great need of professional employees, five thousand young Chinese seemed to have no future worthy of their skills.[6] Lei Jieqiong (Kit King Louis), a sociology graduate student from the University of Southern California in the early 1930s, made a similar observation of American-born and American-reared Chinese in Los Angeles: although many Chinese youth had absorbed American ideas, attitudes, and customs, the dominant society denied them acceptance; college education failed to become a social mobility channel for them. Lei wrote: "But the door of occupational opportunity seems closed to them on account of their physical characteristics. They cannot attain the social and economic status in the American community which they desire."[7] To avoid being trapped in a segregated labor market, many educated Chinese returned to China.

However, "push" factors alone are insufficient to explain why some American-born Chinese returned to China. We need to find out what kind of social conditions drew the American-born Chinese back at that time, and to understand the linkage between China and Chinese America. Since the Opium

War in 1839–40, China had become a semicolonized country subject to a great deal of Western political and economical dominance and cultural influence. Through unequal treaties, imperialist powers opened coastal cities to international trade, established foreign settlements, and obtained extraterritoriality for foreign citizens in China. These powers collected and controlled Chinese customs duties on import and export goods. International banks, commercial firms, and factories sprouted like mushrooms in Chinese urban centers.

Christian churches and schools also appeared. "By 1905, Protestant missions had 389 'intermediate and high schools and colleges' with fifteen thousand students."[8] Beginning in the south, these missionary schools spread into northern, southwestern, southeastern, and central China. Some of these schools, with a curriculum heavy in Western culture, gradually expanded into colleges and universities, each with an attached high school section. The most well-known included Lingnan University (Canton Christian College), St. John's University in Shanghai, Jinling Women College, and Nanjing University, Yanjing University in Beijing, Qilu (Cheeloo) University in Shangdong, and Huazhong University in Hubei.[9] At the same time, modern schools and colleges began to appear in China. By 1930s, some of these institutions, like Nankai University (attended by Arthur), or Beijing Union Medical College (where Elbert worked) had become first-tier, full-fledged universities, attractive to Chinese youth both in China and overseas.

Returning to China to take advantage of these educational and professional opportunities was a pragmatic consideration for many foreign-born Chinese youth during this period. Knowledge of both English and Chinese became a useful mechanism for the second-generation Chinese Americans to ensure their social mobility in a racially defined society. Some, like Arthur, initially went back to study Chinese culture and language but decided to stay longer for advanced education. For American-born or -raised Chinese youth, attending schools in China meant reverse migration and acculturation into the culture of their ancestors. However, their return to China was not necessarily permanent. Many might go back to their homes overseas after awhile. But life in China often gave them a sense of belonging and a new cultural identity.

Family Letters and Immigration Files as Research Data

The documentation of the Chang family history is mainly based on Sam Chang's collection of family letters, speeches, poems, soliloquies, pamphlets, placards, posters, flyers, and farming notes, and of his personal reflections on cultural and political events of his times. Recently released immigration documents such as the Records of the INS–Los Angeles District Segregated Chinese Case Files at the National Archives and Records Administration at Laguna Niguel, California, and immigration files at the National Archives–Pacific Sierra Region, San Bruno, California, are also crucial parts of the original data.[10] Hundreds of immigration forms, memos, and interview transcripts of Chang family members and their relatives make up such documents. The files tell us how each of the Chang family members—father and son, husband and wife, brothers and sisters—handled tough questions, resisted psychological pressure, and collectively protected the family interest as they went through the grueling immigration interview process for landing or for a reentry permits before a planned visit to China. More significantly, the INS files help us better understand the subjective meaning of Chinese migration and the specific strategies used by Chinese in the immigration process, when we compare and verify information in the files with that in the immigrants' letters. Through such files, we have also obtained minute information about immigrants' family relationships, the social landscape in their home villages or towns, and their business operations in the United States. No other kind of documents would contain, for example, the floor plan of a residential house in Guangdong, the number of wells, ancestry halls, and schools in a rural village, or the multiple names of a male Chinese immigrant. We could probably write a most detailed social history of Chinese immigrants based on the INS files.

Chang's family letters fall into three parts. The first section includes his letters to his children and other fairly immediate relatives such as brothers, cousins, and nephews. There are about nine hundred such letters, copied down by him in eighteen student notebooks. The second section includes more than a thousand outgoing letters of Chang to members of his clan and friends, as well as his essays, poems, and recollections on both Chinese and American life and culture. The third part of the collection consists of about three hundred incoming letters from Chang's children, relatives, and friends. Sam has left us a gold mine of firsthand material that reflects the attitudes and perceptions of the Chinese about their life in the United States. (In this book, translations in English of Sam's letters attempt to match the style of his draft letters in Chinese.)

In immigration studies, aggregated data, demographic statistics, and structural determinants such as economic cycles and social ecology only allow us to make hypothetical assumptions about goals and motivations of immigrants. But migration is a careful decision and immigrants are calculating individuals who base decisions on evaluation of the situation at home and abroad. Immigrants' letters offer insights into personal motivations and aspirations, and help us answer specific questions about why some individuals chose to migrate while others from the same family or region did not. Sam Chang's letters, for example, indicated that his second brother remained in China to take care of the family property and wealth while other family members explored opportunities abroad. Sam later sponsored his second brother's children's immigration to America. In the Chang family history, migration was obviously a collective endeavor based on the interest of the entire family. While working overseas, immigrants also wanted to maintain their link to home in case migration did not work and they needed to return.

Family letters are also important as firsthand research data. There has been a growing tendency to use Chinese-language materials for research in Chinese American studies; this tendency reflects limitations of previous scholarship, which was often based on English-language materials. Many such studies are at best a record of what happened to the Chinese, rather than of what they achieved. In such studies, Chinese perceptions of life in America were seldom noticed. As Yong Chen points out, "Yet, through words and expressions in various written documents, ranging from elaborate wedding announcements and obituaries to letter and diaries, we can glimpse the immigrants' feelings of joy and sorrow, their beliefs about life and death, their concepts of time and space, and their sense of identity."[11] Chinese-language materials link our research directly to Chinese life and community. In Asian American Studies, our research is deeply committed to our community. Since the validity of our research depends on perceptions of the people that we do research for, community-based research is essential for an accurate interpretation of the Chinese American experience.

Letters are one of the few sorts of documents that allow us to penetrate the meaning of the immigration experience for individual Chinese. Using such Chinese-language materials, we can express and explain the sensibility and perceptions of the Chinese and write history from their perspective. Sam Chang's letters, for example, demonstrate that he was very pessimistic about immigrant life in America, regardless of the Chang family's successful herbal and farming businesses. He believed that the life of the Chinese in America represented a downward rather than upward mobility, in terms of social status. As the Chinese were treated as an inferior race, he observed, his children had low self-esteem. (In fact, this was one reason he sent them to China for education.) Family correspondence is also a vehicle of moral education in Chinese family culture. The Chang family letters illustrate how parents passed on family history, instilled family values in their children, and inspired the children to study and work hard to live up the older generation's expectations. Letters by Sam and his children truthfully reflect the aspirations, frustrations, and motivations in their transnational life. As historical data to document personal insights and feelings, family letters are more objective than memoirs or interviews, since these latter often reconstruct past events on the basis of memories and feelings, and are often meant for a public readership. Yet, like memoirs or interviews, letters reveal personal perceptions that enable us to find the subjective meaning of a group's experience.

Immigrants' letters are also a valuable source for studying the process of migration. Ties among family, wider kin, friends, and hometown people form the social networks to sustain and expand chain migration. Family letters are instrumental in chain migration, providing information and coaching in the immigrant social network. These letters inform potential immigrants about local conditions in the receiving country, advise them how to travel, where to find jobs, and how to locate friends and places to stay upon arrival. And correspondence is not one-way communication; information, ideas, and feelings are exchanged back and forth. Sam Chang's family correspondence was not communication between two individuals but a network of communication among more than a dozen people, to whom Sam constantly offered advice and suggestions on when, how, or whether to come to America.

Letters have been the primary source in many immigration studies. A classic example is William Thomas and Florian Znaniecki's 1918 multivolume study *The Polish Peasant in Europe and America*.[12] In more recent decades, scholars have not only used letters as the primary source for research but also translated and published them.[13] However, little existing Chinese American scholarship has been based on personal letters. The Chang family letters are among the few firsthand written documents left by pioneer immigrants that allow us to penetrate the meaning of the immigration experience for individual immigrants.

Significance of the Chang Family History

Rather than a straightforward, one-way trip from one side of the Pacific to the other, the Chang family history was a long, complicated transnational circular migration during which family members constantly considered factors that might affect their life and what strategies to adopt for the best interest of their future. This history illustrates how a Chinese family system could function as a social institution that transcends national boundaries.

The transnational experience of the Chang family demonstrates that immigrants were not people displaced from one set of social relationships and absorbed into another; instead, Chinese immigrants and their families were capable of maintaining involvement in both China and America for a prolonged period.

Focusing on the Chang family history, this book explores why some Chinese immigrants pursued a transnational family life, how transnational social and cultural networks helped in their family businesses and children's education, and in what way the transnational family pattern represents some creative and adaptive strategies used collectively by Chinese immigrants to insure their survival and social mobility in a hostile racial environment. My theoretical framework is to view Chinese American experience as a history that transcends national boundaries. It was the circular migration as a whole, rather than one locale, that provided the setting in which many Chinese organized their family life and developed their world outlook and ethnic identity. From a de-nationalist perspective, this book emphasizes the multiple social relationships the Chinese have maintained in China and America, and explores in depth the meaning of transnational family experience for the Chinese.

Chapter 1 looks at the Chang family's origins, and helps readers understand the cultural roots of the Chinese and social environment of Guangdong that sent hundreds of thousands of immigrants to the United States, and elsewhere, in the nineteenth century. Chapter 2 describes Yitang as the pioneer immigrant of the Chang family, and shows how the Chang family network was transplanted and expanded from China to the United States. Chapter 3 focuses on the herbal business of Yitang, and through his experience examines herbal medicine as a transnational culture. Chapter 4 uses Sam Chang's emigration story to illustrate how social instability in China and family networks in America played roles in immigration decisions among the Chinese. Chapter 5 focuses on Sam's asparagus farming as a family business. Chapter 6 explains the importance of education in Chinese family culture; Sam and his wife closely followed the educational progress of their children attending schools in China and the United States. Chapter 7 describes linkages between China and the Chang family, explains why the younger generation of the Chang family returned to China for education and occupational opportunities, and explores how China remained a cultural home for them.

CHAPTER 1

Origins of the Chang Family

$\mathcal{L}$ike most early Chinese immigrants, Sam Chang's family originated from a narrow region along the Zhujing (Pearl) River Delta in Guangdong Province. The Chinese immigrants from this region further divided themselves based on three geographic districts—Sanyi, Siyi, and Zhongshan County. Sanyi included the districts (or counties) of Nanhai, Panyu, and Shunde; Siyi included the counties of Xinhui, Taishan, Kaiping, and Enping.[1] The family letters and other documents, together with the INS testimony transcripts, enable us to trace the family's origin from Yitang, the first member of the Chang family to immigrate to the United States, to Chunli, and then to Zhandong, and thus to see a sketchy three-generation genealogical history of the Chang family in Guangdong. The story is detailed enough to inform us, as we put pieces of information together, of some of the most important aspects of family culture in rural Guangdong—such as the inheritance system, patterns of residence, kin relations, and other key factors affecting the structure and size of a rural family. The story also demonstrates the importance of ancestral halls, village schools, rural markets, and other social and economic institutions and events for the rural population in Guangdong.

The Chang family lived in Niushan ("Cattle Hill") Village, Kaiping District. The village had about four hundred houses (families), four ancestral halls, and two to four schools, though not all of the schools were operating on a regular basis. Among several rural markets, the nearest to the village was called Yung Ku Market, operating year round. There were four wells that supplied water for village residents. In front of the village was a river, which could be used for irrigation or boat transportation to Guangzhou city. At the back of the village was a long brick wall with several gates. The Chang house was located in the heart of the village and was about one block away from the nearest gate. There were several family clans in the village. The Chang clan was not the most prominent, as it did not own a big ancestral hall. Nor did it run the best school in the village.[2] In nineteenth-century Guangdong, ancestral hall and school often represented the power and status of a clan in a rural village.

In the stereotypical image of a Chinese rural population, peasant families toiled for generations in carefully cultivated, tiny rice fields for survival. A harmonious extended family of several generations lived under one roof. Sons revered parents, wives obeyed husbands, and brothers assisted each other in family affairs. Such an image stands for perpetuity and the changeless nature of the Chinese family culture. However, life in rural Guangdong resembled nothing like this picture. D. H. Kulp's research on the Chinese countryside in the 1920s has noted that a nineteenth-century Guangdong rural village could have clerks, salespersons, merchants, fruit dealers, carpenters, doctors, tailors, teachers, and others in addition to farmers.[3] Diversified commercial activities, prevalent lineage organizations, and a competitive social environment characterized Guangdong. In agriculture, cash crops had begun to replace self-sufficient farming. Although the Zhujing Delta produced silk and sugar-cane, other hilly areas grew tea, tobacco, and various fruits. The Delta was one of the richest agricultural areas in China.

In sharp contrast with the stereotypical image of rural China, the Chang family history is marked by volatility and eventfulness. It shows how a small, modest family could grow in wealth, fame, and size through hard work, frugality, and good investment by the first and second generations, then sink into poverty and shame from a later generation's extravagant life style and a heartless scramble for family property among male descendents of that generation. In rural Guangdong, family life was often subjected externally to market forces, and internally to conflicts among siblings over property. A Chinese rural family could experience a considerable social ascent or descent within a short time. Hugh Baker writes that the rise and fall in family fortunes meant society was like a seething cauldron, with families bubbling to the top only to burst and sink back to the bottom.[4] Family was the cornerstone of the Chinese social structure, and family history reflects changes and continuities in Chinese society. Placed in a larger historical context, the dynamic rise and fall of the Chang family helps clarify the competitive social environment of Guangdong that sent hundreds of thousands of immigrants to the United States and elsewhere in the mid-nineteenth and early twentieth centuries.

Zhandong as an Ancestor

Living sometime approximately between the 1780s and 1830s, Zhandong Chang was the eldest son of a well-to-do farmer's family and had five brothers.[5] Although information about him is slight, descendents in the Chang family referred to him as the founder of the family's wealth. Zhandong married Nie, daughter of a well-to-do family in the neighboring rural town Beizha, who bore him one son and two daughters.

In a letter to his children, Sam Chang explained why Zhandong deserved great respect in the family history:

> Zhandong inherited a farm from his aging father that produced no more than a hundred *dan* of grain [one *dan* equals approximately 185 pounds]. But he worked hard, lived a thrifty life, and was able to build his fortune up to one thousand *dan* of grain a year. That is his first achievement. Second, he was well educated, knew law, and could write legal complaints for relatives and friends. Third, he knew how to deal with the local tyrants when they tried to take advantage of his wealth, and so avoided a lot of trouble. Fourth, he viewed polygamy as the root of misfortune. Although he was the wealthiest man in the village and had only one son and two daughters, he did not marry more wives for more sons. Fifth, though he could inherit the best house of the family as the eldest son, he gave it away to the widow of his half- and fifth brother out of respect for his father's wish, and chose a smaller house for himself. Sixth, as the eldest son, he made sure that the six brothers remained close and friendly long after their parents passed away. Seventh, he lived a decent life-style. Opium-smoking relatives and gambling relatives always stayed away from him. Eighth, in addition to farming, he ran a reading class and taught children of the clan until he was old. We later generations should learn the above eight qualities from him. Although he lived only about fifty years, he was a very happy person and enjoyed a relaxing time in his later years.[6]

Family history is always important in Chinese culture. While some families composed and preserved books of genealogy, many others probably passed stories of their ancestors orally from generation to generation. Sam's letters to his children, for example, contain many anecdotes and events concerning his ancestors. In a bit of exaggeration, a British diplomat in early twentieth-century China recalled that "the commonest Chinaman can trace his descent back by memory from two hundred to five hundred years, or even more by referring to his 'genealogy' book at home."[7] In Sam Chang's collection, there is no formal genealogy. But the summary of eight personal qualities of Zhandong in the above letter indicates that Sam probably knew a great deal about this ancestor.

Although not a detailed biography, the letter was long enough to portray Zhandong as smart, educated, and a responsible farmer. Revealing important aspects of Chinese family culture in rural Guangdong, Sam's writing indicates what kind of qualities and moral character could help village men succeed, what kind of knowledge and skills were considered useful, how a farmer of middle echelon handled social relations in the village and kinship relations within the family, and what ethic and moral principals were considered to guide such relationships. Writing this letter to his children from California, Sam's appraisal of Zhandong reflects his perception and understanding of Chinese family culture; in his depiction, Zhandong was not a stereotypical Chinese landlord who had sought a family life in which three generations lived under one roof. Raised and educated during a transitional period of China at the turn of the century, and working and living in the United States as an immigrant, Sam, in his comments on his ancestor, aimed to pass on family history and instill important family values.

In the letter, Sam did not begin his discussion with Zhandong's role as a model of filial piety. Instead, he ranked Zhandong's economic success above any other accomplishment. According to the letter, when Zhandong inherited a piece of land from his father, his farm only produced about a hundred *dan* of paddy rice per year.[8] Since the average annual yield of paddy rice per *mu* (one-sixth acre) in Zhujing Delta was between two and four *dan*, it can be assumed that the size of Zhandong's inherited land was twenty to thirty *mu*.[9] In the early nineteenth century, one *dan* of grain could feed an adult male for a hundred days, or sell for three hundred copper in cash. An agricultural laborer's monthly wage was only between two hundred and four hundred fifty copper in cash.[10]

As the equal inheritance rule in Chinese family culture determined that Zhandong's share was similar to that of each of the other five brothers, his father had probably owned one hundred and twenty to one hundred and eighty *mu* of land, which was a fairly large property. Although Zhandong's share was modest, it was much above the self-subsistence level. By 1821, population pressure became heavy, with the ratio of population to land increasing almost 25 percent from 160 persons per square mile in 1787 to 192 persons per square mile in 1812. There was 1.67 *mu* of cultivable land per person in 1821, below the national average of 2.19 *mu* in that year.[11]

Zhandong was already in his late twenties when he received his share of his father's estate, and he retired from farming in his mid-fifties. Thus, in less than thirty years, he was able to expand his land property to ten times what he had inherited. Considering that arable land was far from sufficient to meet the needs of the local population in Guangdong, his success as a farmer was very impressive.[12]

The letter provided no details of how he accomplished this success, except in praising his fugal life style and hardworking spirit. His rapid accumulation of wealth, however, seemed only possible in a cash-crops-oriented area like Guangdong. According to China scholar G. William Skinner, some speculative agribusinessmen were able to expand their landed property and became rich within a short time because the commercial marketing system was well developed and organized in rural Guangdong.[13] Zhandong was not a self-sufficient farmer who worked solely to feed himself and his family, but probably a landlord who grew crops for sale.

Sam listed Zhandong's education and legal knowledge as his second most important achievement. Although presumably not scholarly enough to pass the civil service examination and earn a degree, he was well educated and could write poems. Another family document described Zhandong as a tolerant person with a resolute temper, wealthy but not malicious, and a highly respected farmer in the village. "When his wealth sometimes made him the target of envious and rapacious people, Zhandong's ability to write legal complaints enabled him to defend himself and gain upper hand in the conflicts with other people during arbitration by the local government."[14] During the Qing Dynasty, the land ownership system, legal codes on landed property, and land sale procedure were complicated. For example, tenant farmers could have permanent access to land as long as they paid taxes. As permanent tenancy became another form of ownership, many land properties could have two or three owners.[15] Zhandong could not accumulate his land smoothly without knowing the law; his ability to write legal document must have been an important skill in handling economic issues. According to James Hayes, most social and economic transactions in Qing China were documented in writing, and writers of such contracts were not parties to the transactions but probably fellow villagers, clansmen, or fellow townspersons.[16] Ping-ti Ho's research on social mobility in imperial China emphasized that literacy was essential for farmer families not only for pursuing scholarly titles but also for successful farm management; and that therefore there was a high degree of literacy among Chinese farmers.[17]

In his letter, Sam also mentioned Zhandong's responsibility to use his spare time to teach clan children and to continue his teaching duties even after he retired from farming. Like many educated farmers, he was probably a part-time teacher, as school was an integral part of the village life in Guangdong. Zhandong's legal knowledge may have been rare among farmers, but many other villagers must have had a functional literacy, considering the popularity of village schools in Guangdong.

That Sam ranked wealth and education as the first and second greatness of Zhandong does not mean Sam regarded filial piety as less important in family culture. In fact, Sam seems highly impressed with Zhandong's kindness toward his brothers. In Chinese family culture, filial piety includes the idea of *xiao ti* (fraternal love). Although "filial" refers to relationship with parents, *ti* means maintaining cordial fraternal relationships. In these, junior brothers should defer to senior brothers, while the latter should display affection and care and set a good moral example in family affairs. For instance, Zhandong set an excellent example of *ti* as he let the widow of his fifth (his half-) brother receive the best house of the family estate in the property division. Since Chinese family culture disapproved primogeniture, every son was entitled to a share of the family property. But, as the eldest son, Zhandong could use his seniority to demand the best land and house. When he gave up such a demand, he acted as a caring and generous brother. Regarding Zhandong as a good role model in family culture, Sam carefully handled his own sibling relationships. When he joined his father Yitang as an immigrant in America, he found that his father's second marriage had added four younger siblings—three stepsisters and one stepbrother. Following the *ti* principle, Sam treated his American-born siblings kindly. Several family photos showed how Sam taught his siblings Chinese language and culture.[18] Sibling relationships remained cordial in the Chang family. Such cordial and close relations were an important factor for the family to survive and succeed in American society.

In his letter, Sam also praised Zhandong's preference for a small family and his commitment to maintain a harmonious family. Chinese family culture allowed polygamous marriage, as the filial piety advocated in Confucianism encouraged wealthy men to marry concubines to have more sons to continue family lines. However, this was not a model that every wealthy man followed, since more sons could result in more competition over family property. Zhandong did not marry concubines and chose to have a small family with one wife and three children, of whom only one was a son.

A small family allowed him to keep his wealth undivided, and to leave his son Chunli a good opportunity to further expand family property. Without several sons as potential competitors for family property, Zhandong also enjoyed a peaceful retirement life. Sam spoke highly of Zhandong's decision not to marry concubines, because he noticed how sibling fighting accounted for the eventual decline of the Chang family's wealth during his father's generation. Sam's letter also mentions gambling and opium smoking in the village—in effect, a footnote on lifestyle in the rural Guangdong and indicator of how widely opium spread in Chinese society in the early nineteenth century.

The Expansion of Family Wealth under Chunli

As the only son of Zhandong, Chunli inherited all the family's land and houses. The Chang family's ascent continued—from the wealthiest family in the village to the wealthiest family in the county. Several family documents mentioned that during Chunli's times the family obtained four thousands *dan* of rice a year, an amount four times larger than in Zhandong's time. For this yield, Chunli probably owned and/or leased up to five hundred *mu* or more of land. No doubt, Chunli's family lived a comfortable life based on rents paid by tenants. In a period when many farmers went bankrupt and peasant laborers could not find jobs, Chunli had tons of grain in the barn and a huge holding of land assets. Family documents indicate that he was known as one of the wealthiest landlords in Kaiping County at that time.[19]

From the late eighteenth to the early nineteenth century, Guangdong was undergoing dramatic demographic changes. Its population grew from sixteen million in 1787 to twenty-eight million in 1850.[20] This was a period in which social stratification increased, with the growing commercialization of rural society in South China. There was a great discrepancy between the extremes of wealth and poverty in the south, by the mid-nineteenth century. The average ratio of land to population in Guangdong was 7.8 *mu* per family, and only one million farmers, of a total 12.5 million agriculturalists, owned their own land.[21] Some 3 to 5 percent of the population controlled about 50 to 60 percent of the cultivated land. Moreover, interregional and international trade led to the cultivation of cash crops in place of subsistence farming.[22] Chunli seems to have been a very capable entrepreneurial landlord to have amalgamated family land holdings into large estates operated by hired peasant laborers.

It is interesting to note that Sam Chang's letter and other family documents referred to the wealth of the Chang family by the amount of grain (as rent) received annually rather than by the amount of land owned. And Sam often referred to his birthplace as Paoxi *xiang* (township) rather than Niushan *cun* (village). Larger than a village, *xiang* hosted markets for bartering, retail venders, or trade on a regular basis. As an administrative unit, the town was recognized as a rural center surrounded by a dozen villages. It was often the focus of the villages' economic and social life in Guangdong, as rural markets were held every few days, bustling with all kinds of business.[23] In fact, there were several markets close to Sam's home village, the largest lying about six *li* to the south (one Chinese *li* is equal to 0.31 miles).[24] Obviously, commercial activities were common among the rural population in Guangdong. According to Skinner, the market town shaped the local social structure and integrated the peasant community into the total society.[25] During the Qing period, markets in rural Guangdong became very specialized, with fruit, grain, silkworm, pig, draft animal, fish, and even fabric markets opening regularly at various locations.[26]

As family wealth grew, the size of the Chunli family began to expand. In sharp contrast to Zhandong, Chunli married four women, three of whom were considered wives and one a concubine. He probably wanted to establish a large family and then expand it into a powerful lineage organization like those of many other wealthy people in the area. Since the seventeenth century, lineage organizations proliferated in Guangdong, the results of social unrest. Pirates sometimes attacked the villagers during the harvest time, armed feuds between Cantonese and Hakka over land disputes were common, and there were frequent physical fights over property between rival lineages or during tenants' rebellions against rent collection. The lineage system was so prevalent that most rural inhabitants belonged to one or two lineages, in that area.[27] As endemic violence was part of rural life in Guangdong, a strong lineage organization was a reliable safeguard.

In Chunli's marriage life, the first wife, Chen, died shortly after the wedding, without bearing any children. The second wife, Wu, bore him five sons and two daughters. Then Chunli married a concubine, Liang, who bore him another five sons and one daughter. The eldest, second, fourth, sixth, and eighth sons belonged to Wu while the third, fifth, seventh, ninth, and tenth sons belonged to Liang. When Wu died, Chunli married Yuan as a wife rather than as a concubine; Yuan bore him another two sons and three daughters. Yitang (1866–1952), Sam's father, was the first son of Chunli and Yuan. When Chunli married Yuan, he was almost sixty years old and Yuan was only nineteen. Chunli granted Yuan a wife status for fear that she would not agree to this marriage as a concubine, given the age gap. The four women bore him a total of eighteen children—twelve sons and six daughters.

Family School and Ancestral Hall as Symbol of Success

With his wealth, Chunli built a family study house, called *Cuncheng Shushi* ("sincerity study house"), which functioned probably both as *citang* (ancestral hall) and as a school for his children and for other children in the village. Chunli owned one of four ancestral halls in the village; even though theirs was not the largest, that they possessed an ancestral hall means the Chang family became, with Chunli as its head, fairly powerful and influential in the village.

Building ancestral halls was an important cultural tradition in Guangdong. Beginning in the seventeenth century, ancestral halls proliferated across the province. As Qu Dajun observed, "Every clans, big or small, have ancestral halls built in grand style and function as lecture room. A clan of thousand people could have several dozens of ancestral halls."[28] Wealthy and powerful families would place their memorial tablets in an ancestral hall, which usually belonged to the lineage or the clan. Tablets in the family shrine could be preserved for at least four generations. Chen Hansheng noted that one village of about seven hundred inhabitants in Guangdong maintained over forty ancestral halls, though all belonged to one clan.[29] An ancestral hall could also function as a meeting hall to discuss clan affairs.

Building ancestral halls did not only display the wealth and social status of a family or clan, but also reflected its worship of ancestors, an important tradition in Chinese society. When immigrants left China and arrived in another country, they continued this custom. Overseas Chinese often had a joss house for praying, if they could not build a temple.

In rural Guangdong, ancestral halls became far more numerous than in many other regions, because of intense competition over land, widespread clan organizations, and epidemic social instability. Many immigration officers noticed this cultural feature of rural Guangdong through their conversations with Chinese immigrants, and therefore questions on ancestral halls became an important component of admission interrogations. Immigration officers routinely asked Chinese immigrants about the number of ancestral halls in their villages as a way to verify if a person was really from a given village. When Yitang sponsored family members and relatives to come to America, this was a crucial question in INS interviews. In one interview, a relative of Yitang acknowledged the existence of two to four ancestral halls in the village. This person pronounced the names of the ancestral halls as "Kay En Doo" and "Tund Sen She Sit"—names phonetically similar to "Kay You Doo" and "Cheung Sing She Sit," names of the two village schools mentioned by Yitang in his own interview.[30]

Ancestral halls in rural areas often functioned as village schools. Japanese scholar Shimizu Taiji noticed that many *citang* were used as classrooms, with *shushi* or *shuwu* ("study room") inscribed on the doors.[31] As social mobility in traditional China was closely linked with education, Chunli sought to elevate his family's status by investing in his children's education, and invited established scholars to teach in the school. With a good education from a village school, children of an ordinary family could take a local civil service examination, which had three levels—preliminary county test (*xian kao*), department test (*zhou kao*), and prefectural test (*fu kao*). If any passed the tests, they would be selected as licensed candidates (*gong sheng*) for the provincial examination (*xiang shi*), held triennially. For more advanced education, students needed to attend a larger, more advanced, and better equipped school, often located in cities, called *shuyuan* ("academy"). (A word-for-word translation of *shuyuan* is "academic institute.") Famous *shuyuan* in Chinese history were usually academies sponsored by leading scholars or wealthy families to train competent scholars. The *shuyuan* originated in the Tang Dynasty as private places where scholars could store books and study, and became popular in the Song Dynasty (960–1275) following the rise of the neo-Confucian movement. Numerous district schools called *shuyuan,* or clan and village schools called *shushi*, like the Chang family study house, existed in Guangdong Province during the late Qing period.[32] Trained at *shuyuan,* students could take a higher level of the examination and earn the scholarly title *ju ren,* then could participate in the national metropolitan (*hui shi*) and palace (*dian shi*) examination to become a *jin shi*, the highest scholarly title, which almost guaranteed a good position in the imperial government. Education, in traditional China led to prestige, power, and wealth.

One scholar contends: "The Canton basin was one of the most academically prestigious areas of the country. During the Ch'ing period, Kuang-chou Fu ranked fifth among the nation's prefectures in the number of chin-shih ['highest degree holder']."[33] After the 1670s, the Qing government created special examination quotas for more developed areas like Guangdong, Zhili, Zhejiang, Shandong, and Shanxi. Sometimes the Qing government also permitted purchase of degrees at the county or district level. Since degree holders belonged to the respected gentry class, a great number of wealthy landlords were interested in buying scholarly degrees. Guangdong had the second largest number of degrees purchased of any province.[34] Of course, village schools could not guarantee the success of every student, but they were the first step to academic success. In addition to having important roles in assisting the local youth to pursue further education for the civil service examination, village schools enabled many rural children to obtain functional literacy.

Chunli established a school in the hope that his children could receive a good education, pass the local civil service examination, and be eligible to hold government offices. Among Chunli's children, his eldest, second, third, fourth, fifth, and sixth sons passed the local civil service examination. Biaobing, his eldest son, became a *lingongsheng* (paid licentiate of the dynasty school), while the other brothers became *fugongsheng* (supplementary licentiates without pay). Only the first-place candidate in a local civil service examination was named a *lingongsheng* and received a government stipend. A *lingongsheng* was also eligible to hold education positions in local government. Chunli's eldest son was appointed as an education official in Shunde County, a neighboring county of Kaiping. Although the status of the scholarly titles was no guarantee of office for the other brothers, it was often a precondition to hold an office. Moreover, the scholarly titles of Chunli's sons raised the family into a privileged social status, the gentry class. Such a family was often exempted from taxes, public manual labor, and corporal punishment in court. The local government also respected the gentry families and treated them as community leaders.[35] Obviously, those sons with scholarly titles brought honor and prestige to the Chang family.

Sibling Feuds over Family Property

Although family wealth reached its zenith during Chunli's time, it began to decline as he grew old. Many factors contributed to the fall of the Chang family, including Chunli's senility, weakened patriarchal authority, and bitter conflicts over family property among his sons. When rent from land became the only source of income, Chunli's sons competed intensely over their father's landed property. The harmonious Chang family became a divided house in Chunli's senior years.

As a son of the youngest wife of Chunli, Yitang was much younger than his elder brothers. However, he was still a competing sibling for family property, because of the equal inheritance principle. Two incidents reveal the intensity of the brothers' rivalry. When Yitang was a teenager, he had a fight with a son of the second brother in school and slightly injured the head of his nephew with a wooden slipper. In revenge, the second brother chased him everywhere and wanted to beat him to death, until Chunli interfered. As Chunli grew senile, and his patriarchal authority weakened, some of the adult sons were rude to him whenever they found him showing special affection to the sons of his youngest wife. On one occasion, Chunli had a birthday dinner and his second son prepared his favorite food, a sea cucumber dish. When Chunli gave a piece of cucumber to Yitang, the second brother rudely shouted at his father: "This delicacy is a special food for you. Not for anyone else. You cannot give it away!"[36] Chinese family politics is delicate yet intensive. On the surface, the second son was competing for Chunli's affection and favoritism; in reality, he challenged Chunli's authority, tried to enforce a hierarchical sibling relationship, and showed his power in family affairs.

Under such circumstances, Yitang's mother Yuan arranged for him to marry a girl named Guan from Langxia *xiang*, Kaiping County, in 1882, when he was only sixteen years old. Yuan was worried about her son's share of family property, with Chunli growing old. After marriage, Yitang could establish his own nuclear family by moving to a room or house that had its own kitchen (or stove), and could officially ask for his share of family property. Guan bore Yitang three sons: Sam (Weixi), Zhongping (Weizong), and Elbert (Weiying).[37] In Chinese family culture, "property division may take place either before or after the death of the father but generally occurs at the time of the marriages of the second and third sons, as harmonious family life is difficult to maintain when married brothers live together."[38] In splitting family wealth, the rules of equal inheritance ensured that the brothers were "equal." All sons, whether the offspring of the primary legal wife or of concubines, had rights in the patrimonial estate and property as long as their father recognized them as sons. According to Qing codes, even a son born of a proscribed sexual relationship (as with a domestic maid) would receive half the share of a legitimate son. The father could not disinherit a son without a valid reason.[39] Contracts dividing family property were one of the most common legal contracts in the Qing Dynasty.

After Yitang's marriage, Chunli decided to divide his property evenly among his sons, though a common practice was to divide property on a ratio of six-tenths to the son or sons of the primary wife, four-tenths to the sons of others. But Chunli's eldest and second eldest sons opposed this decision, and wanted to maintain the land property under the extended Chang family system. Both, as mentioned above, were degree holders; they were the most powerful brothers in the family. In Guangdong, land property was sometimes owned by a lineage or clan, due to a scarcity of arable land. The two eldest brothers probably used this argument to seek control of family land. Faced with this opposition, Chunli insisted that one piece of his land be divided as a base to supply staple food to each son and his family. However, the family estate was not officially divided.

Chunli died when Yitang was eighteen years old. After Chunli's death, the family conflict intensified. The second eldest brother sometimes physically attacked Yitang and his mother when feuds arose. On one occasion, there was no food left in Yitang's house, as the two eldest brothers ordered the tenant farmers not to give his household any grain. As the family was starving, Yuan went to the farmland allocated to them by Chunli and cut the crop herself. When the second eldest brother heard this, he led a dozen of his family members and relatives to rush to the field and beat Yuan with bamboo sticks. One family letter described the incident:

> After they beat Yuan with bamboo sticks, there was blood all over her. Then they shouted: "What is the point of killing this useless woman? Let us get rid of her son." The second eldest brother chased Yitang with knives in both hands. Yitang ran as fast as he could. He fled to a small hill but was blocked by a deep pond. As he jumped over the pond, he rolled down the hill and lost consciousness. Fortunately, someone saved him.[40]

It was a savage family battle. Professor Ping-ti Ho writes that the custom of equal inheritance in Chinese society frequently gave rise to property disputes among brothers. Widows with minor sons often found it impossible to ward off the encroachment of rapacious brothers-in-law or other kinsmen. Ho cites an example in which a boy was thrown into the river by his uncle and was only saved by a neighbor.[41]

The physical attack on Yitang by his elder brother is a vivid example of the intensity of competition among male siblings. Such competition reflected the inner contradiction in the Chinese family system. On the one hand, brothers had an equal claim to the assets of their family. According to Qing law, all male descendents had the right to divide family property in land, house, and movable property such as furniture, clothing, livestock and so on. On the other hand, brothers were hierarchically ranked siblings. Following the *ti* principle, younger brothers were supposed to display the same obedience to older brothers as they showed to their father. This contradiction between status inequality and economic equality made fraternal relations a key issue in family politics.

The incident also reflects the disadvantage of junior brothers in family fighting under the Qing legal system. The Qing law coded that killing an older sibling be punished with beheading. By contrast, older siblings guilty of killing younger siblings were usually sentenced to penal servitude or banishment.[42] Such discrepancy in punishment probably encouraged the elder brothers to use physical assault in family feuds. Dispute over the division of property; clashes over the support and treatment of parents, and irresponsible behavior of a brother fragmented numerous Chinese families when aging parents lost their authority.

Though Yitang narrowly escaped being lynched, the battle for family property was not over. As the second eldest brother was so merciless in family disputes, Yitang and the other eight brothers formed a united front and addressed themselves as the Nine Families, while the second eldest brother banded with the eldest and seventh brothers as the Three Families. The Chang brothers did not necessarily band with each other on the basis of maternal ancestors. It was the nuclear family rather than the extended family that was the preferred unit of consumption, production, and property ownership. The united front of the Nine Families was based on similar visions of how to divide family property. The ultimate goal in the property division was a larger share for the nuclear family.

The Decline of the Family

Male descendents' fights over property was the root cause of the Chang family decline. In the same letter, Sam concluded, "While Chunli has a high reputation, he is not as great as Zhandong even though he lived seventy-nine years old with four-thousand *dan* of farm wealth and eighteen children. He did not divide his property earlier and was very unhappy during his last years."[43] The size of the family was difficult to support. When the collected rent was divided among each family within the lineage, each son received only a modest amount after expenses were deducted. In another letter to his cousins, Sam Chang wrote:

> Our marriage tradition is very different from the Western people. In the West, even if you have a millionaire father, you will not marry until you acquire a career to support yourself. The parents do not give money to children to encourage early marriage. And, after marriage, the children and parents live in separate houses so that there will be few family conflicts. In our country, however, parents want

their children to marry early. They do not mind if there is enough to eat for the family, but only care for the vanity of having grandsons. Life in a Chinese extended family is like a hell. The rich, big families can just produce a few parasites for the human world. Take our ancestor Chunli's family, for example. Each son's family received two hundred *dan* of grain per year. After some processing of the grain, there was about one hundred and twenty *dan* left, and forty *dan* would be used to feed the domestic animals. So each family only had eighty *dan* left. If one *dan* was worth two dollars, each family had about one hundred and sixty dollars a year. The children's education cost about thirty dollars, clothing thirty dollars, social activities twenty dollars, and medicine twenty dollars. Not much was left. Yet many of our clan people lived a befuddled life, only interested in getting concubines, opium-smoking, and gambling.[44]

Sam's writing not only criticized the extended family residence pattern that encouraged many of Yitang's brothers to depend upon wealth left by the older generation, but also revealed his observations of Western family values.

But residence patterns were not the sole reason for the decline of the Chang family. As the above letter indicates, many of Yitang's brothers failed to adapt to the changing Chinese society and develop a skill or competence with which to support their families. After the imperial civil service system was officially abolished, the traditional *shuyuan* were gradually closed or transformed into modern schools. The scholarly degrees held by Chunli's children, and the classical Chinese education they had acquired, were not useful anymore for upward social mobility. To maintain their elite social and economic status, Chunli's children needed to learn alternative skills or professions.

As Sam pointed out, gambling, opium smoking, and concubines were common life styles for the rich in traditional Chinese society. Such life styles often contributed to the decline of an elite family. For example, local bandits once held Yitang's third eldest brother. While the other family members tried to raise funds for his release, the captured brother's own son attempted to use the money raised—to marry a concubine. In this case, the father's life was less important than the son's lust.[45] Several letters in the Sam Chang family collection described similar examples, and indicate that many children and grandchildren of Chunli failed to learn a useful skill, while living a parasitic life. Spoiled by affluent circumstances, they relied entirely on the wealth left by Chunli Chang, and had no aspiration to further develop family wealth. In later years, as the Chang family declined, two of Sam's aunts actually died of hunger.

Conclusion

Instead of self-sufficient farmers, Zhandong and Chunli Chang were probably speculative, entrepreneur landlords. Their life stories allow us to see important characteristics in rural Guangdong. Rural markets were important commercial centers; schools were popular in villages, as social mobility required education and literacy played an important role in daily farming activities. The rise of the Chang family wealth enables us to see the ancestral hall and village school as two important institutions in rural China. While an ancestral hall was a symbol of wealth and power, school functioned as a pipeline to deliver more talented children to advanced education away from home. As the ultimate goal of education was to pass civil service examinations and become government officials, school life acquainted rural children with a national culture and prepared them for sojourning life in the future. Education in a way linked the rural society to the outside world, and shows how Chinese society was relatively open, less stratified, and status-fixed than in stereotypes. But family was the foundation of both institutions.

The fall of the Chang family wealth allows us to understand how filial piety and moral obligation to the family bound male siblings together and gave them a sense of roots and identity. Equal inheritance rules, on the other hand, embroiled male siblings in intense competition for parental favoritism and family property. In a polygamous family, concubines or younger wives were often bullied when the patriarchal head of the family passed away, though theoretically their sons were also entitled to family property. Since diminution of family land tended to cause inevitable decline in social and economic status, family members needed either to compete vigorously in farming management and capital accumulation or to seek alternative means of social mobility. Such alternatives included entry into officialdom through education, entering professional and business careers, or becoming craftsmen and other specialists, either locally or elsewhere. With a long and historic contact with the outside world, migration could certainly become another rational choice for people in rural Guangdong.

CHAPTER 2

Yitang as a Merchant Immigrant

*Y*itang left his home village for Guangzhou (Canton) in 1884. However, his departure did not necessarily mean a breakaway from his family roots and kinship relationships in his home village. Nor was his leaving entirely due to the intense family feuds; in fact, his mother, wife, and children still lived in the home village. Yitang's venture into the urban, and later overseas, arena of opportunity was more embedded in the Chinese sojourning tradition, a quest for social mobility. In Chinese culture, ambitious men often spent their formative years away from home—studying (or taking examinations as scholars), holding office as government officials, or engaging in business in metropolitan centers. A successful scholar, businessman, or laborer sojourning away from home often obtained respect from fellow villagers, as he brought home money and fame. The structure of social hierarchy, and the family system in Chinese society, encouraged or pressured ambitious young men to explore such opportunities in other places and to strive for success. And if Yitang successfully established himself elsewhere, this could improve his embattled position as a son of the youngest wife of Chunli.

Yitang left home at eighteen years old and found a job as an apprentice in an herbal store in Guangzhou. According to an immigration file, he was a "drug merchant at Yuk Gee Hong, Canton, China; and also once worked in Yu Sin Chung Co. a clothing store in Hong Kong, China."[1] Another immigration file for Yitang indicated that his father-in-law, Quan Quock Sing, operated a Wing Hing Lung store in Hong Kong.[2] In spite of its different spelling, this is probably the same store that Yitang had worked in, in Hong Kong, after he left his home village. His apprentice position in the herbal store indicates that he had obtained some medical knowledge before he left home. In traditional Chinese society, many families possessed herbal medical knowledge, to take care of their own health problems, and would pass it on from generation to generation. Yitang had probably learned the skill from Chunli, and now used it to find his first job away from home.[3] While working as an herbalist, Yitang also tried to get an assistant position to a Chinese diplomat in the United States.[4] Failing to get the diplomatic position, he went to Hong Kong to do silk import-export trade for awhile, then returned to Guangzhou to continue his herbal business.[5] Apparently a government job was still attractive to Yitang, as he was an educated person from a gentry-landlord family background. The United States was also a familiar name in Guangdong, as many Cantonese had migrated there since the early 1850s. In fact, migration was one of the major reasons the Chinese government agreed to establish diplomatic relationship with the United States, in 1878, and sent diplomats there. Racial riots against the Chinese and racist immigration laws in America were urgent issues to be negotiated and handled between the two governments. Most early Chinese diplomats sent to America were Cantonese in origin.

Yitang was the only son of Chunli to translate his herbal medical skills into a profession. Although herbal medical skills were useful in maintaining the health of family and friends and, of course, oneself, the social status of herbal physicians could not be compared with positions as government officials and did not command the same respect in Chinese society. While other sons of Chunli were thus not interested in learning herbal skills, Yitang understood the potential of such a profession and the market demand for medical care.

In late nineteenth century, the metropolitan Guangzhou possessed a booming medical community. John Kerr, a longtime missionary in Guangzhou, wrote a guidebook to the city that included a long list of Western medical hospitals and Chinese herbal dispensaries.[6] Sponsored by wealthy merchant guilds, and sometimes called charity houses, Chinese hospitals also functioned as orphanages, served as homes for disabled people, or provided free meals for beggars. Fangbian yiyuan ("Convenience Hospital"), one of the largest charity houses in Guangzhou, received over ten thousand patients annually.[7] Although Yitang did not work for these medical institutions, his herbalist career in Guangzhou was successful. Shortly after he opened his own business, he sent for two nephews from the home village to work as assistants. With the profit from the herbal business, Yitang was able to purchase several housing properties in the city and bring his children from the rural village to live, and attend schools in, Guangzhou. In his career choice, Yitang demonstrated a greater flexibility and motivation than his brothers as he explored opportunities outside the home village. It is this greater flexibility and motivation that later led him on the path of migration while most of his other siblings remained in China.

While working as an herbalist in Guangzhou, Yitang kept watch for education opportunities for his children.[8] To adapt to social changes in Chinese society, his children, he made sure, received an education different from his schooling in the home village. The traditional education provided by the Chang family school was no longer adequate for a good career in early twentieth-century Chinese society. The late Qing government carried out a series of social reforms including education reform, and the government itself began to take graduates from the new schools for employees. Yitang was fully aware of such social changes, and, with his herbal income, sent his children to the newly established modern schools. His eldest son, Sam Chang, first went to an occupational school in Hong Kong, studying mathematics and business English for a year. Later he gained admission into the Police Academy of Guangdong. Yitang's second son, Weizong, went on to the College of Administration and Law (Zhengfai Xuetang), the most famous modern school in Guangdong Province in the 1910s.[9] Both sons found very good jobs, after graduation. Sam became a police judge for the Guangzhou city government and Weizong served as a local government judge in Zhaoyangluo District. Yitang's migration from the rural area to the city provided opportunities of social mobility for his children as well.

In 1900, sixteen years after he settled down in Guangzhou, Yitang decided to move again, this time to the United States. Sam Chang's letters offered no explanation on Yitang's motivation to go abroad. Considering his successful herbal business, he was obviously not pushed by poverty or unemployment. A family flyer on his seventieth birthday celebration attributed his motivation to a sense of responsibility and obligation to the Chang clan. According to the flyer, before Yitang left for America, the clan requested him to return to the home village and manage the clan property, since the eldest brother had long been away from home, serving the government in another county. The flyer indicatd that the Chang clan's economic situation in the village had become troubled while Yitang's herbal business prospered. Yitang's response was that he found his herbal business too small to meet the financial needs of the Chang clan, then over one hundred people. As he had heard that "the United States was the richest country in the world, he decided to explore opportunities for the clan across the Pacific."[10]

Although the flyer did not specify why Yitang went to America, it described his trip as an effort to help the Chang clan's economic situation. Yitang left not to get away from home, but to increase his power in the Chang clan. Even though he had conflicts with his siblings, he remained interested in family and clan affairs. His herbalist career in Guangzhou had already gained respect from his siblings and their families in the home village. Moreover, Yitang was still entitled to an equal share of his father's landed property, and, unless he stayed involved in family affairs, he could not have complete control of his share. When the Chang clan requested him to return, this acknowledged how his successful herbal business had enhanced his position. If he could further expand his herbal business across the Pacific Ocean, he might gain more power over lineage affairs. Thus, instead of a reckless break from old social relations, migration was, for Yitang, a rational choice based on aspirations for social advancement, and an endeavor for the collective interest of the family.

At the time, California was a familiar name to most people in Guangdong. Many Chinese had migrated there as early as the mid-nineteenth century. A trip from Guangdong to California was not too inconvenient; monthly and bimonthly transportation service from Hong Kong to San Francisco was available year round. A one-way trip took about thirty-five to forty-five days and cost between forty and sixty dollars, a considerable amount for a working-class immigrant but manageable for a merchant like Yitang. Even after the U.S. Congress passed the Chinese Exclusion Act of 1882, American shipping companies still advertised in Chinese newspapers. In the early twentieth century, they even updated their fleets with larger and faster ships, such as the *Mongolia* and *Manchuria*.[11]

When Yitang left Guangzhou, he was thirty-four years old and a family man with a wife and three sons. With a thriving herbal business and several housing properties, he had already established a comfortable home for his family in Guangzhou. Obviously he did not plan to go to California as a laborer. Nor did he intend to settle there. In fact, Yitang's departure to Los Angeles paralleled in intent his migration from rural Guangdong to Guangzhou city. It was not so much an escape from poverty but an attempt to explore opportunities. Many Chinese immigrants at that time shared a similar goal. Their migration to the United States was not to relocate their home but to improve their social status.

Yitang in Los Angeles

Yitang arrived in California a fairly experienced business man. In addition to running his herbal medicine store in Guangzhou, he had traveled to

Hong Kong and accumulated trade and sales experience there. Like many Cantonese immigrants at that time, he had social networks in California to assist him. His wife had a relative in San Diego who could provide necessary information and accommodation upon his arrival.[12]

Interestingly, it is not family documents but Yitang's immigration files that provide an accurate record of his arrival in California. One of his files recorded that he was granted a Section Six certificate and left Hong Kong on 17 May 1900. The certificate was marked with a notation "Admitted Jul 6 1900 Br. S.S. STRATHGYLE San Diego, California W. W. Bowers Collector."[13] This certificate is a key document in Yitang's immigration papers. A "Section Six" certificate was issued only to merchant immigrants and, according to immigration laws at that time, merchant Chinese were still allowed to enter America. Yitang had to show this certificate every time he applied for a reentry permit so that he and his family members might visit China. The certificate was also a key document when he sponsored family members and relatives to come to America.

Yitang went through an immigration interview, in which he provided three names to the Immigration and Naturalization Service (INS) officer: Cheung Tsoi Shan (Zhang Caichen), Cheung Yick Hong (Zhang Yitang) and Cheung Pang Bing (Zhang Pengbing). In Chinese family culture, a man often has more than one name. Probably, "Cheung Tsoi Shan" was the name by which Yitang was addressed in his nuclear family, "Cheung Yick Hong" was used as his courtesy name on a formal occasion, and "Cheung Pang Bing" was his clan name. In immigration interviews, officers always asked Chinese men to state all their names, as a way to check their true identity.

Yitang landed in San Diego, carrying bolts of silk. The trip was uncomfortable as the ship was crowded, and he became seasick. On his first night's arrival, Yitang stayed with a distant relative who seemed to run a gambling joint, and had to wait until the games were over and then sleep on one of the tables.[14] Whoever that relative was, his aid indicates the importance of social networks in the migration process. It was not clear why Yitang carried bolts of silk. Perhaps he wanted to start a silk business, because of his clothing merchant experience in Hong Kong, or perhaps he merely used the silk to demonstrate his merchant status, as U.S. immigration laws strictly forbade the entry of Chinese laborers. It is also not clear why he entered the United States through San Diego, as Chinese travelers usually landed in San Francisco. In any circumstance, Yitang was very fortunate to be so smoothly admitted. His merchant status played a crucial role in his interview procedure in 1900.

Apparently unimpressed by San Diego, Yitang went north to Los Angeles. According to the 1900 Census, only 293 Chinese resided in San Diego, whereas Los Angeles had about 2,111 Chinese, constituting the fourth largest Chinese community in the United States.[15] If Yitang planned to practice herbal medicine in the Chinese community, Los Angeles was certainly a better choice. After he arrived in Los Angeles, Yitang joined an herbal business called Dun Sow Hong Company (Zan Shou Tang) located at 306 Marchessault Street, Los Angeles. The company had nine partners; most had invested in the business with $500 to $850, except Hom Dy Mon (Tan Jiman), the manager, and Yitang, a new partner, both of whom invested $1,000. The total capital was about $6,600.[16] Although Yitang was a new partner, most of the partners were probably not herbal physicians and only invested in the company when they found the herbal business profitable. A couple of partners also had "Chung" (Chang) as last name, and could be distant relatives who encouraged Yitang to purchase shares from a former partner. Although newly arrived, Yitang could play a vital role in the business, as a veteran herbal physician with sixteen years' practice in Guangzhou. He could bring over new medical knowledge or new herbal formulations. His experience in Guangzhou might help boost the store's reputation, as he could promote himself as having been a master herbalist in Guangzhou. When accepted as a partner, Yitang was able to gain a foothold in America and eventually establish his own herbal business in the Los Angeles area. His immigration status also became secure, since the INS recognized a herbalist career as having merchant status.

After spending four years in Los Angeles, Yitang went back to China for a visit. Some family documents provide a typical Chinese reason—to see his aging mother and the rest of the family. In his application for a reentry permit in May 1904, however, Yitang indicated that he wanted to bring over his third son Elbert (Cheung Tseung Yit, or Weiying). In a notarized statement, he described his son as an eleven-year-old boy born in 1894 and presently living in Niushan Village, Guangdong. He wanted the boy to "obtain an education in the English language, in order that he, the said Cheung Tseng Yit, may become a merchant."[17] To bring over his third son for an American education was probably Yitang's real purpose. To pass the arduous immigration process, he needed to convince the INS officers that he held merchant status himself and his son would become a merchant, as well. Yitang's decision to bring over Elbert indicates his confidence that he could make a living and raise a family as an herbalist in America. After four years' stay in America alone, he felt it time to bring over family members.

When Yitang returned to Guangzhou in 1905, his eldest brother had already died. But the second eldest brother still tried to get a larger share of Chunli's property. The Nine Families originally asked Yitang to negotiate a truce with the second eldest brother.[18] But the Three Families refused to compromise, and demanded land from the Nine Families. In fact, Yitang's return inflamed new conflicts, because the Three Families viewed his return as a move to continue the fight for lineage property. The Chang family feuds continued to be bitter and brutal. The second brother's son knew some local bandits and could get their assistance in the feuds. The two sides sometimes fought in court and sometimes resorted to physical battles. Each side also attempted to establish its own governmental connections. In one fight, the Three Families had the third and fifth brothers arrested by the county government. But, in another case, the Nine Families convinced the provincial authority to rule that family property should be divided evenly among the children of the spouses of Chunli, and that children of the first wife should not get twice as much as children of the succeeding wife and concubine. As the Three Families colluded with the local bandits, the family feuds sometimes escalated into military battles. Each side armed themselves with weapons. Each also had connections with the local government. In some feuds, bandits' attacks were invited by competing Chang family members or by other clans because of conflicts over land or housing property.[19]

In another county court fight, the Three Families, with their connections to county officials, had a brother in the Nine Families arrested. Seeing that bribery was helpful, the Nine Families used money to free the arrested brother and build up connections with government officials. When they could not win the fight in court, the Three Families contacted local bandits for possible revenge. To protect themselves, the Nine Families built a watchtower or a blockhouse against the bandits' attacks. They stayed in their houses by day but slept in the blockhouse at night. One day, the Nine Families caught an agent sent by the Three Families to steal weapons from the blockhouse, and had him executed by the county government. In revenge, the Three Families let the bandits kill two adult members of the Nine Families. Other members of the Nine Families were scared by this brutal revenge. To escape further bandit attacks and battles with the Three Families, dozens of the Chang clan fled the countryside. Yitang lent several thousands of Chinese dollars as a way to help them settle in Guangzhou, Hong Kong, or to emigrate abroad; many members of the Chang clan did go overseas. Yitang secured the loans by becoming mortgagee of his relatives' land. Some of these relatives eventually paid back their debts. Others forfeited their homes and property to Yitang, because they lacked cash and so had to give up their real estate properties.[20] Ironically, while Yitang's emigration experience helped him gain greater entitlement to land holdings in the Chang clan, the possibility of returning to the home village for retirement became slim because of the intensity of lineage conflicts.

The history of Yitang Chang's family illustrates how family politics affected life among rural people in Guangdong, why kinship organizations were important, and how such organizations were formed, split, and re-formed according to the interest of each nuclear family. In the Chang clan, though Chunli's sons shared one ancestor, the Nine Families and Three Families split into two kinship organizations and became two antagonistic groups. In another family letter, Sam mentioned that his wife's family was also divided into two factions, and that each side built its own blockhouse for self-protection.[21] Each side sometimes hired bandits to make surprise attacks on each other, especially when a member of the opposite faction was on his way to collect rent from tenant farmers or from housing property in the city.[22] Merciless infighting among male siblings, fragmentation of family property, and the continual splitting and regrouping of family or lineage organizations characterized rural life in Guangdong.

The bitter Chang family feud was one of the general symptoms of social disorder in Guangdong, which included opium smuggling, gambling, theft, prostitution, kidnapping, banditry, clan/lineage feuding, and warfare over land between the Cantonese and *Keijia* (*Hakka*, or "guest people"), an ethnic group that migrated to Guangdong from the north. According to historian Hugh Baker, rural Guangdong in the nineteenth century experienced serious social violence: "Fighting over water rights, over territorial boundaries, over personal insults, over business transactions in the market, over ritual benefits, over attempts to exploit or to throw off exploitation, over almost anything, could break out suddenly or could take place sporadically between long periods of smoldering distrust."[23]

Clan wars sometimes involved bandits, usually displaced peasants or unemployed urban laborers who carried out robbery, killing, or kidnapping at random. During this precarious period, it was also common practice for local bandits to kidnap family members of overseas Chinese and demand ransom money. Chinese language newspapers in the United States frequently carried news about kidnappings or robbery of overseas Chinese families in Guangdong Province, during this time. More organized outlaws had more permanent bases in the mountainous areas. Farmers in the rural area had to pay protection fees to keep the bandits away. The gentry and merchants often developed their own militia. As clan battles and ethnic warfare were endemic in Guangdong, villagers erected watchtowers, iron mail gates, high walls, mud embankments, and arms warehouses, and hired semiprofessional fighters.[24] The Kaiping area still preserves thousands of watchtowers built in the first half of the twentieth century.

In July 1906, Yitang returned to Los Angeles with his third son Elbert (Weiying). Elbert was eleven years old and had attended a village school for two years. However, he was rejected for admission when an immigration doctor diagnosed him as having symptoms of tuberculosis, and returned to China. The following year, Yitang's wife Guan (Quan) died of an illness. Elbert tried to join his father again in 1907. This time, he gained entry after being detained at the Angel Island immigration station for a few days. He traveled to Los Angeles from San Francisco by train. After his arrival, he first attended Grand Avenue School, then went to Polytechnic High School.[25] As Yitang wanted his son to study medicine, Elbert spent two years at the University of Southern California for premedical courses. Around 1918, he went to Georgetown University medical school in Washington D.C., and received his medical degree in 1923.

Upon Yitang's return from China, he continued his herbal medical business in Los Angeles. Family documents indicate that he was a hardworking physician. By day, he mainly served the non-Chinese patients in his residence/ office on Ninth Street. In the evening, he rented an office room above Tsui Fai Low Restaurant in Chinatown.[26] As mentioned earlier, the Chinese population in Los Angeles was just over two thousand by 1900. The Chinese concentrated in two areas, Chinatown (next to the plaza known as "Negro Alley"), and an area east of the Adams Boulevard district. As the plaza was Los Angeles's business center, Chinatown developed into a tourist center that served both Chinese and non-Chinese. By 1910, it was not only a residential area for the Chinese but had at least fifteen restaurants, many gift shops, grocery stores, herbalist offices, and Chinese organizations. The Chinese community in the East Adams Boulevard area, which gradually expanded to Ninth Street, consisted mainly of farmers or laborers in the produce business.[27] As Yitang did not have a car yet, he took a bus from Ninth Street to Chinatown. He worked there from seven in the morning to nine in the evening. Most of his evening appointments were with Chinese patients, as Chinese small businessmen and laborers had not finished work until then.[28]

Yitang's Second Marriage

Yitang's herbal business also gave him an opportunity to establish a new family. He became acquainted with the family of his second wife, Nellie Yee, through his service in Chinatown. When Nellie's elder sister was sick, Yitang paid a house call, since women in Chinatown usually remained at home, especially at night. According to Nellie, Yitang knew her father long before he met her, and left a good impression on his future father-in-law. Nellie's recollected in an interview that Yitang "didn't smoke and didn't drink, he was a good man. He was educated and could take pulses, he was a doctor."[29] But, as was common in traditional Chinese culture, Nellie did not see her prospective husband before the marriage. When Yitang came to see Nellie's eldest sister, who was very sick, Nellie only heard him walking upstairs.[30] Nellie's father soon sent a relative to ask if Yitang would like to marry his youngest daughter. As his wife in China had passed away, Yitang happily agreed.[31]

Yitang married Nellie Yee (Yu) on 2 June 1910. He was already forty-four years old, while Nellie was twenty-two. During this period, women only made up a small percentage of the Los Angeles Chinese community. The U.S. Census of 1910 recorded 2,455 men but only 147 women.[32] Yitang was fortunate to be able to form a new family. Restrictive immigration laws made it very difficult for Chinese immigrants, even merchant-class immigrants, to bring their wives and children to America. Meanwhile, many laboring-class Chinese in America were too poor to support a family and thus had had to leave theirs in China.

Yitang's herbal store and his stable income as a merchant assured Nellie and her parents that he could raise a family. In 1900, forty out of the fifty Chinese families with children in Southern California were headed by businessmen. By 1910, 90 percent of Chinese children were growing up in business families. The average age difference between Chinese husbands and wives in Los Angeles in 1910 was 14.4 years.[33] Yitang and Nellie's marriage is fairly representative of Chinese families in Los Angeles at that time.

Nellie was born on 24 September 1888 in Ventura, California. Her father, Qizhang Yu (Yee Yee Hay or Yee Kay Hung), had emigrated from Taishan County to the United States in the 1860s. Yu was a skilled labor immigrant. He had been a carpenter in China, but learned cooking skills in Hong Kong before he arrived in the United States. He married Chen (Chun), a Chinese woman from Nanhai County, in Ventura. They had two sons and two daughters. But the eldest son died shortly after birth, and Nellie's mother passed away when the girl was only six years old. In the United States, Yu worked as a cook for Chinese tenant farmers. He usually went out with the labor gangs to harvest wheat in Ventura County in the summer, and did not come home until September.[34]

After her mother passed away, Nellie stayed with her eldest sister, Emily, who married Lum Joe, a Chinese cook working for a white Los Angeles city official, Mark Jones. When Nellie's father retired from cooking, he settled down in Los Angeles and lived with Emily and Lum Joe in Chinatown. They rented a house at 521 Apablasa Street, which, together with the streets Marchessault, Alameda, and Los Angeles, housed many Chinese families and businesses.[35] Nellie's father was already over seventy years old and only did a little carpentry. Emily worked at home. She sewed buttons and made cigarettes, mainly for Chinese customers. Nellie remembered her sister bringing cases of tobacco home, sprinkling it with tea, mixing it well, and then covering it with a lettuce leaf or a piece of cloth until it was damp. Then Emily would cut papers into small pieces, roll cigarettes with tapes, heat them up with some paste, and put bundles into a pack. It sold for one dollar per pack. When Nellie stayed with her sister, she helped with rolling cigarettes and with family chores.[36] Nellie belonged to one of the few laboring-class Chinese families in the Los Angeles area. Her life tells us that, instead of going to school, children of such families often worked at home with their parents.

Nellie's life indicates that Chinese American women often lived in seclusion. Influenced by traditional Chinese culture, young and unmarried women avoided public social life. Even the grocery shopping, Nellie recalled, was done by her father, her brother, brother-in-law, or the children of her elder sister. Occasionally, Mrs. Findlay, a white missionary woman in Chinatown, also came to help with the shopping. Nellie seldom went out of her house, because there were frequent "tong wars" in Chinatown, in which Chinese gang organizations fought each other over drug or prostitution or smuggling.

While living with her sister, Nellie had a famous downstairs neighbor, Wu Panzhao (Ng Poon Chew)—a well-known Chinese American newspaper operator of the turn of the twentieth century. At that time, Wu was operating a translation business and running a newspaper called *Wah Mei Sun Bo* (*Chinese-American Morning Paper*).[37] On Sunday, Wu would bring Nellie and her brother, together with his own children, to a Chinese Presbyterian church and Sunday school on Wellington Street. Such activities were meant not only for religious but also educational purposes, as public schools were not open to Chinese children in the late nineteenth century. Nellie's parents also had Mrs. Findlay teach her at home. Findlay taught many Chinese women English, and even arranged for Chinese children to attend public schools once the racial environment improved. With Findlay's assistance, Nellie was able to complete a third-grade education and was probably one of the small percentage of Chinese women who could read and write. The 1900 census indicates that 73.6 percent of Chinese females in California then could not read or write English.[38] However, scholars should be cautious when they interpret the level of English proficiency among Chinese American women, and should not ignore the fact that many public schools in the late nineteenth century did not accept Chinese children. In 1884, Chinese parents Joseph and Mary Tape fought a hard legal battle to get their daughter admitted into a public school in San Francisco. Although the Supreme Court ruled in the parents' favor, San Francisco's city government built a segregated school in Chinatown for their daughter and other Chinese children.

Contact with the Christian religion influenced Chinese American lifestyle, as well. The marriage of Yitang and Nellie followed both Western and Chinese traditions. At the wedding, Nellie wore a Chinese wedding gown and headdress. Both Chinese and white guests were invited.[39] The couple was married by Edward Locke, a Methodist minister.[40] Her marriage to Yitang, an immigrant not eligible for citizenship, also meant Nellie would lose her U.S. citizenship status. In October 1932, Nellie petitioned for her citizenship and was approved, following the amended Immigration Act of 1922.[41]

After his second marriage, Yitang moved to a slightly larger house, on Hill Street. Growing up in a working-class family, Nellie had little difficulty adjusting to a working woman's role after marriage. She quickly learned how to handle almost every aspect of the herbal business while being responsible for the heavy household chores such as cooking and laundering. Although Nellie was born in the United States, she followed her mother in speaking the Four-District dialect, and probably could read a little Chinese. As a daughter of a laboring-class Chinese immigrant, Nellie's life reflects how an American-born Chinese woman had to obtain education outside of American public schools and had to learn Chinese to work in an ethnic business.

Ties with Home

With a new family, Yitang found that his life in the United States became stable. Nellie bore him four children: Lillian (Qiaoxin or Kow San) on 31 March 1911, Arthur (Weixun or Wei Soon in Cantonese) on 31 December 1913, Marion (Qiaoshang or Kow Shung) on 8 October 1920, and Marie (Qiaozhuang or Kow Shung) on 6 April 1927. By the time the last two daughters were born, the family had moved to 1322 South Hill Street.[42] By 1910, the average number of children per Chinese family in Los Angeles was 2.7.[43] Many a working-class Chinese American man in Los Angeles at that time had no family, or had a wife and children left in China.

With income from the herbal business, Yitang was not only able to raise a fairly large family but also to invest in an asparagus farm of twenty-five acres in North Hollywood, around 1915, in partnership with some relatives. When Sam Chang, his eldest son, arrived in the United States on a government mission that year, Yitang requested him to stay and assist in the family business. In a "chain migration" pattern, Yitang was also able to sponsor several dozens of relatives to the United States. One family document listed sons or grandsons and their wives of Yitang's first, third, fourth, fifth, and sixth elder brothers. Usually he sponsored male descendants of the Chang lineage and provided them with employment in his herbal business and asparagus farms.

As an herbalist, Yitang fit the category of merchant immigrant defined by the INS agency and had a right to bring his family members to America. However, many of the relatives he sponsored were not immediate family members. Yitang had to create false identities for them as immediate family. This is a typical "paper son" strategy used by many Chinese immigrants during the Exclusion period. Relatives or friends entered America in the name of immediate family members of a merchant immigrant or of an American-born Chinese. They were only sons or daughters of such Chinese on paper. Two relatives were admitted in the names of Yitang's sons in the early 1910s. One used Sam Chang's name and another used Yitang's second son Weizong's name (Chang Weizong or Cheung Tseng Gip).[44] Weizong never came to America, and passed away in 1927, while Sam came as a government official, without Yitang's sponsorship, and used a different name. As Sam and Weizong were holding good government jobs at that time, Yitang probably did not intend to bring them over. However, each time a relative came, Yitang had to make a personal testimony in front of immigration officers and find white witnesses to testify for his merchant status. Sponsorship was a complicated process and meant risks and obligations. Sponsored relatives were supposed to work in the Chang family's herbal or farming business. As Yitang and his relatives pooled their financial and manpower resources for economic survival, mutual help expanded and strengthened kinship solidarity. After Yitang's male relatives established their own businesses or purchased property, they could send for their wives and set up their own families.

Yitang could also create or purchase "paper son" slots, and provide opportunities, for his fellow villagers to come to America, though they needed to pay a fee for his sponsorship. In a letter of 1925, Sam wrote to his niece,

> The paper for your father's entry into America includes two sons. I have consulted with an attorney in San Francisco and was informed that we could use both slots. So ask your mother to sell one slot in the village at two thousand Hong Kong dollars. The buyer should pay the transportation and attorney fee in Hong Kong himself. It should be a one-time full payment to your mother with no refund if the buyer cannot get admitted. If we take care of everything, he should pay twenty-eight hundred to three thousand Hong Kong dollars and it can be paid after he arrives in America. If someone wants to buy, he should send a photo to me so that we can process the paper work. If you cannot sell it, I can find someone here to help sell it.[45]

Obviously, the letter refers to the "paper son" slots the Chang family created after Yitang had migrated to America. It is not clear if the Chang family made a deal or not. But the letter shows how Chinese immigrants sponsored their fellow countrymen during a period when a "paper son" slot was one of the few strategies Chinese could use in migrating to America. Many families in Guangdong used this strategy to successfully send young people to the United States during the Exclusion. As Madeline Hsu pointed out, the strategy illustrates "the losing struggle of government agents to impose rigid, nation-centered boundaries on the more fluid cultural, social, economic, and political realities of people who move around."[46] Although coming from an educated merchant background with a strong sense of family honor, the Chang family members, like other Chinese in America, did not see "paper son" as an ethical issue. It was simply a necessary mechanism to get relatives and friends over to America. After those relatives arrived, they naturally banded together, with Yitang as the lineage leader.

Yitang's herbalist career in Los Angeles and sponsorship of relatives to America greatly built up his reputation in his lineage and home village. Around 1916–17, Yitang's relatives in China proposed to build an ancestry hall in the village to honor his sponsorship of relatives to the United States and his financial assistance in times of difficulty. As mentioned before, building an ancestral hall for an outstanding member of the lineage is an important Chinese tradition and was especially prevalent in Guangdong, as lineage organizations used the ancestral hall to strengthen kinship solidarity. It is interesting that it took about the same time (sixteen years) for Yitang to establish himself in Los Angeles as for him to do so in Guangzhou. Migration to America in this way paralleled his migration from a rural village to a city in China. Both were endeavors to explore opportunities away from home, and in each it took considerable time to establish himself in a new social setting. But kinship relations and commitment to home remained unchanged. To his relatives, Yitang's migration displayed his courage and vision; and his personal achievement was also a collective asset to the Chang lineage. For Yitang, his American journey gave new opportunities for his herbalist skill and ambition to pursue a successful career. Instead of a break from home, Yitang's emigration was a bridge that enabled the kinship network of the Chang family to transplant and expand itself from China to the United States.

After proposing to build an ancestral hall in Yitang's honor, the lineage collected money to buy a piece of land, plant trees along the side, and name the plot Huai Yuan (the Beholder Garden). Sam, as the eldest son, was invited to write a biographical sketch of his father, to be engraved on the tablet in the temple. The tablet listed the following as Yitang's great achievements:

> When he heard that America was the wealthiest country in the world, my father decided to go there alone. He did business there for three years, until he needed to come back to take care of his aging mother. He also sent his children to modern schools, as he believed that only reforms could make China strong. Following father's instruction, Weixi went to the Advanced Police Academy of Guangdong; Weizong went to the Guangdong College of Law and Administration. Weiying went to the medical school at Georgetown University. Weixun and Qiaoxin graduated from Los Angeles High School in the United States. When father was thirty-eight, he returned to the United States. He has been in America for sixteen years and has managed to bring twenty to thirty relatives to America.[47]

To have an ancestral hall built in his name was indeed a great honor for Yitang. Only men of outstanding achievement or contribution to the lineage or clan were considered to deserve such an honor. In most cases, an ancestral hall was constructed after a person's death. Out of high respect to Yitang's contributions to the Chang clan, his siblings and their family members built a hall in his honor while he was still alive. Following Chinese tradition, Sam listed the education of Yitang's children as his first important achievement. In Chinese culture, a successful man was not completely successful unless he raised his children well and saw them through a good education. This indicates how important education of children was as a parent's responsibility and obligation in Chinese family culture.

Sponsorship of relatives to America became another important accomplishment of Yitang. In Chinese society, a clan not only represents kinship relations but also functions as a social organization. In the case of the Chang family history, evidently the Nine Family members attempted to unite with Yitang as the center, when they decided to build an ancestral hall in his name. If the scrambling for clan property made the Chang clan a divided house, Yitang's migration abroad helped family members to reorganize. When bandits attacked the Nine Families members and drove them from their home village, Yitang's financial assistance helped them to settle elsewhere, or to immigrate to the United States through his sponsorship. This shows how rural people of the same ancestry grouped and regrouped themselves from time to time according to social circumstances and economic interests. As Frederic Wakemen points out, "Since the tablets hung in the cz-tang [or ancestral hall] had none of the immanent sanctity of the actual ancestral tablets in the domestic shrine, they represented ascribed social values, not personal religiosity. These tablets actually conferred genuine social status on those enshrined there, and on their descendants who came to pay ritual respect."[48]

More than a symbol of kinship solidarity, an ancestral hall was often used as a meeting place for clan affairs and a school for the clan or village children. Yitang later asked his relatives to use his ancestral hall as a free classroom for the children of the Chang lineage and children of poor families. Such generosity further enhanced his reputation in the home village. As the tablets listed Yitang's migration abroad as a great accomplishment, it demonstrates how people in Guangdong valued migration as another social mobility channel, like attending schools for civil service examinations, pursuing government positions, or engaging in domestic or international trade. As with these channels, personal success achieved during overseas migration was often viewed as an achievement benefiting the clan collectively.

CHAPTER 3

Herbal Medicine as a Transplanted Culture

*W*hen Yitang became a partner of the Dun Sow Hong Company and began his promising career as an herbalist in Los Angeles, the market in Chinese herbal medicine was thriving. Yitang practiced herbal medicine for almost fifty years. This profession allowed him to claim membership in the immigrant merchant class, gave him the right to sponsor other family members to America, and enabled him to see all of his children and most of his grandchildren through college. The herbal business played a key role in the immigration history of the Chang family. As mentioned in the previous chapter, Yitang successfully brought over his third son Elbert and two other relatives. With profits from his herbal business, Yitang invested in a farm and helped his eldest son Sam establish merchant status so that Sam could bring over his wife, daughter, and two children of Yitang's second son. Although the monetary value of the Chang family farms was higher than that of the herbal store, Sam claimed he was an herbalist, rather than a farmer, in his immigration testimony, since farming often involved manual work and thus the INS was more likely to grant merchant status to herbalists than to farmers. The special nature of the herbal business, as well as the privilege provided by its merchant status, gives it a unique interest among stories of family life and success in the early Chinese American community.

Yitang's herbalist career represents a tale of personal success while revealing details of an important occupation in Chinese American history. Although little has been written about them, Chinese herbalists were a significant part of American medical history during this period. They provided an almost indispensable medical service to both the Chinese and the non-Chinese communities in California from the mid-nineteenth century to the first half of the twentieth century. The history of herbal medicine shows how an ethnic culture gained foothold in American society. Early Chinese immigrants in the second half of the nineteenth century possessed desirable labor and professional skills when they worked in mining, agriculture, manufacturing, trade, business, and railroad construction; however, when recessions occurred, racist social movements quickly drove them into ethnic ghettos. They were then forced to engage in whatever menial and service occupations white people were unwilling to pursue; as a result, Chinese typically found themselves working as laundrymen or cooks. Ironing and cooking became trademarks of their ethnicity even though many Chinese picked up these skills only after arriving in America.

Herbal medicine, however, was a true ethnic skill. A journal article of 1899 claimed the herbalist as "the only professional man who has invaded our shores from the Flowery Kingdom."[1] In spite of finding themselves in a society hostile to their ethnicity, many Chinese herbalists still managed to become successful petty capitalists through their thriving businesses. Herbal medicine is one of the rare instances in which the Chinese made their living with a true ethnic skill for a prolonged period.

The history of Chinese herbal medicine in America is also of interest because most of the clients of the herbalists were Caucasians. Herbal medicine clearly demonstrates a point of intersection between mainstream America and Asian culture, and shows how Caucasian patients adapted themselves to an Asian therapy.

Chinese herbal stores began to appear as soon as the Chinese arrived in the United States. Medical knowledge was popular in Chinese society, as medicine had long been considered a "benevolent art," and medical skill was important for the proper fulfillment of filial duties in Chinese family culture. Many literate Chinese immigrants probably possessed some medical knowledge and knew how to cure minor disease or injury with herbal medicine.[2] In 1964, the Son Loy Company of San Francisco donated to the Chinese Historical Society of America three sub-basements' worth of personal items belonging to Chinese pioneers who had left them with the store for safekeeping at the turn of the century. Of the many boxes and trunks opened for examination, almost all contained some Chinese herbs or medicines.[3] Early Seattle Chinese immigrants benefited collectively from an herbal recipe book that contained the best personal recipes of the members of the Chinese community. Although the book originally belonged to the Wah-Chong Company, founded in 1868, it was community property and served everyone when no professional herbalists were available.[4] Both of these examples demonstrate the popularity of herbal medical knowledge among Chinese immigrants.

According to Paul Buell and Christopher Muench, herbal doctors were among the early Chinese immigrants who arrived in the 1840s and 1850s.[5] Among the eighty-eight San Francisco Chinese businesses listed in a business directory in 1856, fifteen were pharmacies and five were herbal doctors. This number was second only to that of grocery stores (thirty-eight).[6] Photos of Chinatown in San Francisco before the 1906 earthquake included pictures of herbal business.[7] Clearly, herbal medical practice was an important part of early Chinese immigrant life.

Historian Liu Pei-Chi (Boji) wrote that every Chinatown had at least one herbalist shop in the late nineteenth century, and many had three to four shops.[8] Fiddletown of Amador County, California, still preserves the Chew Kee Herbal Shop as a historic site. This store was established by herbalist Fund Jong Yee in 1851 and operated for fifty-three years. During the Gold Rush, approximately five thousand to ten thousand Chinese miners lived in Fiddletown.[9]

The herbal trade was transnational by nature, and a highly specialized business, requiring the manufacture of medicine from hundreds or even thousands of indigenous herbs gathered on the mountains and in the valleys of China. To facilitate passage of Chinese medicines through U.S. customs, the San Francisco Chinese Chamber of Commerce published a booklet of forms and labels for twenty-three basic types of herbs. The book was entitled *Liang Yao Zhao Zhi,* which roughly translates as "Food and Drug Labels."[10] As early as 1878, there were eighteen wholesale herb companies in San Francisco's Chinatown, which imported herbs from China and distributed them to Chinese herbalists throughout the United States.[11]

Herbal practice also developed in states other than California. An article, "Chinese Drug Stores in America," in the *American Journal of Pharmacy* of December 1887 noted that there were at least four herbal shops in Philadelphia and: "day and night their clerks are busy, weighing and pounding and tying up packages for the relief of their suffering countrymen."[12] This article provides a fairly detailed description of how herbal medicine operated in America, and appears based on careful observation of Chinese herbalists in the metropolitan cities of the East Coast. *Overland Monthly,* a San Francisco–based journal, carried an article in 1869 that noted: "The Chinese, wherever they go, are followed up pretty closely by men professing to be skilled in the healing art." It adds, "Judging from the number of their apothecary stores, one would suppose that the Chinese were large consumers of medicines."[13] In more recent scholarship, Jeffrey Harlow and Christine Richardson have researched Chinese herbalists in Oregon, and Paul Buell and Christopher Muench have written about herbalists in Seattle and Idaho.[14] Clearly, herbalists were always part of the Chinese immigrant community.

The service provided by herbalists was a source of cultural comfort to the early Chinese immigrants. Patients could communicate easily with the physicians about their symptoms; besides, drinking herbal tea was a familiar treatment used by the Chinese for several thousands of years. According to Chinese historian Liu Pei Chi, early Chinese immigrants believed in Chinese traditional medicine far more than in Western medicine—hence the rise of herbal shops and practice.[15] Chinese immigrants usually tried herbal medicine first, unless the sickness required surgery. However, Western medicine was not totally foreign to the Chinese, especially to those from the Guangzhou area. There, missionary hospitals had begun to appear during the 1840s. By 1905, there were 166 Western hospitals and 241 clinics in China. Meanwhile, China established a number of Western medical colleges.[16] In his book *A Guide to the City and Suburbs of Canton,* the early missionary doctor John Kerr recorded many medical institutions affiliated with Western missionaries.[17]

It should be noted that herbal medicine was probably the only treatment available to the early Chinese immigrants in America. These immigrants were denied access to public medical facilities and treatment, while simultaneously accused of harboring hidden threats to American health. Public health issues were often the most powerful arguments brought forward to exclude the Chinese during anti-Chinese campaigns. Racist Caucasian doctors blamed the Chinese for "ignoring all laws of hygiene and sanitation," and "thereby endangering the welfare of the state and of the nation."[18] Chinese passengers were regularly subject to medical examination upon entry into this country; Chinatown was frequently inspected for disease and placed under quarantine. These tactics were intimidating and humiliating to the Chinese community.[19] Several times, Sam Chang expressed his resentment over this harassment. In 1922, he wrote:

> Recently the new quarantine officers at the customs were even stricter than before. Many Chinese passengers were denied entry. In the past, people sometimes could use bribery to get in, but not anymore. Anti-Chinese movements are also rampant in Mexico and Canada. In this chaotic world, Chinese belong to a weak nation and cannot go anywhere.[20]

In 1870, although San Francisco's Chinese population constituted five per cent of the total city population, only a token number were admitted into the health facilities operated by the city and county.[21] The Chinese patients were usually "shunted off to a smallpox or pest hospital or to a special building, originally operated exclusively for the Chinese and later designed as the Lazaretto or Lepers' Quarters."[22] Under these circumstances, the Chinese community was compelled to take action on its own.

By the late nineteenth century, San Francisco's Chinatown had become the largest Chinese community in America. In order to meet the needs of their own people, each clan or district organization set up a clinic for its own aged and ailing members.[23] The Chinese Six Companies also had planned to establish a general hospital in Chinatown as had the French and German communities. But the city authorities repeatedly rejected and delayed the plan. Finally the Chinese Six Companies managed to establish a Tung Wah Dispensary, which opened in 1900 at 828 Sacramento Street.[24] The dispensary hired both Western physicians and Chinese herbalists. After a legal battle, Chinese herbalists were allowed to treat some diseases.

While the Six Companies were fighting hard to set up a general hospital for the community, individual herbalists opened their own practices to serve the needs of Chinese patients. As Chinese communities expanded, more and more professional herbal doctors, herbal stores, and dispensaries appeared. Most of the practitioners were professionally trained herbalists, although some individuals had obtained herbal knowledge informally. The professionals were often descendants from a long line of herbal practitioners or had studied under master herbal scholars in China. In Yitang's case, herbal medical knowledge was a family tradition. He had already practiced herbal medicine in Guangzhou before his arrival in America. His son Sam Chang had also spent a few years of study under Guan Chengbi, a famous herbalist in Guangzhou in the late nineteenth century, as part of his education.

Crossing Ethnic Lines: From Chinese to Caucasian Clientele

After opening practices in the Chinese community, Chinese herbalists started to attract Caucasian clients as well. Inadequate Western medical facilities, and the inability of Western medicine to effectively treat some diseases, as well as a lack of standardization of medical practice, were the main reasons for the prosperity of herbal businesses among both Chinese and non-Chinese communities. All kinds of alternative medical practices existed in the nineteenth century, and Chinese herbalists were not the only practitioners of unorthodox medicine. As William G. Rothstein has pointed out, "Before the twentieth century, very few curative or ameliorative therapies existed, and patients had little reason to prefer physicians' services to other treatments. Many patients used traditional medications."[25] Beginning in the early twentieth century, however, unorthodox medical practices performed mainly by Caucasians, such as chiropractic or botanical healing, gradually achieved legal status, while the Chinese herbalists were never granted licenses to conduct medical diagnosis. Since a medical practice required licensing, most herbal physicians promoted their business as selling herbs, although in fact they offered medical diagnosis and therapy.

Ironically, herbal medicine is not a folk practice. In China, the Chinese refer to Chinese traditional medicine as "zhongyi" (Chinese medicine) and medical practice developed in Europe as "xiyi" (Western medicine). While not the world's earliest recorded medical system, Chinese medicine is "the oldest continuous surviving [medical] tradition, rivaled only by Ayurvedic medicine in India. . . . The earliest surviving pharmacopoeia, the Pen-ts'ao ching attributed to Shen-nung, was probably compiled in the first century B.C."[26] Through centuries of empirical experiments, Chinese medicine developed into a systematic body of medical knowledge, with complex theories and with specializations such as pharmacology, pulsology, acupuncture, and moxibustion. Diagnostic methods include visual observation, inquiry into case history, auditing symptoms, and the taking of the patient's pulse, or pulsology.[27] According to Buell and Muench, although there were all kinds of health practitioners in the western United States and Canada, "the traditional Chinese physicians were a vital part of the health care system for all of the frontier community. Chinese and non-Chinese alike employed their services, often preferring the Chinese medical approach to that of their Western doctors."[28]

It was usually the more established and aggressive Chinese herbal physicians who marketed their profession to Caucasian patients. An article, "Chinese Physicians in California," in *Lippincott's Magazine* in 1899 noted that mediocre herbalists did not attempt "to ply their vocation among the whites, but wisely confine their 'practice' to their own people."[29] As early as 1858, the herbal physician Hu Junxiao, also known as Wo Tsun Yuen, of San Francisco's Chinatown used English-language signs in his shop to attract Caucasian patients. According to Liu Pei Chi, the most famous herbalist at that time was Li Pu-tai (Li Potai) from Shunde County, Guangdong Province, who arrived in California during the late Gold Rush period. Li opened an herbal office in San Francisco on Washington Street, and had patients coming all the way from the East Coast. His office schedule was always booked. The same 1899 article from *Lippincott's Magazine* claimed that Li was "the first doctor to leave his countrymen and to go boldly among the whites, advocating his system of medicine and establishing a lucrative practice among Caucasians." The article also noted that Li's son and nephew were Chinese physicians in Los Angeles who spoke English readily and whose practice was exclusively among English-speaking people.[30]

In fact, many herbalists, like Li, had more Caucasian than Chinese patients. Barlow's book noted how herbalist Ing Hay began to increasingly cater to Caucasian clients as the Chinese population declined in East Oregon around 1900–10.[31] In 1933, herbalist Fong Wan wrote, in the foreword of his book *Herbal Lore*:

> The demand of Americans for Chinese herbs has for several years been steadily on the increase. Consequently, whereas some forty years ago the sale of Chinese herbs in the United States was confined almost wholly to the Chinese population, at the time of this writing, the American patrons far outnumber the Chinese.[32]

The growth of Caucasian patients shows the effectiveness of herbal medicine and its increasing popularity in American society.

In a book on Chinese herbalists in Oregon, Jeffrey Barlow and Christine Richardson noted that herbal medicine was far more successful in treating the ills and injuries of the frontier region than were the ministrations of conventional physicians at the turn of the twentieth century. Although Western medicine was helpless before the winter flu, herbal medicine kept the Chinese highway builders from becoming bedridden and enabled them to keep up with their demanding work schedule. Moreover, none of the Caucasian patients of the Chinese herbalist in John Day died during the 1915 and 1919 flu epidemics, which caused thousands of deaths in nearby Portland. Herbal medicine also cured patients suffering from meningitis, lumbago, mumps, colds, stomach ailments, hemorrhaging, and influenza.[33] In fact, Chinese herbal medicine is based on time-tested theories and has a long tradition of dealing with epidemics, which is probably why it was so effective a therapy for flu patients in Oregon.

Herbal medicine was not totally foreign to Caucasian Americans. As a social movement to oppose orthodox medicine, botanical healing, with its prominent leader Samuel Thomson, was quite popular in the early nineteenth century. But medical practice became more and more standardized in the second half of the nineteenth century, as Western medical schools, journals, and organizations were gradually established.[34] Traditional practitioners then came under increasing pressure from those practicing orthodox medicine. It is all the more remarkable that, in spite of this, Chinese herbal medicinal practice continued to grow, especially when one considers the racism toward the

Chinese at the time. It could have been quite a challenge for a Caucasian to trust, and take herbal teas, from a Chinese person. Herbalist Tan Fu-yuan claimed in his book that, "as a rule, Caucasians have been unwilling to consult us until they had tried every other form of medical treatment within their reach. Therefore, it may be said that all of the cures which we have made have been cases given up by other doctors."[35]

The effectiveness of his therapy helped an herbalist to win over not only Caucasian clients but also their friendship. Yitang invited some loyal clients to testify as witnesses in his immigration cases. The fact that they were white was of great help. Yitang's wife Nellie and son Arthur recalled, in their interviews, detailed information on how Yitang successfully treated some Caucasian patients.[36] Nellie remembered several difficult cases Yitang had handled. In one, a Caucasian man working for the Union Pacific Railroad had a boil in his chest. After four operations by Western physicians, his incisions from these operations on the boil still would not heal, but after seeing Yitang, at the recommendation of a friend, he was cured in two months. The Chang family also remembered "a coughing girl," the only daughter of a Caucasian woman: although several Western physicians had diagnosed her as having an incurable cough, the coughing girl became "a chubby girl" after taking Yitang's herbal tea. In the early 1930s, stomach ailments were common in California. Booklets by Chinese herbalists contained a number of testimonies from patients with stomach trouble. Many patients of Yitang also suffered from this problem. A stage manager at the Orpheum Theater and his wife came in together for treatment. The wife had such a badly upset stomach that she could not fall asleep and would pace around all night. After seeing Yitang several times, both were cured. Such patients were so impressed by Yitang's therapy that they became family friends. They brought their families to visit Yitang, and some were invited to attend Yitang's wedding party. Many of them began to take Chinese herbal teas for all their colds and coughs.[37] Writings by herbalists Tan Fu-yuan, Tom Leung, and Fong Wan also contain statements by their patients, who claimed that they received successful treatment when Western doctors could not cure their illnesses.

It is worthwhile to point out that Chinese herbalists treated Caucasians of both sexes. In an advertisement in the *Los Angeles Times* of 9 August 1887, an herbalist put "diseases peculiar to women" as one of his specialties. In another commercial, an herbalist listed the name of a supposedly well-known local Caucasian lady as one of his references.[38] In his book *Herbal Lore*, Fong Wan included a brief testimony by a Caucasian woman who explained how she got rid of several breast lumps after taking Fong's herbal medicine.[39]

In both Tan Fu Yuan and Tom Leung's books, there are sections on women's diseases. Garding Lui's book offered a theoretical explanation for women's health problems, in common language. The herbalist Ah-Fong of Idaho claimed women's diseases—including venereal diseases, infertility, and amenorrhea—as one of his specialties. Yitang took women patients, as well. That Chinese herbalists highlighted the treatment of women's diseases in their commercial promotions reflects that gynecology and obstetrics were important specializations in Chinese herbal medicine. Publication of medical texts, including herbal prescriptions on women's diseases, proliferated during the Qing period.[40] Many herbalists probably had read or possessed such prescriptions and could offer therapy to American women, while Western doctors felt helpless to treat certain symptoms.

In addition to the effectiveness of herbal medicine, there are several explanations for why Caucasian female patients went to see Chinese herbalists. One can certainly see the attraction for women of the noninvasive examination, in the form of feeling the pulse or observing the tongue. Herbalists usually did not ask a woman patient to undress in order to check their body. Delivering a baby was usually done by a female midwife rather than by a male herbalist, in Chinese society. The objective and nonmoralistic approach of the herbalists toward sexual matters, along with the social distance between the Chinese and the Caucasian community, would be other key reasons for Caucasian women's patronage. The unencumbered sex education and health advice to women in Garding Lui's book, and the sketch of the female body (reprinted from an ancient Chinese medical encyclopedia) included in Fong's book, clearly demonstrate both these points, as well as the professional attitude of the herbalists toward their female patients.[41] Health care provided by Chinese herbalists to white women illustrates a meaningful breakthrough of Chinese culture into American society. Chinese medicine was accepted, as an ethnic therapy, by both Caucasian male and female patients, during a period when Chinese males, like African Americans males, were often viewed as sexually interested in white women and thus threatening to white racial purity. Herbal medicine represented a genuine aspect of Chinese culture to ordinary Americans, a counterbalance to the stereotyped images of Fu Manchu villains from Hollywood movies, or of Chinatown as an exotic tourist destination.

Yitang and Other Herbalists in Southern California

As family, clan, and friends were the basis of social networks for Chinese immigrant communities, it is not surprising that some famous herbalists were related. Tan Fu-yuan was Li Pu-tai's nephew, and became his assistant in 1891. After Tan established himself in Northern California, he moved to Southern California with Li's son and opened an office in Redlands in 1893. Tan attracted many patrons and aroused jealousy from Western doctors, who began to attack his methods, and Chinese traditional medicine in general, as pseudoscience, in the *Redlands Citrograph,* the local newspaper. But the *Leader*, a rival local newspaper, published testimonials from Tan's patients warmly acknowledging his skill as a physician. Ironically, this pen war increased Tan's reputation and brought him more clients. In 1896, Tan opened another office, called Foo and Wing Herbal Company, in a large Victorian house at 903 S. Olive Street in Los Angeles.[42] He also had offices in Oakland and Boston. In 1899, Tan Fu-yuan sent for his cousin Tom Leung to be his assistant. Leung was a smart young man. In a few years, he quickly learned how to prescribe and dispense herbs, and was promoted from a cashier to vice president of the company. In 1914, Leung built a twenty-thousand dollar residence and office at 1619 W. Pico Street, and in 1918 he set up another office, at 711 South Main Street.[43]

It is difficult to determine the precise number of Chinese herbalists during this period. According to Garding Lui's 1948 estimate, there were more 120 herbalists in California by then, and one third were in Los Angeles.[44] Lui's estimate, while not necessarily accurate, indicated a prosperous herbal market in Southern California. Although it is hardly possible to verify Lui's estimate, the 1913 *International Chinese Business Directory of the World* listed twenty-eight Chinese herbal physicians in Los Angeles City.[45] This cannot be the complete number, as, for various reasons, many herbal physicians were not listed. In 1933, Chinese herbalists in Southern California had a professional conference in Los Angeles; although there was no written record, the photo of the conference (see the illustrations section of this book) included thirty-five herbalists of Southern California.

Yitang Chung's name was missing in the 1913 directory. A probable reason was that he was very careful about publicizing himself, to avoid harassment from Western medical organizations; however, he did advertise his herbal business through flyers and local newspapers. Meanwhile, the Din Au Tong store mentioned on the list is located at the same street address as Dun Sow Tong, in which Yitang was a partner in the 1900s; by 1913, the business may have been purchased by another herbalist and changed to a new name. While twenty-eight may not be the definitive count, there were at least several dozen Chinese herbalists in the Los Angeles area.

Using the 1913 *International Business Directory,* and assuming that at

TABLE 1   *The 1913 Directory*

Business	Address
Chinese Medical Co.	955 S. Hill St.
Bow Sui Tong, Drugs	319 S. Marchessault St.
Chinese Herbal Co.	433 S. Hill St.
Chinese Tea and Herbal Co.	1049 S. Main St.
Dai Sang Tong, Drugs	323 Marchessault St.
Din Au Tong, Drugs	306 Marchessault St.
Tom She Bin and Sons, Physicians	145–47 W. 22nd St.
Wong Company Sanitarium	713 Main St.
Fong Sue Nom, Physician	208 Marchessault St.
Foo and Wing Herbal Company, Medicines	903 S. Olive St.
(having moved from its old location, 929 S. Broadway)	
Gee Ning Tong, Drugs	514 Los Angeles St.
H. T. Chan, Physician	1045 S. Broadway
Hong Wo Tong, Drugs	212 Ferguson Alley
Kam Brothers and Co. Physicians	603 S Olive St.
Lum Wing Yue, Chinese Tea and Herbal Co.	819 S. Hill St.
Mon Yick Tong, Drugs	304 Marchessault St.
Mon Yuen Tong, Drugs	319 Apablasa St.
Po Sang, Drugs	320 Marchessault St.
Po Sow Tong, Drugs	319 Marchessault St.
Quan Tong, Herbal Company	716 S. Hill St.
Suey Gee Tong and Co., Drugs	757 N. Alameda St.
Sun Kam Lee and Co., Teas	418 W. 7th.
Wah Young Herbal Company, Drugs	936 S Broadway
Wing On Tong, Drugs	302 Marchessault St.
Yee Sing and Co., Drugs	322 Marchessault St.
Yick Yuen Tong, Drugs	759 N. Alameda St.
Young Woo Tong, Drugs	315 Apablasa St.

Source: International Chinese Business Directory of the World, 1413.

that time most Chinese people resided mainly on the Los Angeles streets of Marchessault, Ferguson, Alameda, and Apablasa, we find that about half of the Chinese herbal offices were located in Caucasian communities.[46] A list of actual companies and their addresses is given in Table 1. Like Chinese laundries and other small Chinese businesses, these offices were situated one block or so apart. This cluster, on a few streets close to downtown, could make the city of Los Angeles an herbal medical hub attractive to patients across Southern California. For example, some of Yitang's patients came from Anaheim in Orange County. Geographic concentration could cause competition but was probably not a major concern to herbalists, as each physician might have his own formulas, passed on from one generation to the next within the family. According to Ralph C. Croizier, "despite the large medical literature, much of Chinese medical knowledge was the private possession of the individual practitioner, who might transmit it to his son or disciple but would certainly not share it with his professional rivals."[47]

U.S. Census data indicate that the Chinese population in Los Angeles City from 1890 to 1920 was only around two thousand, dispersed in several neighborhoods rather than concentrated in Chinatown.[48] One can infer that, given the small size of the Chinese community, the large number of herbal physicians on the list strongly indicates that herbalists catered to the needs of both Chinese and Caucasian communities and many herbalists had more Caucasian than Chinese patients. According to historian Carey McWilliams:

> Much of the early medicine of the region was a combination of folk-healing, quackery, and superstition. Chinese herbal doctors still did a lively business when I first arrived in Los Angeles in 1922. . . . As late as 1870, Southern California had only one doctor in attendance at the annual meeting of the State Medical Society, and a local society was not formed until 1888. The vacuum created in the medical art was filled by Chinese herbal doctors, faith-healers, quacks and a miscellaneous assortment of practitioners.[49]

Here, McWilliams noted not only the medical market for Chinese herbalists, but also the existence of other nonorthodox practitioners. It is interesting to note that McWilliams himself was probably a patient of the highly regarded Yitang. The children of Yitang and Sam remembered McWilliams as an acquaintance of the family.[50]

Lack of Western medical facilities and doctors was likely the primary reason for the rise of Chinese herbal medicine among whites in Southern California. When Yitang became a partner in Dun Sow Hong Company (Zan Shou Tang), located at 306 Marchessault Street in Chinatown, he probably treated more Chinese than Caucasian patients. He soon opened his Chinese-American Herbal Corporation, at 917 South Hill Street outside Chinatown, so that he could attract more Caucasian patients. Since herbal medicine was part of his family tradition and he had already practiced it in China, he was confident of his skill and naturally wanted to expand his clientele base into the Caucasian community. His son Arthur recalled that Yitang "had more Caucasian customers than Chinese."[51] His wife Nellie also said that, in the first few years, her husband's patients were Chinese and later most were white: "Hardly any Chinese came."[52] As mentioned, Yitang's contemporaries, the herbalists Tan Fu-yuan, Tom Leung, and the son of Li Pu-tai, all had more Caucasian clients than Chinese. The herbal medicine business was also unique among Chinese businesses in that many practitioners had white partners. In Yitang's Chinese-American Herbal Company, four of eight partners were Caucasian.[53]

During Yitang's career, the Chang family moved several times but always lived outside Chinatown. He once established his herbal office in a shopping center on Ninth Street. Although there were Chinese and Japanese produce distributors, and a number of middle-class Chinese families, located there, the area was essentially a white neighborhood. Chinatown in Los Angeles was a community that survived without a large Chinese labor force, and it had a greater social acceptance by mainstream society and more frequent interactions with the non-Chinese community than had most Chinatowns of the period.[54] Different from other Chinese populations in the United States at that time, many Chinese in Los Angeles chose to live outside Chinatown. The third largest Los Angeles produce market, at Ninth and San Pedro Streets was mainly owned by Chinese and Japanese farmers and agribusinessmen; many Chinese merchants' offices and herbal shops in the area served both Chinese and Caucasian clients. William Mason noted that throughout the 1920s the Chinese were spreading from the old Chinatown into other parts of the city. The Chinese with families preferred to live in residential districts; only old single men still clung to the old Chinatown.[55]

As an experienced herbalist, Yitang had a variety of substitute formulae when a particular substance was not available. In addition, he established a working relationship with other Chinese herbal doctors in Chinatown in order to have a supplementary supply of herbs. Because of the long tradition of herbal medicine in China, trade in medicinal herbs was a highly specialized field, and was usually operated by people with herbal knowledge. As herbal medicine was also popular in other Asian countries, a few Japanese merchants also engaged in the herbal import business. Imports, however, did not always arrive in time.

Profits, Partners, and Promotion

Family documents do not have a record of how much Yitang made each month or year, though we can find some income figures from the immigration files on the Chang family. In an interview, Yitang stated that he spent two thousand dollars in 1906 to acquire the stocks of the Chinese-American Herbal Cooperation from a man called Mock Ku Yen, and that, under Yitang's own operation, the business revenue was about eight thousand to nine thousand dollars, with 20 percent profit, in 1910. He paid himself seventy-five dollars a month as salary and usually paid an assistant fifty dollars per month. In addition, he could have a dividend profit of three to four hundred dollars for every thousand dollars he had invested in the business.[56] Although he was not so rich as Li Pu-tai, Yitang was, as previously noted, wealthy enough to provide his family with a comfortable life and to see all his children through college. When business was good, appointments in his office were always full. Patients came from other towns—or even from other states, as the transcontinental railroad had been completed.

Yitang did not charge for a diagnosis, as he was fully aware that he was not a licensed doctor. He made his profit out of selling herbs. Usually he could provide one to two week's prescription for a patient. A week's prescription was about eight to ten dollars.[57] This was probably the standard charge by most herbalists during that period, other than to treat a symptom that required rare and expensive herbs. According to *Herbal Lore*, Fong Wan in Oakland charged the same price. Tom Leung, Yitang Chang's contemporary herbal physician and close friend, also charged ten dollars per week.[58]

Although not every herbalist became wealthy in America, herbal medicine was essentially a profitable business. Many herbal physicians lived a much wealthier life than did the average Chinese. Li Pu-tai was one of the wealthiest Chinese in San Francisco, with a yearly income of seventy-five thousand dollars. His office hours were often completely booked up, and many patients came from other cities or even other states. With his profits, he even built his own joss house, where he prayed for blessings from the god of wealth in Chinese culture. Li was also known as a notorious gambler and sometimes bet one thousand dollars in a game.[59] Fong Wan was a wealthy herbalist in the 1930s. His residence office on Tenth Street in Oakland was a big mansion with fancy furniture and ornaments. It was so glamorous that it attracted hundreds of visitors who just wanted a look at his house. One of his attendants' sole jobs was to take visitors on tours of the house. Tom Foo Yuen (Tan Fu-yuan), Tom Leung, Tan Fei-xuan, and Yitang Chang of Los Angeles, and Su Shao-nan of Denver were only a few of the famous Chinese herbalists of the time; each often had more than one office, and all built residential offices spacious even by contemporary California standards.

Some successful herbalists may have had the largest clientele, Chinese and non-Chinese, among all medical practitioners in the region at that time. Commenting on Tan Fu-yuan's company, the 1899 article in *Lippincott's Magazine* claimed that, with the possible exception of one or two well-advertised doctors, Tan had more patrons than any of the 350 physicians in Los Angeles. As poor people could not afford the high medical charges de-

manded by the herbalists, many patients were the well-to-do and their families—women, businessmen, lawyers, journalists, even physicians.[60]

The economic success of these herbalists reflected a pattern of medical practice different from that in China. For example, pharmacist and
pulsologist were often separate occupations in traditional China. The most
prestigious doctors in China were scholar-physicians who only offered their
services in royal courts or practiced their profession as a benevolent skill
among families and friends. Other practitioners made diagnoses, wrote prescriptions, and charged a therapy fee. In America, however, an herbalist was,
in the first place, a merchant. Although some herbal stores only sold herbals
according to prescriptions, most herbalists ran their own stores, wrote the prescriptions, and sold herbal medicine all at the same time. Pulse diagnoses
were usually free, because Chinese herbalists understood that they were not
allowed to practice as doctors. The herbalists were engaged in every aspect
of the trade from building commercial networks through the importation of
herbs to advertising their professions. In targeting Caucasian clients, some
herbalists actively used commercial advertising, publicizing their busines in
local newspapers. According to Ray Lou, commercial advertisements for Chinese physicians began to appear in Los Angeles local newspapers in the early
1870s; beginning in the 1880s, some included sketches of themselves mea-
suring the pulse of Caucasian patients. Some advertisements ran as large as
a half-page. It is certain that the herbalists also treated Mexican patients, since
some of these ads were printed in Spanish.[61] Although Yitang did not publi-
cize himself as a physician, his herbal business did advertise in local newspapers under the company's or his Caucasian partner's name. During his short
and unsuccessful herbalist career in Salt Lake City in late 1910, Sam Chang
advertised in almost every local newspaper. Among Sam's collection of family
papers, there are advertisements in Japanese and Greek. At the turn of the
century, Los Angeles had a fairly large Japanese community; in Salt Lake
City, there was a Greek community of considerable size.[62]

For commercial reasons and to defend themselves against racial stereotypes, the herbalists published books and pamphlets and distributed all
kinds of flyers. Tom Foo Yuen, a well-known herbalist in Los Angeles, published a book in 1897, *The Science of Oriental Medicine, Its Principles and
Methods*.[63] His former partner and later competitor Tom Leung published a
booklet called *Chinese Herbal Science* in 1928.[64] In Northern California,
Fong Wan of Oakland published his *Herbal Lore* in 1933.[65] And Lui Garding,
another Los Angeles herbalist, published *Secrets of Chinese Physicians* in
1943.[66] In plain and straightforward English, these books explained the

history, theory, and practice of Chinese herbal medicine. Leung's book even advocated establishing a college of herbal medicine. These books contained endorsements, support, and praise from Caucasian patients. More than commercial promotions, the publications were intended as rebuttals of racist criticism. Sensational newspaper writers of the nineteenth century often presented Chinese herbal medicine as relying on superstitious beliefs and involving sharks' fins, spider's eggs, dried toads, or dragon bones. The herbalists' printed materials reflect their resilient efforts to promote Chinese herbal medicine to American society as legitimate.

Working with Caucasian partners, along with hiring Caucasian interpreters and receptionists, was another strategy to reach Caucasian clients, and was a common practice among the more established herbal physicians. However, some interpreters that the herbalists hired knew little or no Chinese, let alone herbal medicine. The Chinese of Yitang's partner, a Mr. Holmes, was good enough to greet Chinese clients in Cantonese.[67] Tom Leung's interpreter, a Mr. Hallow, could not speak Chinese at all.[68] Such "interpreters" functioned more nearly as cultural intermediaries for the Caucasian clients.

The herbalists also liked to have Caucasian partners with medical licenses. Some herbalists hired Mexican women who could speak both English and Spanish, to target Mexican clients. And Caucasian employees could help the herbalists communicate with local newspapers about advertising, and with the courts, police, and attorneys when unfair charges were imposed on them.

When Yitang started his business, he chose Holmes as his Caucasian partner. Holmes had worked with a couple of Chinese herbalists and knew a little Cantonese. He was also a chiropractor, apparently, as he offered spinal adjustments in the advertising flyers. In the advertisement, Holmes was presented sometimes as the superintendent, or manager, and sometimes as a physician, while Yitang Chang was always the manager; with Holmes's license, Yitang's herbal business could take patients. Caucasian partners also played a role that no Chinese partner could play. They could serve as white witnesses in immigration issues. When Yitang applied for his reentry permit in 1904 for his visit to China, he submitted notarized testimony of three Caucasian friends. In 1911, Yitang applied for the admission of a relative who had landed on September 22 and was detained at Angel Island. In his testimony, Holmes claimed that he had known Yitang for eight years, and that Yitang was "the herbalist of the Chinese-American Herbal Co. for which I am the manager; and he attends to the buying and importing." Holmes also handled the leasing agreement of the company, as Chinese partners might have a hard time leasing or buying property in a white business area, especially after California passed the Alien Land Act in 1913. Yitang confirmed that Holmes had attended to leasing, when immigration officers interviewed him. In the testimony, Holmes had no hesitation to call himself a physician, but Yitang always carefully described himself as an herbalist with no right to diagnose patients but only the right to sell herbal medicine. However, the issue of merchant status was more important than the issue of medical titles, in immigration testimony. Mr. Knell, another white witness, accidentally referred to Yitang as a doctor several times in his testimony, but apparently in this instance it did not cause the immigration officer to fault Yitang. Of the eight partners of the Chinese-American Herbal Company operated by Yitang, four were Caucasians.[69]

Interestingly enough, chiropractice was also an alternative healing practice at that time. All practitioners not trained in medical schools following the orthodoxy medical principles transplanted from Europe were labeled "quacks" or "folk doctors," though, before the twentieth century, orthodox physicians, represented by the American Medical Association, could do little about these practitioners. Therefore, Chinese herbalists were not the only practitioners of unorthodox or nondominant medicine when they brought their profession to the United States. Commercial advertisements by the herbalists often appeared side by side with those of chiropractors. There were cases of chiropractors opening a practice together with a herbalist, such as that of Holmes working with Yitang for several years.

Beginning in the early twentieth century, however, healing systems performed mainly by Caucasians, such as chiropractic or botanical healing, gradually achieved legal status, while the Chinese herbalists were never granted licenses to conduct medical diagnosis. Hundreds of chiropractors were arrested for practicing medicine without a license in the early twentieth century. To fight for their legal status, Chiropractors Association of Alameda County, California, requested its members to protest by going to jail rather than paying a fine. In 1923, when public opinion favored the chiropractors, the governor of California pardoned all jailed chiropractors.[70] It is worth mentioning that there were Chinese chiropractors as well.[71] The shared alternative medical perspective served as a basis for the cooperation between herbalists and chiropractors.

Herbal Medicine as a Family Business

The herbal business is not a labor-intensive profession, but an herbalist still needs assistants to prepare and dispense medicines. In China, a pulsologist would only do diagnosis, leaving such miscellaneous tasks to a pharmacist. But herbal practice in America could not afford such specialization, so many herbalists hired assistants. The 1887 article "Chinese Drug Stores in America" noted that in Philadelphia clerks working in herbal shops were responsible for bookkeeping and preparing and dispensing medicine.[72] Nevertheless, in most cases, herbal medicine was a family business, using unpaid or underpaid family members.

Before he married Nellie, Yitang ran his herbal shop by himself. As a hard-working physician, he ran two offices—one on South Hill Street and another, above Tsui Fai Low Restaurant in Chinatown, for appointments in the evening. He took a bus to get there, and worked there from 7:30 p.m. to 9:00 p.m., when most Chinese small businessmen and laborers had finished work. His herbal business became a family affair after he married Nellie Yee. As an American-born Chinese woman, Nellie spoke, and had a reading knowledge of, both Chinese and English.[73] She played an indispensable role in Yitang's store. While remaining responsible for the heavy household chores such as cooking and laundry, she quickly learned how to handle almost every aspect of the herbal business. She knew how to read prescriptions in Chinese, and to take out the exact amount of herbs from the right drawers, wrap them up, and hand them to the clients. It was by no means an easy job. In the herbal room, she needed to identify the right herbs among hundreds of drawers labeled in Chinese characters.[74]

As herbal tea tasted bitter, many Caucasian patients found it difficult to drink. Yitang made herbal pills covered with honey, as an alternative for these patients. Making pills was a labor-intensive job. The grinding tool was a heavy implement of iron. Because it looked like a boat, with a cylinder in the middle and two handles on the sides, Yitang's family referred to it as the "rocking boat." Grinding was arduous work that required the use of feet or knees to propel the handles over and over until the herbs were ground almost into powder. Sometimes a hired relative did this work; sometimes it was done by Yitang. When Yitang's feet and knees grew weak, Nellie took over the job. She always wore low-heeled shoes to work the "rocking boat." The ground powder was poured through a sieve and mixed with hot honey, before it was thoroughly steamed. The family would then shape the medicine into small balls, barely bigger than green beans, in pans, and let them gradually dry. If some were not dry enough, the family would heat them briefly in the oven. Once the pills were complete dry, the family would put them into little bottles and seal the bottles. The pills were more convenient than herbal tea, as the patients did not have to cook the medicine; patients could also consume them with water, as the pills still tasted a little bitter. Many patients, however, adapted themselves to the herbal medicine; they would come every year during the flu season, buy packages adequate for several weeks, and then cook the medicine at home. Some patients requested medicine be sent through the mail when they moved out of the Los Angeles area. There were also patients who sought consultation and treatment through correspondence.[75]

Yitang bought herbs from wholesale dealers in Chinatown or imported herbs from China himself. In immigration testimony, Sam Chang indicated that the family herbal store purchased herbs from a company called Dock On Chung Company in Hong Kong, the Jop Lon Tong and Jon Ming Tang company in San Francisco and a wholesale herbal company called Tai Wo Tong (Tai Wu Tang) in Los Angeles.[76] Sometimes wholesale companies delivered the herbs; sometimes family members needed to pick up the supply themselves. After Nellie married Yitang in 1910, the family lived outside of Chinatown, moving among locations at 917 South Hill and elsewhere.[77] Although she hardly had gone out of doors before marriage, Nellie learned how to drive in order to pick up the herbs. Yitang purchased a car for the business but, after a car accident, was nervous about driving. He asked Nellie if she dared to drive; if she didn't, he would sell the family car. Nellie replied, "It seems so easy to drive a car. I might as well learn." To Yitang's great surprise, Nellie got her driving license after a month's practice with her brother Bill. With her driving skill, Nellie helped deliver medicines to patients, buy groceries, drive the children to school and bring back heavy loads of medicine from Tai Wo Tong in Chinatown. Nellie was one of the few Chinese women who could drive, during that period. With this skill, she became more active in social affairs, and in the months before the United States entered the Second World War she took part, with other Chinese American women, in the protests against American scrap iron exports to Japan.

Often, Yitang's house also served as a residential office. At their home on South Hill Street, the family lived upstairs, while downstairs Yitang had a spacious five-room office. Two rooms were used as waiting rooms; in another, Yitang took the pulses of patients and wrote prescriptions. In yet another, he administered medicine or had patients take medicinal teas. The stove in the family's big kitchen had six burners, which could cook up to seventeen or eighteen pots of medicine in one afternoon. For each patient Nellie would pack a week's prescription into seven paper bags. Medicine was cooked on a slow fire in numbered pots, for forty-five minutes to an hour, then administered in beautiful porcelain bowls. Yee Pai, son of Yitang's third elder brother, helped pour the tea and took it to the patients, who already could smell the unusual aromas wafting from the stove. Some patients drank the hot herbal tea like soup, spoonful by spoonful. Others waited for it to cool enough to gulp down. More experienced patients would pick up a whole week's prescription and brew the medicine themselves. Yitang would provide specific directions on how to cook the herbs.

When the living room was full of patients waiting for medicine or treatment, Yitang's daughter Lillian and son Arthur might go downstairs and chat with them. Sometimes they helped serve crackers so that the herbal soup would not taste so bitter for a patient. Although they were still young and often would be holding a toy while talking to patients, they knew this was their family business. As Nellie helped make pills with "the grinding boat" and the sieve, Lillian and Arthur also learned how to shape the pills with their hands. When Holmes left the business and as they grew a bit older, they helped interpret for their father. Having been involved in the herbal business, Yitang's American-born children were also exposed firsthand to an important piece of Chinese culture. A Chinese family business was not merely an economic entity, but also an ethnic cultural island. Since an herbal store, laundry service, gift shop, grocery, or bakery could function simultaneously as living quarters, the Chinese language, culture, family values, and traditions were transmitted there though interactions between parents and children. When children reached school age and acquired English fluency, they in turn became interpreters for their parents in the family business and a bridge to mainstream American society. Surrounded by a hostile racial environment in the larger society, family life offered mutual support in the business and fostered close relationships among family members.

Restrictions on Herbal Business

An ironic challenge to Chinese herbalists was the fact that their profession represented Chinese culture. At the same time that their white patients accepted and preferred herbal medicine to Western medicine, Chinese culture was regarded as an inferior culture in American society. In their practice, the practitioners needed to emphasize their ethnic background as a proof of their authenticity. Most herbalists would claim that their skill was a family tradition for many generations, or that they had learned the skill from a master scholar in a royal medical college. Famous herbalists in Southern California, like Tom Foo Yuen or Tom Leung, claimed they had been trained and served in the Imperial Medical College of Peking (Beijing) before their arrival in America. (However, even Tom Leung's children were suspicious of that claim.)[78] In their offices, some herbalists wore Chinese robes and round Mandarin hats as a trademark for their profession, while others would hang framed certificates of a medical degree in fact been issued by friends in the Chinese government. There did seem too many royal doctors for one emperor, among the Chinese herbalists.

Yitang used a more American style to approach his clients. He often dressed up in a three-piece suit in his office, thus looking more like a Western professional. Many other herbalists, especially those with more white patients, also wore Western clothes at work. In the newspaper advertisements, photos of herbalists in traditional Chinese clothes often existed side by side with photos of those in Western suits. The Mandarin hat and robe looked theatrical and eccentric in twentieth-century Southern California, but it was one approach that worked for some herbalists anxious to show their authenticity as true Chinese doctors.

Being an alternative therapy and an ethnic practice competing for American patients meant that the image of herbal medicine suffered from all kinds of distortion and prejudice. As noted, Chinese herbalists carried out persistent campaigns against stereotypes and distortions of herbal medicine. They published books, wrote articles in newspapers and journals, and made extensive use of the testimonies by their Caucasian patients in courts, to defend the effectiveness of herbal medicine. In Los Angeles, Tom Foo Yuen was repeatedly attacked by Western medical organizations. Dr. P. C. Remondino, then president of the Southern California Medical Association, made a vicious attack on Chinese herbal medicine. Tom replied in the *Los Angeles Times* of 15 August 1895 with an elaborate article defending such medicine; the deep anger and resentment he felt resonates through the article. This article caused Remondino to write another offensive article, to which Tom further replied. The debate aroused a great deal of attention.[79] After this debate, Tom wrote, then published in 1897, a booklet called *The Science of Oriental Medicine.* In their writings, herbalists carefully explained the history, theory, and function of herbal medicine and presented it as a medical science as respectable as Western medicine. To prove their point, the herbalists quoted prestigious Western academic sources. For example, in the first chapter of *The Science of Oriental Medicine,* Tom Foo Yuen quoted an article from the *Encyclopedia Britannica,* which praised the Chinese as first-rate artists in every kind of manufacturing and noted that "their physicians have a thorough knowledge of the virtue of herbals, and an admirable skill in diagnosing by the pulse."[80] Both Tom Foo Yuen and Fong Wan argued that Chinese herbal medicine had a longer tradition and more sophisticated theory, than Western medicine, and was more effective in dealing with many difficult symptoms. Tom wrote:

> The Oriental system has cured thousands of cases of various forms of disease, which had been abandoned by other doctors. This has been established beyond the possibility of dispute. In fact, we prefer to treat so-called incurable cases. As a rule Caucasians have been unwilling to consult us until they had tried every other form of medical treatment within their reach. . . . In other words, we have lived in Southern California long enough to establish a reputation, and to secure a following.[81]

Testimonies by Caucasian patients were used as evidence to prove the effectiveness of Chinese herbal medicine. To defend themselves from racial stereotypes, the herbalists often emphasized that common white people were ignorant of the greatness of Chinese civilization and failed to distinguish the educated, elite Chinese from the low laboring classes. Presenting themselves as high-class Chinese, the herbalists pointed out that the herbal physician was a respected professional in China. One cannot help noting that this argument displays little concern for the sensibility of working-class Chinese.

As mainstream medical organizations, with the endorsement of local government, viciously distorted herbal medicine as a pseudoscience and suppressed it harshly by enforcing "medical care" laws, Chinese herbalists were often engaged in legal battles. The article "Chinese Physicians in California" noted that Chinese herbal medicine was not recognized by law in California, and the judicial records of the state showed that herbalists were often arrested and fined for their practice. The pioneer herbalist Li Pu-tai suffered from a great deal of harassment from Western medical professionals and law officers in his early years of practice. Later he used his friendships with Senator Leland Stanford and Governor Mark Hopkins to obtain some protection.[82]

Fong Wan of Oakland was another famous herbal physician during this period. As one of the most established Chinese physicians in the San Francisco area, he was known as the "King of the Herbalists." From 1915 to the mid-1930s, he received several thousand patients and became one of the most well-known and wealthiest Chinese herbalists in the area. His success earned him not only fame but also envy. According to his book, Western doctors launched a great campaign against Chinese herbalists from 1929 to 1932, and involved people from all walks of life. For example, the postal masters sent fraudulent orders, for the purpose of entrapping the Chinese physicians, and examined the return letters for negative information to use in legal testimonies. Fong Wan was repeatedly sued by envious Western doctors, and had to appear many times in both local and federal courts. At a federal court on 29 July 1931, Wan was indicted on sixteen counts of criminal and other charges. Pharmacologists, postmasters, professors, chemists, and physicians were all brought to the court to testify against him. Hiring his own lawyers, and using many favorable Caucasian patients' testimonies, Wan was proved not guilty. During his career, he went through and won dozens of medical cases. In 1925, when an Anti-Herbal Bill was introduced into the State Assembly, Fong Wan went to Sacramento and presented the arguments and facts instrumental in having the bill withdrawn.[83]

Yitang Chang and other Chinese herbal physicians in the Los Angeles area, also, had to deal with extensive legal harassment, at that time. The herbalists deposited money in banks and hired lawyers, to help bail them out if they were arrested during a suit. Like Fong Wan, they used Caucasian patients' testimonies, and hired Caucasian lawyers for their defense if they had to appear in court. For example, Tom Leung used to hire Thomas White and Paul Shenck as his attorneys. Both were famous Southern California lawyers of the period.[84] Sam Chang's daughter remembered that Yitang had consulted on legal issues with Carey McWilliams, who was not only a historian but had a law degree.[85]

The herbalists used different strategies to resist racial harassment. Yitang's friend Tom Leung was a very aggressive herbalist. He was arrested numerous times on the charge of practicing medicine without a license, but he did not give up using the "Doctor" title until the late 1920s, and even published a book in 1928, *Chinese Herbal Medicine*, to spread his reputation and vehemently defend his profession. The book *Sweet Bamboo*, by his daughter Louise Leung Larson, contains a vivid description of how Chinese herbal physicians in Southern California were harassed at that time:

> Father did well as an herbalist, too well, in the opinion of the American Medical Association and the Board of Medical Examiners. He and the other Chinese herbalists in Los Angeles at that time were accused of practicing medicine without a license because they used the title "Doctor" and felt the pulse as one way of diagnosis. Papa was a special target and was arrested over 100 times on the misdemeanor charge. . . . The police, at times, used stool pigeons—people pretending to be patients—and would arrest Papa after the usual consultation. Sometimes a whole squad of police would arrive in a patrol car and raid our home. I came to view the AMA and the Board,

as well as the police, as our mortal enemies. Papa was unflappable, even the time when he was hauled off in the patrol wagon. He had set up a routine for these crises. As soon as the police came, the secretary phoned A. C. Way of the First National Bank to arrange for bail.[86]

Only after Dr. Leung ceased to call himself a doctor and changed his company name to "Leung Herbal Company" did the harassment gradually decline.

Yitang Chang was also repeatedly charged by local medical organizations in Los Angeles for claiming to be a physician without a doctor's title, and the organizations demanded he stop his medical practice, in accordance with California law. Yitang dealt with the harassment by keeping a low profile. His son Arthur recalled: "There were medical societies questioning father whether he treated patients or not. He always said that he was an herbal seller. He never advertised his business. Other patients referred all his patients. He did run into some trouble before but he got out of it."[87] Yitang's children remembered that their home was searched and a large, tall policeman frisked their father though no one was arrested. To carry out his herbal business, Yitang applied for a license as a drug store. He also worked with Holmes, whose chiropractor's license gave the business some excuse to take patients and diverted the attention of medical organizations. Seldom did Chang advertise his business in newspapers, as he sought his new clients through referrals by his old patients.

The Western Medical Association (the western arm of the American Medical Association) was not the only organization to chase after herbalists. The INS, as noted, regularly questioned the herbalists, in immigration testimonies, about their profession and to see if they followed the law. When Yitang and Sam appeared in the INS office for interviews, the officers often asked them if their herbal business provided medical service. Both always carefully emphasized that they only sold herbs and did not practice medicine. In an interview in 1926, for example, the officer specifically challenged Sam by asking "Do you ever render any professional services, that is acting in the capacity of a physician down there?" Sam categorically replied, "No, we sell herbs, that's all." Checking their professional service status, the agency sometimes sought an excuse to reject Yitang or Sam's qualifications to sponsor family members to America. In another question, the officer asked: "What class do you cater to principally?" Sam replied: "Both to Chinese and Americans."[88] Obviously, catering to Caucasian clients was an important criterion to measure an herbalist's social status. Serving Chinese as major clients could be interpreted as associating with lower-class people and might be cause to disqualify Sam's merchant status. The above two questions to Sam by INS officers show how narrowly herbal medicine was defined as an economic niche for the Chinese and how carefully they had to tread in the prejudiced environment of the times. By his low profile and by offering service to both Caucasian and Chinese patients, Yitang survived racist harassment and carried out his herbal business until the late 1940s. During World War II, the Japanese invasion of China had already disrupted the herbalists' business to a great extent, as the herb supply was cut off, especially after the Japanese occupied Guangdong and Hong Kong. But it was especially after the Trading with the Enemy Act was passed in December 1950 and trade between the United States and China was suspended, that many Chinese herbalists had to discontinue their business. In the year before his death, Yitang was bedridden with swollen legs, probably due to a heart problem. When he died in 1952, the Chinese herbal business was already shrinking rapidly. It was done in, not by discrimination but by the federal ban on Chinese imports that followed the establishment of the People's Republic of China in 1949.

The history of herbal medicine demonstrates how Chinese immigrants used an ethnic skill to create a lucrative and respected career outside the limited sphere of menial labor jobs typically open to them at the time. One has to admire these early herbalists, for theirs was also a profession carrying great risk. As with any doctor's practice, the responsibility of dealing with human health and lives was great, and any failure or problems in the herbalists' treatment could result in a harsh response. The challenges that the herbalists had to meet and the obstacles that they had to overcome illustrate how Chinese immigrants creatively explored their economic opportunities and vigorously defended them when threatened.

Equipped with an ethnic medical skill, relying on family labor and transnational networks, and taking care of patients of all ethnic groups, the herbalists became among the few immigrant professionals to successfully break into the American medical market. Their success is not a "melting pot" story, with immigrants assimilating into mainstream society, but a story of reverse assimilation, in which white Americans opened up to, gained a greater appreciation for, and reaped benefit from another, in this case Asian, culture.

CHAPTER 4

Between Troubled Home and Racist America

Sam's Educational Background

In June 1915, Sam Chang, Yitang's eldest son, visited the United States as a senior officer of the Guangzhou Police Bureau. Upon his arrival, Sam stayed in the New China Hotel in San Francisco for a few months, as he was also in charge of supervising the Chinese Exhibition at the Panama-International Exposition. In March 1916, he arrived in Los Angeles to join his father, and studied at an English-language school. Then, in the summer of 1917, he left for the East Coast and visited New York, Washington, D.C., Philadelphia, and Pittsburgh, as well as Canada, to learn about U.S. and Canadian police systems and facilities.[1] This education was the main purpose of his trip to America; as a senior police officer on a government mission, he did not plan to remain in America as an immigrant.

Sam was born in 1886, Kaiping County, Guangdong Province. In a letter of 1921, he wrote briefly about his educational background:

> From thirteen to fifteen, I studied in the home village. At age eighteen and nineteen, I was not in good health and also busy with family affairs so I did not go to a university. . . . I received some education from thirteen to twenty, six years altogether. I had a mediocre teacher for three years. Then, I learned a lot during the two years I studied with my fifth uncle-in-law. I also studied in Guangzhou for one year. From six to twelve, I studied *Hongpi Shu* (*The Red-Paper Books*) at home but my teacher did not even know *Sishu Wujing* (*The Four Books and Five Classics*). . . . When I was age twenty or twenty-one, the Imperial Examination System was abolished. . . . Although I liked to read books, I had no friends or good teachers who could help me pursue serious academic study. . . .

I studied business for one year in Hong Kong where they taught me only some mathematics and English. Then I studied at the Guangdong Police Academy for two years. I also studied medicine. After working for the government, I have been very busy and have had little time to read books.[2]

The books mentioned in Sam's letter were classic texts used in Chinese traditional schools. The *Four Books* (*Sishu*) include *The Great Learning, The Doctrine of the Mean, The Analects of Confucius,* and *The Analects of Mencius.* The *Five Classics* (*Wujing*) includes *The Book of Songs, The Book of History, The Book of Changes, The Book of Rites,* and *The Spring and Autumn Annals.* In the rural areas, however, such texts often appeared in cheap red paperback editions without annotation, and were accordingly referred as "Red Paper Books." According to the letter, Sam as a rural youth during this transitional period still read classic Chinese literature—sometimes with a hired teacher at a village school and sometimes simply with a scholarly relative. According to another family document, he also had opportunity to study classic Chinese literature with Qu Yuchao (Au Yue Chiu), a famous scholar in Guangdong Province. Sam loved writing poetry and composed hundreds of poems, though he never published them.[3] In addition to learning classical Chinese, Sam studied herbal medicine with Guan Chengbi, a famous herbalist in Guangzhou city.

Sam did well to adapt himself to a changing Chinese society. As the letter indicates, he began to study modern subjects such as English and mathematics at urban schools when the traditional civil service examination system was gone. While widely read in Chinese classics like Confucian and Tang poetry, and writing classic poems himself, he also had strong interests in the writings and ideas of the reformists at the turn of the twentieth century like Kang Youwei, and Liang Qichao, or of the later political leaders and literary giants like Sun Yatsen, Hu Shi, Chen Duxiu, and Cai Yuanpei, and translations of Western political and literary writings. His family letters also indicate that he was well read in Western literature. By this time, many Chinese journals and newspapers carried translations of Western fiction and poetry; in fact, translation of Western literature became a popular literary genre in China at the turn of the twentieth century.

Sam was married in 1904. His wife, Zhiyuan Cen, was born in 1885 in Enping County and was one year older than Sam. Cen's family was much wealthier than the Chang family.[4] Coming from a rich family, Cen knew how to read and write. Since girls' schools were rare in rural Guangdong when

Cen was a child, her family hired tutors at home so that their girls as well as their boys could receive an education. Cen was able to write letters to her children and relatives when she and they were apart. Sam and Cen married young, but they did not have children until seven years later. Their first child was born in China in 1910, named Tingxun, and came to America in 1929, where he adopted "Tennyson" as his English name. Their second child was Yuhua, a daughter born in 1912, who became "Constance" after she came to America in 1923. Sam and Cen also had two children who died in infancy.

Sam decided to stay in America when Yitang requested he help the family business in Los Angeles. What he probably did not realize was that he would stay in the United States for the rest of his life and never have an opportunity to visit his home country. As a scholarly immigrant, Sam wrote many reflections about Chinese life and work in America and numerous letters to his children, siblings, other relatives, and friends. He passed away in 1988 in Los Angeles, at the age of 102. Sam in his lifetime witnessed and experienced many stages of the local Chinese community's development. His writing enables us to understand how Chinese immigrants and their family members perceived their life in America, what kind of information, emotions, and opinions were exchanged among them, and how and why they maintained a transnational family life.

Sam's knowledge about Chinese culture, his keen interest in current events in Chinese society, and his love of China greatly influenced the younger generation of the Chang family. He often tutored his American-born and -raised siblings and children in Chinese language, encouraged them to know both Chinese and American culture, and advised them to find a career in China after completing their college education in the United States. Under his influence, many in the younger generation of the Chang family traveled back and forth across the Pacific to pursue their education and careers. Ties between the Chang family and China were never severed.

Sam's Police Career in China

Sam's training at the Police Academy in Guangdong came at a critical juncture in Chinese society. A modern police system in China did not come into being until the late Qing period. Following a memorial by Yuan Shikai, the Qing court issued an imperial decree in December 1902 that each province set up a police bureau after the Japanese model. But the Imperial Court did not set up a Police Ministry until 1905.[5] Guangdong, however, organized its own Central Police Bureau in 1903 in Guangzhou, and divided the city into five administrative districts with three thousand police officers.[6] The Guangdong Police Academy was probably established a few years later. Sam attended the Academy around 1910 and graduated in 1912.[7] He was among the first cohort of police officers in modern China. According to some relatives and friends, Sam was one of the best of the Academy's graduates and became a capable police officer in Guangzhou after his graduation.[8] However, in his immigration files, the Academy was actually called "Self-Government Reform Association School," which probably later changed its name into Guangdong Police Academy. The "Self-Government Reform Association," established in 1907, was an elite social organization that consisted of senior local government officials and gentry scholars, and played a significant role in social and political reforms in Guangdong in 1910s as the Qing government increasingly lost control of many provinces.[9] Sam's major subject was "self-government;" and his "special area" was "police system." Sam "was appointed as a member of the Police Bureau on October 16,1912, holding a position defined as police judge who would hear cases and pass judgment on offenders. In 1913, he was appointed an official of the second class, first section, third district, his commission being signed by the late Commissioner of Police, Cheng King Wah (Chen Jinghua)."[10] Sam was probably in charge of one of the five districts in the city.

Unfortunately, Sam's police career started in the most turbulent period in modern Chinese history. The Qing Dynasty having been immersed in political, economic, and foreign crisis for a long time, its fall was only a matter of time. On 10 October 1911, a group of revolutionary-minded soldiers launched a sudden revolt in Wuchang, Hubei Province. Shortly after the Wuchang Uprising, fifteen provinces in southern and central China declared their independence of the Qing court. On 1 January 1912, the Republican government was established in Nanjing, with Sun Yatsen as provisional president.[11] Sun did not have a strong and reliable military base. Many of his followers were opportunists more concerned with personal ambition than with the goals of the revolution. The former imperial elites and officials of the independent provinces also watched for an opportunity to become local warlords, rather than being firm supporters of the revolution. Other than in ending the Qing dynasty, the Republican Revolution of 1911 was inconclusive, and it was weak in many ways.

In the new Guangdong Republican government, Chen Jinghua, a key leader in the Republican revolution, became the superintendent of the police department.[12] As a professionally trained police officer and a local Cantonese, Sam soon became a key senior aid to Chen, who made the police department a powerful and efficient organ of the revolution. During its two-year rule, the Republican government carried out reform programs ranging from the discarding of the queue to new health and sanitation standards. Policemen sometimes forcibly removed the queues of those who did not voluntarily do so, and often enforced the new policies that required the registration of doctors, medical schools, and midwives, and the segregation of disease carriers. Other health measures included barring the collection of human waste during daylight hours, as many houses had no private toilets and depended on nearby farmers to collect their waste at dawn. In the early Republican years, theft, opium-smoking, gambling, prostitution, and banditry were common in the city. The most difficult task facing the new government was to enforce the ban on opium-smoking and gambling, an important source of revenue for the Guangdong Government since 1900.[13] As Sam described his position as a "judge in the police department," his responsibility was probably to handle many such judicial affairs.[14] Being a senior aide, Sam assisted Chen to quickly eliminate much of this crime.

Sam found it especially difficult to deal with corrupt officials and warlords. Two examples demonstrate the difficulty faced by Sam as a police officer. In one incident, Sam's plainclothes agents caught Li Xiuyu, superintendent of Guangdong's head customs office, smoking opium. As Li was a high-ranking official, many people interceded on his behalf after his arrest. But Sam still fined Li five hundred dollars for illegally smoking opium.

A second episode involved Sam's dealings with abusive warlord soldiers. Yuan Shikai, who betrayed first the Qing court and then the Republicans, was China's strongman during the early Republican days. With his own military base in northern China and the support of Western powers, Yuan forced the Qing court to give up, then forced Sun to give away the Republican presidency. Moreover, Yuan wanted to become the new emperor of China. But he needed money to build up his military strength in the north to wipe out the Republican forces in the south. In spite of repeated protests by the Republicans, Yuan Shikai finally obtained his much-wanted Reorganization Loan from the Five-Power International Consortium in April 1913 and was ready to confront the revolutionary government in the southern provinces.[15] To avoid a civil war, the Republicans appealed to the Western powers to cancel the loan. But the foreign consortium paid the money four days after Yuan signed the contract. Yuan immediately nominated his own officials in southern provinces. In desperation, the Guangdong Republican government declared its independence of Yuan's regime on July 18, and engaged in a civil war with Yuan. Lacking financial and popular support, the Republican local government collapsed within a month. Yuan appointed Long Jiguang, a war-lord in Guangxi Province, as the new military governor of Guangdong Province. In August, Long's five thousand Guangxi troops forced their entry into Guangzhou.[16] Sam and his police colleagues had a hard time dealing with the abusive behavior of Long's soldiers.

One of Sam's poems reflects upon his police career during that period.

> New and fragile the Republic was born.
> Harnessing the lawless became a heavy duty.
> Crime and violence occurred day and night.
> But few fugitives escaped from justice.[17]

Sam wrote the following explanatory note to the poem,

> Upon Yuan Shikai's order, Long Jiguang's troops entered into Guangdong. The troops were abusive. One day the local people were so mad that they captured a military rapist and sent him to the Police Bureau for punishment. But the rapist's fellow soldiers forced their way into my office and threatened me at gunpoint. Fortunately the Battalion Commander, Feng Baosheng, and his men came to my aid and saved me from the danger.[18]

Although Sam behaved quite heroically in front of such abuses, the local police force was, generally speaking, helpless when military forces became villainous. Since Guangdong and Hunan Provinces were the hometown of many Republican leaders, such as Sun Yatsen, Huang Xing, and Hu Hanmin, Yuan Shikai hated these two southern provinces in particular.[19] Upon his order, the counter-revolutionary revenge was extremely violent in these two areas.

It was during this period that China witnessed the rise of military warlordism.[20] Long became an agent of Yuan Shikai and carried out his orders to persecute the revolutionaries. His troops marched into Guangzhou, removed all the previous Republican reform measures, and canceled Guangdong's autonomy. Chen Jinghua died a mysterious death after Long invited him to a dinner. Under Long, none of the new governmental appointees, from the provincial to the district magistrate level, were Cantonese.[21] Sam remained at his police position until he left Guangdong in 1915. There is no apparent reason why Long spared him during the purges of 1913. One possibility was that he was not a political appointee but a professional police officer. Moreover, when Long took over the provincial government, the Guangzhou police and the Guangdong local army were still powerful military forces. The local political and military forces wanted to remain autonomous of both the Republicans and Yuan Shikai's government. While these two armed forces were not in active support of the Republicans during the war with Yuan Shikai, some local troops did resist Long's Guangxi army's invasion of Guangdong Province. When Long's soldiers confronted Sam (in the incident here referred to), the Battalion Commander Feng who came to his rescue was probably an officer of the Guangdong army. Long Jiguang and Yuan Shikai acted skillfully to avoid an open confrontation with the local army, in order to win their potential support.

Although there is no information about how active Sam Chang was in Republican politics, it was possible that he knew some of the Nationalist leaders at that time. According to one source, Hu Hanmin, a leading Republican, recognized Sam's ability and reputation as senior police officer, and had him assigned to a mission learning about police practices in the United States.[22] Hu was the governor of Guangdong from 1911 to 1913, and appointed Chen Jinghua as the superintendent of the police department.[23] After the Republican government collapsed, Hu and all the Republican leaders fled to Japan. Even though Sam was a civil service officer rather than a politician, the above poem and the incident it describes indicate his anger at the abusive behavior of Long's army. His anger, combined with Long's attempt to eliminate all local Cantonese officials, may have contributed Sam's desire to leave his position, though he still intended to return and did visit a number of American police facilities after he arrived in the United States. The poem and his government mission also confirm that Sam was a high-ranking police official in Guangzhou. An ordinary police officer would not have had such authority even if he wanted to handle some of the tough cases. At Sam Chang's eightieth birthday party, in 1965, several guests spoke highly of his police career in their speeches. A few Chinese newspaper articles about him also described this period of his life. The guest speakers and newspaper articles especially praised Sam's heroic performance against Long's troops. In carrying out his police duty, Sam did not back off, even when the warlord's soldiers threatened to shoot him.[24]

When Sam came to the United States in 1915, his ranking was high enough to represent a local Chinese police department in a foreign country. His immigration files also indicate that he came to study the police system and government management, was financially able to make the contemplated trip, and was provided with a draft for fifteen hundred dollars. The photo in his immigration files shows Sam in a fashionable suit with a black tie. His passport issued by the Guangdong government clearly indicated that Sam was not a laborer immigrant, and had a property in Guangzhou worth twenty thousand U.S dollars. In compliance with the 1882 Chinese Exclusion Act, he belonged to an exempted class, and his background had been verified and certified by the American consul's office in Guangzhou. The passport also noted that he had a scar on his upper lip and a mole on his left check.[25] Although a Chinese identification document, the passport recorded certain physical features of Sam. This was probably required by the U.S. immigration authority to prevent fraudulent use of his identity.

One year after Sam Chang left Guangdong, Yuan Shikai died in Beijing. China reached the zenith of political chaos. Long's Guangxi soldiers became even more abusive toward the Cantonese. According to one account:

> While the soldiers acted cowardly on the battlefield, they acted arrogantly toward the civilians. . . . Looting, burning, raping, and killing were regular features of the conduct of most Chinese soldiers. . . . Although provincial troops sometimes committed acts of violence against their own people, the most flagrant cases usually occurred when an army operated in another province. . . . In Kwangtung during 1919–20, Kwangsi troops also behaved very badly.[26]

Under such conditions, it became unlikely that Sam could return and assume his previous government position.

Sam's Decision to Stay

In contrast to the chaotic Chinese politics and precarious situation in his home village, Sam found, in America his father had established a prosperous herbal business and had invested in an asparagus farm that had the potential to expand. By the time of Sam's arrival, Yitang had already sponsored several relatives to California and established a new family. His herbal business had several branch offices. During this very busy period, it was natural for Yitang to request Sam to stay and help with the family businesses. While the political chaos in Guangdong did not provide a strong incentive or good opportunity for a return, Sam's sense of filial piety to his father, and of obligation to the Chang family, were also important considerations in his decision to remain in America. Indeed, in the eulogy at Sam's funeral in 1988, a relative recalled Sam's commitment to his father's businesses as filial.[27]

As Sam had received herbal medical training previously, he first tried practicing as an herbalist. In the winter of 1918, he went to Salt Lake City to open a branch office of Yitang's Chinese Herb Company. He brought with him a relative who served as his assistant and interpreter. As the Chinese population was less than two hundred in Salt Lake City during that period, he mainly targeted non-Chinese patrons.[28] He rented a three-room office at 69 East Second South Street and advertised his business in local newspapers. In these advertisements, Sam emphasized that his herbal company had existed for eighteen years, with two offices in Los Angeles and another in Reno. With some exaggeration, Sam presented himself as one of the former leading herbalists in China for the treatment of asthma, blood poisoning, kidney and bowel troubles, rheumatism, diabetes, and lumbago. One advertisement read, "former sufferers of Utah have prevailed upon us to open a branch here, so that their friends could be treated without leaving their business, besides eliminating the great expense incurred through travel."[29] Sam's advertisement indicates some of the typical symptoms that Chinese herb medicine dealt with in the American West.

While advertising his business in mainstream American newspapers such as *The Salt Lake Mirror*, *Salt Lake News*, and *Salt Lake Herald*, Sam also tried to target immigrant communities. One of his promotional pamphlets read, "A great many people of all nationalities have tried our natural teas and herbs treatment with excellent results."[30] As there were a large number of Greek mining workers in Utah, he advertised in a local Greek-language newspaper, *Greek Daily*.[31] He similarly promoted his business in a Japanese-language newspaper published in Los Angeles but distributed in Salt Lake City. In this latter newspaper, Sam mentioned that he had experience treating Japanese patients in Los Angeles.

Unfortunately, Sam's herbal business was unsuccessful in Salt Lake City. The failure of any herbal business in America could be due to many factors, including inadequate expertise and business experience as an herbalist, insufficiently timely supply of herbs, and local attitudes toward the influence of Chinese culture on the local communities. A year later, he returned to Los Angeles.

Yitang then asked Sam to manage the asparagus farm, in which he had invested with other relatives, sometime around 1915–16. The farm was about twenty-five acres in size, located at 4660 Whitsett Avenue in North Hollywood. Yitang had previously hired someone else to manage it, but this person did a poor job. When he attempted to hire an experienced asparagus farmer named Liu Xipu, they could not make a deal as Liu asked for a monthly salary of forty dollars—five dollars higher than the norm.[32] Thus Sam took over the management. Although Sam possessed no farming experience, he was a filial son and was committed and obligated to see the family business succeed.

Reunion with Wife and Daughter

In 1923, Sam bought over his wife, Cen, and daughter Constance, as he prepared for a long stay in California. Meanwhile, he had heard that the forthcoming 1924 Immigration Act would severely restrict future Asian immigration to the United States. Even a previously exempted class such as merchants and their family members could be denied entry. By the time Sam began to arrange for his wife and daughter to come to the United States, the racial environment in California was also a serious consideration. Beginning in 1919, California witnessed a renewed agitation against Asians. Although the racist agitation mainly targeted the Japanese, it affected other Asian groups as well. In 1922, Sam began to urge his wife to join him in California, after he learned of new anti-Asian laws being proposed in Congress. Meanwhile, he planned to sponsor two sons of his second brother Weizong (Zhongping, as another name) to America in the names of his own sons. Since Yitang and Sam had decided that Weizong should stay behind to take care of family property in Guangdong, they felt that they should bring some of Weizong's children over. While attending school, the boys could also help in the family business. However, preparing the immigration papers and coaching for the immigration interview was a tedious process during the Chinese exclusion period. Upon entering the United States, Sam's wife and the children could encounter all kinds of questions, and be rejected by immigration officers for a variety of reasons. In February 1923, Sam wrote to Tennyson:

> You must have received my letter and "coaching paper" for your mother, Yuhua, Tingqu, and Tingwei. Ask your mother to memorize the content of the papers. Our attorney is a very careful man. He used to work at the immigration office in Washington, D.C., and is familiar with the immigration process. He has prepared two copies of our documents. If the ship company takes away one copy, we shall still have another copy for ourselves.[33]

Although Tennyson was only thirteen years old, he was the eldest son and had responsibility in family affairs, especially when Sam was away. Sam wrote most of his letters home to Tennyson. In the letter, Sam did not explain why the ship company would take away passengers' immigration documents. It was probably a measure to prevent Chinese passengers from reviewing the content of documents during the journey.

Obviously, the Chang family had created "paper son" slots for Tingqu and Tingwei, sons of Sam's brother. On the immigration papers, the two boys were listed as sons of Sam, and Tingqu became "Tingmao," the name of Sam's first son, who had died in infancy. In another letter, Sam told Tennyson:

> As Tingqu will come to America in the name of Tingmao, your mother will be sad because the name reminds her of our dead son. According to Chinese custom, we do not like to mention the name of a dead child, as this causes sadness. But in America, . . . after a baby child has died, a family, whether Westerners or Chinese, hang the child's picture on the wall. When somebody asks about it, the family will explain who the dead is and express their sadness, and is willing to talk about the child when visitors ask questions. The people seem to have an open attitude toward this matter.[34]

As Sam's wife had been living with Weizong's family since he had left China, Tingqu and Tingwei knew her well. Through some coaching, they were supposed to be able to act genuinely as the real sons of Sam and his wife. Ironically, the more closely they feigned, the more pain they would cause in Sam's wife. As the letter indicated, the name "Tingmao" would remind her of the real son she lost in the past. In Chinese family culture, the death of family members is a sad topic and should not be brought up until absolutely necessary.

Although Sam's letter constantly compared differences between Chinese and American culture and discussed various social issues, ethics, and political events, he made no ethical comments on "paper son" strategy. Obviously, he did not view this strategy as a deception but as a useful means to get family members admitted. When sending for the two sons of his second younger brother, Sam simply followed what everybody else did, in the Chinese immigrant community, and was mainly concerned about the technical aspects of the process. In the same letter, Sam advised his family to purchase first-class tickets, to reduce potential harassment. He informed them:

> I hear that the customs staff has changed and the new doctor is very harsh on new immigrants and rejects many of them because of liver and lung diseases. In the past, people used money to get admitted. Now it is difficult. . . . So Yuhua and others should come as soon as possible. . . . Several months ago, a young man from Enping County came to America. The customs officer asked him if he could read and write and if he had been to school. He said yes and so they thought he was from a wealthy merchant family and let him in. Yuhua should know the importance of claiming herself as a school girl.[35]

Here Sam reminded his family that the social status of an immigrant was important. To present themselves as merchant class Chinese, they should use first-class accommodations and the kids should claim to be students.

In another letter, Sam provided more in-depth advice to his family on their trip to the United States.

> Recently, many friends told me that the new immigration and customs officers are very strict. In the past, some people could ask our counselor or local Western missionary to act as sponsors so that they would be allowed to land first and go through the examination later on. Now this arrangement is no longer possible. When your mother and sister arrive, they will be taken away to the Angel Island immigration station for an eye, liver, and lung examination, and could be interrogated from two or three days to one or two months. A weak nation has no diplomacy to speak of. Coming from a weak nation, there is no point buying first-class tickets as you have to go through various examinations anyway. Take the second-class tickets and save several hundred dollars for other use. The ship will provide meals. Second-class accommodations are best on Japanese company ships. Four people will share one room that is clean and little different from the first class. On the American ships, a dozen people share one room, though there is improvement recently. On new ships, second-class ticket passengers will also share a four-people room. It is better to take an American ship. American customs officers are sensitive about American shipping companies' interest and there is a growing hatred for the Japanese in America now.[36]

In preparing his family's trip, Sam kept himself posted on any news regarding immigration. Whether the information was about the arrival of new INS officers or the differences between taking American and Japanese ships, it could have impact on the immigration process that his family had to go through. Through such detailed information, the letter psychologically prepared his family for a tough interrogation procedure and coached them on how to respond to various situations. Even the choice of steamships was an immigration consideration for Chinese passengers. Although Japanese ships provided better service, the Chang family could not take them because the family had to be sensitive to American economic interest and the increasing racial resentment against Japanese immigrants in California. As mentioned in the previous chapter, Sam used this strategy to win the sympathy of American immigration officer in his testimony.

Sam's letter also reflects the national sentiment of Chinese immigrants. The key remark is: "Weak nation has no diplomacy to speak of." Most Chinese immigrants were familiar with this phrase as it linked racial practice in the United States with international politics. From their perspective, discrimination against the Chinese was mainly due to the fact that China was a weak nation. Since the Opium War, this statement became a well-known saying among the Chinese when they referred to unequal relations between China and the West. As a weak nation, China had to accept whatever foreigners imposed on her. The West and the imperialist Japan could bully China any way they liked—from trade privileges to unequal treaties or an aggressive war. When Chinese people went overseas and experienced unequal treatment, they believed this was due to the weak international standing of China.

The most useful immigration strategy for Sam's family, however, was to memorize the family history, so as to pass the interrogation at the Angel Island. The rest of Sam's letter demonstrates to what extent the family members needed to remember their life history:

> Your mother should discuss it carefully with your twelfth granduncle, second uncle, and Uncle Haisheng. According to the coaching paper, it will be perfect for your mother, Yuhua, Tingmao, and Tingwei to stay in the same room. In the coaching paper, I said Tingwei is seven years old. The attorney made a mistake when he wrote six on his passport. Our attorney said he would try to do something about it. . . . Your mother is from Fu-qing-li. Your maternal grandpa is Cen Xuchu. Your mother should say she is illiterate. If they ask why, tell them that the countryside is traditional and backward, without a girls' school. Yuhua is studying at Cai-zhi-tang School, with an annual tuition of ten dollars. Mao started schooling at eight and Wei at seven. I have already put this information in the coaching paper. If asked why Mao started schooling at eight but Wei at seven, tell them that Mao was in poor health at seven and therefore he started one year late.[37]

According to the letter, every detail matters. Sam's family members could not afford a single mistake, whether about the exact amount of school tuition or about why a kid had started school one year late. The interrogation was like a psychological game played between Chinese immigrants and immigration officers. Any hesitation, fear, or inconsistency would cause problems. Two years later, in another letter to a relative, Sam wrote: "I hear there is new equipment at the immigration station. There are some wooden pieces like majiang game units that the officers will ask you to use to demonstrate the layout of your village and what your house is like."[38] While the immigration officers attempted to catch every loophole during the interrogation, Chinese immigrants, young and old, man and woman, tried to make every move correctly.

To play safe, the immigrants sometimes provided answers to fit a stereotype about the Chinese. Sam, for example, asked his wife to say that she was illiterate though she was not. Coming from a wealthy rural family, she had learned how to read and write with a family tutor. After she arrived in the United States, she was able to write letters to her son who stayed behind in China, and later to her daughter when she was sent to China again for education. In a family letter, her son Tennyson (Tingxun) wrote:

> Dear Father and Mother: You must have received the sixth letter of mine, dated May 16. No big change has occurred in Tianjin now but the school is stopped as the students are uneasy about the war. Sister Yuhua told me that mother has written to us. I did not know that mother could write. I thought Yuhua had written for mother in the past. Now I read mother's letter, I find her Chinese writing very smooth.[39]

To immigration officers, Cen had to lie about this part of her life to fit the stereotype that every Chinese woman was illiterate. Interestingly, even her own son did not know she could read and write until they were separated and had to communicate in writing. In traditional Chinese society, some women were literate because their parents hired private tutors at home. Evelyn S. Rawski pointed out that "information from the mid- and late nineteenth century suggests that thirty to forty percent of the men and from two to ten percent of women in China knew how to read and write." She also noted that the 1896 census for Hawaii reported 25 percent of the Chinese female immigrants were literate. [40] You Chung Hong, an INS interpreter who helped interview many Chang family members, once testified in his own immigration matters that his mother, an immigrant, could read in Chinese.[41]

Son as Partner on Paper

In order to apply for his wife and daughter, Sam had to reestablish his immigration status, from a government visa to a merchant visa. On 6 November 1923, Inspector J. C. Nardini, along with You Chung Hong, then an INS interpreter and later a well-known Chinese American civil rights lawyer, interviewed him. As was routine, Nardini began by asking him to list all his names. In Chinese family culture, a man could have multiple names—a given name in his nuclear family, a generation name used in the clan, a nickname employed by his parents and neighbors. Some educated men also had a courtesy name for social occasions or scholarly writings. In their interviews, Chinese immigrants sometimes listed all the names they had used, and sometimes added explanations of each. In his interview, Sam replied to Nardini, "Chang Wei, boyhood name; Chang Sue Yick, married name; and Chang Sheong Peoy, choice name; no other names."[42]

Sam deliberately withheld "Chang Wee Chee" (Zhang Weixi), his given name, as it had already been used by his father to sponsor a relative. When he entered America in 1915, Sam presented himself as "Chang Wei" instead of "Chung Wee Chee." He also purposely changed the spelling of "Chung," which is how Yitang spelled his last name, to "Chang." Obviously he did not want to appear related to Yitang when entering as a government official. In this interview, Sam's goal was to present himself as a business partner, rather than son, of Yitang.[43] By withholding his given name, he could cover his real identity. In any Chinese government record on a family, or in a Chinese family document such as a genealogy, there is no such a thing as "choice name" unless it is an equivalent of the given name; and there is no such category as "married name" unless it means "courtesy name." Sam or other immigrants probably created name categories that sounded familiar to INS officers, rather than list their names according to Chinese family culture. In Sam's situation, "Chang Sue Yick" (Chang Siyi) is actually Sam's courtesy name, used on public and social occasions or in scholarly writings or formal letters to intellectual or government friends. "Chang Sheong Peoy" (Chang Xiangpei) is a name used in his lineage to indicate the rank of his generation. Moreover, "Zhang" was a popular family name in Guangdong, China, though some immigrants spelled it "Chang" and others "Chung."

When INS officers demanded all names from Chinese immigrants, they probably believed that the more information they had, the more easily they would be able to find loopholes. However, without an in-depth knowledge of Chinese family culture, the officers could only mechanically compare all the names in various versions of a testimony. They were not able to discern family relationships to tell the true identity of Chinese immigrants, even if all names were provided. In Sam's case, he did provide most of his names, but the INS officers still failed to find out who he really was and that he was related to Yitang, due to their inadequate knowledge of Chinese culture.

Even though Sam could cover his true identity in the INS files, using a false name was embarrassing and painful for a Chinese immigrant, especially for an educated person like him. Regardless of what he said at the interview, Sam continued to follow Chinese family culture and properly use his multiple names in his letter writing. He used "Xiangpei" when he wrote to his fraternal cousins and uncles. He used "Weixi" when he wrote to his brothers. And he used "Siyi" in his letters to friends and intellectual acquaintances, and signed it as his pen name in the poems and essays written in his spare time. Although he presented himself as "Chang Wei" in his immigration files, his family, relatives, and friends never addressed him by that name.

Naming is an important component of Chinese family culture. Multiple names like Yitang's and Sam's reflect social relations in China, and each name is meaningful in its own way. While a courtesy name symbolizes respect and friendship among friends, a given name embodies affection between parents and children. As a name given by his parents and always used in family circle, "Weixi" represents a family bond between Sam and his parents and siblings. When Sam passed away in 1986, his eulogy used Weixi as his name.[44] Within the nuclear family, Yitang and his first wife called Sam "Weixi," his second brother "Weizong," and his third brother "Weiying." Arthur, son of Yitang and Nellie, though born in America, still follows this tradition, even in 2004, as his Chinese name is "Weixun." *Wei* is the middle character in all these men's given names.

A clan name represents kinship relationship in an extended family. Yitang's clan name is "Pengbing," with *bing* shared by all male members of Yitang's generation. "Yitang," like "Siyi," is a courtesy name, meant to be addressed within the circle of his elite and educated friends and acquaintances. In the Chang lineage history, Sam's name was "Xiangpei" with the last character *pei* to indicate the rank of his generation in the clan. Sam shared the *pei* character with all his male cousins, just as Yee Pei, a hired relative in the herbal business, was the son of Yitang's third brother, Xiubing. The character *pei* indicates that Yee Pei belonged to the same generation as Sam.

Among the next generation, Sam's son Tennyson was called Tingxun, with *ting* his generation character. He shared this character with all his male cousins. Sam's daughters' names all shared *yu* (which means "jade" and is *Yook* in Cantonese Romanization) as their female generation character. For example, Constance's Chinese name was "Yuhua" while Estelle was called "Yuchu" and Joyce was "Yuchzai." All female members of this generation used the *yu* generation character.

As name is such an important signifier in Chinese family culture, Chinese immigrants sometimes extended the social meaning of a family name and creatively used it to develop and consolidate ethnic networks. Early Chinese immigrants usually grouped themselves according to their clan, lineage, or place of origin. Clans with large memberships could form associations based on real blood relationships, but small clans sometimes banded themselves on a basis of fictional kinship. For example, there was a Longgang Association (Lung Kong) in every major Chinese community, which consisted of people who shared the surnames Liu, Guan, Zhang ("Zhang" could be spelled as "Chang or Chung"), and Zhao. The relationship among members was not based on kinship but derived from a famous legend from the Three Dynasty period (220–65). Most Zhang families in the Los Angeles Chinese community including the Sam Chang family belonged to this association.

In the interview, when asked how he became a partner of Yitang's herbal company, Sam replied that he acquired Jung Way Chee's share for five hundred dollars and Jung Chung Jig's share for five hundred dollars. "Jung Way Chee" could be also spelled "Chang Weixi," and transliterated into the same characters in Chinese language. Obviously, this is Sam's given name, given to a person sponsored by Yitang to enter into America. When the officer asked Sam if he rendered professional services, Sam replied, "we do not render any medical services because we are not licensed to do that under the State laws." Officer Nardini also asked about the major clients of the business. Sam replied that the business served "all nationalities." It is clear that Sam understood perfectly the nature of the interview and the restrictions on operation of a Chinese herbal business in America. Then the officer questioned Sam in detail on the business aspects of Yitang's company, including the salaries of the employees, the monthly rent, the insurance rate, the dividends for both active and silent partners, and the supply sources of their herbs. Sam smoothly provided all answers.

At the end of the interview, an INS officer usually asked if there was anything more that the interviewee desired to say. Although most people said no, to stop short the process, Sam replied:

> I desire that the record be sent to San Francisco without delay. My children are very young and not accustomed to be confined by the authorities. They sailed third class because they were not able to secure second-class accommodation on this particular line. We could have done so on the Japanese line, but we didn't want to do so because that is not patriotic.

Perhaps Sam's police background gave him courage and confidence to add this explanation of his family's trip. But his reply informs us how Chinese immigrants paid attention to every detail in their immigration process, including the arrangement of their transportation to accord with the nationalistic sentiment of immigration officers. Sam handled the interview well. In a note to his testimony, Nardini wrote, "From the appearance and use of the Chinese language, according to the interpreter, the witness is undoubtedly a high-class Chinese."[45]

Yitang and two Caucasian friends also needed to testify in support of Sam in the application process. Yitang testified for Sam on the same day. Having testified many times in immigration matters, he was confident and smooth in his answers and convincingly assured the INS officer that Sam was a merchant and a genuine partner of his herbal business. However, it must have been a trying moment when Nardini pointed to the photo of Sam and asked who that person was. Yitang provided a short and probably a painful answer: "Chang Wei, my partner." The father-and-son relationship was covered in the short answer. But the mutual obligation and commitment to family interest was deepened, as both Yitang and Sam understood that passing Sam off as "Chang Wei" in the testimony was crucial to the collective interest of the Chang family. The officer also asked Yitang to describe how much money Sam invested as a partner, what his role was in the business, where he ate and slept, how they operated cash flow, and what the previous year's business transaction totals were, as well as what the rent came to, the salaries of the partners, the business's former name and partners, and the location and exact address of the company. As an extra check on Yitang's family situation, Nardini asked several specific questions on other family members and their whereabouts. During the exclusion period, the INS agency was deeply suspicious of the Chinese family network. In this case, the officer wanted to find out if those still with Yitang were genuine family members. As an experienced witness who had probably been interviewed a dozen of times by then, Yitang replied readily.

On the next day (November 7), the INS officer interviewed two white witnesses—a Mr. Sollinger and a Mr. Payne. Sollinger was a forty-five-year-old salesman for a tire company and had lived at 1535 East Forty-seventh Street for many years. He claimed that he was Yitang's client, visiting the herbal company at least once a month, and had known "Chang Wei" for two-and-a-half years and Yitang for seventeen years. Fully aware of what the INS officers wished to know, he testified that the herbalists sold herbs, tea, and rice, never performed any manual labor, and never engaged in any "objectionable features of restaurant, hotel, lodging, barber, pawn, or laundry business." Any form of the work named could be associated with manual labor and cause trouble for the Chang family. Still not satisfied, Nardini categori-cally pressed on: "Are you familiar with the meaning of the word 'merchant' as applied in these cases?" Probably overwhelmed by the question, Sollinger said no. The officer explained: "A merchant is a person who buys and sells merchandise at a fixed place of business, which business is conducted under his own name (or in a firm name in which he may be a member) and while conducting said business does not engage in the performance of any manual labor except what is necessary to run the business as a merchant. Now, then, from your knowledge and observation of Chang Wei for the past year can you say that he qualifies as a merchant?" Sollinger's answer this time was far more reserved and cautious: "When I am not there I cannot say what he does, but I believe that he devotes his time to that business." This cautious answer reveals the pressure he felt from Nardini's stern inquiry. But Yitang and Sam had to go through numerous such inquisitive interrogations.

Payne, another middle-aged man, was also a customer who had known Yitang over twelve to fifteen years and Sam for three to four years, though this was the first time he testified for the Chang family on an immigration issue. He easily located the company at 126 West Fourteenth Place, Los Angeles, claiming that he visited them a couple of times a week, or sometimes once a month, though he lived in Anaheim in Orange County. He testified that Yitang had cured him, his wife, and his children after he switched from Dr. Wong, another herbalist. The whole family trusted herbal medicine. As a first-time witness, Payne had a couple of slips of the tongue. Several times he referred to Yitang as "Dr. Jung Hong." But when the officer followed up and asked, "Did he practice medicine with your family?" Payne, probably hav-ing been coached not to describe Yitang as a doctor, immediately added, "No, he simply sold us herbs." When the officer pointed out Yitang's photo and asked his identity, Payne naturally responded, "He is the doctor." This was how, as a customer, he usually addressed Yitang.

On the third day, Nardini wrote a two-page detailed report on the en-tire investigation. Among many other things, the report indicated that Sam appeared to be a high-class Chinese and well-educated in the Chinese lan-guage. This is probably the key statement, as it confirmed Sam's class back-ground as a merchant. The report also indicated that Yitang had corroborated the statement of "Chang Wei" in every respect. Both white witnesses were qualified. In addition to taking the interview testimony, Nardini, accompa-nied by You Chung Hong, the Los Angeles official interpreter, had visited the premises of Yitang's company on 5 November, one day before the inter-view, and found that both Yitang and Sam were there. He noticed no changes in the premises since his previous visit. After scrutinizing every detail of the Chang family life and business, the officer concluded in the report: "From the evidence produced [and] the appearances and demeanor of the witnesses there is no question in my mind of the mercantile status of Chang Wei for the statutory period and longer."[46]

On 21 November 1923, Sam's wife Cen ("Som," in immigration files) arrived in San Francisco with their daughter Constance and two boys of Sam's second brother. At the Angel Island Immigration Station, two INS inspectors, one stenographer, and a Chinese interpreter made up a Board of Special Inquiry. During the interviews of the Chang family, this board used three interpreters, switching them from time to time. As the INS agency did not trust its Chinese staff, it used such a measure to prevent the interpreters from possibly aiding the immigrants. The agency interviewed everyone, including Sam and his Chinese witness. Both of them came from Los Angeles to San Francisco to pick up Cen and the children. For verification purposes, some of the questions the agency asked were similar to those that Sam had been asked in Los Angeles, as the transcript of that interview had already been forwarded to San Francisco on November 8. Most questions, however, were different. Sam's response strategy was straightforward. Regarding his alleged parents and his wife's parents, he simply replied that they had all passed away, so that the officers could not test the children about their names, ages, and whereabouts. It is very unfilial for a Chinese to say that his or her parents are dead when they are still alive. But Sam had to overcome this scruple to protect the children's and family's interests in the interview. Regarding his second brother's children, Sam insisted that he did not know their names and age, as they were all born after he left China. He wanted to maintain some flexibility if the family needed to bring other children of Weizong to America.

Sam's wife Cen handled all the questions well. The board asked about ninety questions, and many were in great detail. Over thirty questions asked that she describe the location, street number, rooms, or the size of the front yard of her house in Guangzhou. One picky question asked her how much space there was between the house and the sidewalk. Cen answered all the questions readily, and also made sure not to leave any opportunity for the officer to test the children with her answers. For example, when the board asked her if her children were acquainted with the families of her brothers, she quickly replied no. As a mother, she tried to protect the children as much as possible in the interview. Having been coached, the twelve-year-old Constance answered questions calmly and was able to remember the names of her alleged maternal grandparents. More important, she needed to remember that her father was a business partner, rather than a son, of her grandfather, in immigration papers. However, the board still found discrepancies in her answers. The Chinese witness for Sam had testified that he visited the family in Guangzhou before their departure. But Constance did not recollect any such visit. This minor discrepancy did not escape the keen observation of the officers. Fortunately it did not impact the admission negatively. The board also asked Constance if she could identify her father's photograph. The question was sneaky and vicious as she was supposed to say yes since this was her own father. But the officer challenged her with the fact that she was only three years old when Sam left China in 1915. Constance had no way to back off and insisted that she remembered seeing him in that year. The officers were not convinced, but let her go anyway.

As for the ten-year-old Tingqu (the alleged Tingmao) and the eight-year-old Tingwei, the interview process was a real ordeal since they had to pass themselves off as Sam's sons. When asked if his alleged father had any brothers or sisters, Tingqu stubbornly relied, "I don't know." When asked if he had any uncle living in Guangzhou, he again replied, "I don't know." When further asked if he had any cousins living in Guangzhou, he said no. It is not clear if he was really confused or if he refused to identify his uncle as his father. But when asked if he knew a little boy by the name Chang Tingdong (Chang Hing Doong) who was his younger brother and stayed behind in China, he surprisingly replied, "he lives on Got Lia Alley, Canton." When asked how he was able to identify his father's photograph, he bluntly answered, "My mother told me." The response of the eight-year-old Tingwei was even more childish. When asked if he knew the names of Chang Tingdong, Chang Yupei (Chang Yook Pei), and Chang Yucui (Chang Yook Chew), Tingwai replied no to all three names though they were his real brother and sisters. When asked who lived on Got Lia Street, he answered the question according to the coaching, "My second uncle." But when the officer asked if he knew the names of his alleged second uncle's children, he listed all the above three names.[47] Whether out of carelessness or other reasons, the Board amazingly let him go.

Although the Board pointed out some discrepancies, in its summary report, it still approved the admission. Sam's family was fortunate to survive the tough interview process. During the Chinese exclusion period (1882–1943), only exempted classes of Chinese, such as merchants and their lawful wives and children, government officials and their families, or American-born Chinese students, could still be admitted into the country.[48]

Cousin Become Son on Paper

In 1925, an even more challenging family responsibility came to Sam. He needed to sponsor his cousin Ruyuan to the United States. Sam had to continuously create "paper son" slots for the family immigration. As a pioneer immigrant of the Chang family, Yitang could use his merchant status to sponsor his third son Elbert and two other relatives in the names Weixi (Sam) and Weizong (Weizong), as the INS agency recorded that he had three sons in China with his first wife. He had also helped Sam to switch his status to a merchant though this required he and Sam cover their father-and-son relationship. Now it was up to Sam to use his merchant status to sponsor relatives. When Sam first arrived in America, he reported that he had two sons—true, though one had died. In 1923, he reported that he actually had three sons, one of them born after he left China in 1915. Two sons of his second brother used these two son slots in 1923, and there was one slot left, as Sam's eldest son, Tingxun, had not come to America. For the collective interest of the Chang family, Sam planned to let Ruyuan, son of Yitang's twelfth brother, use Tingxun's name on paper. Sam began to discuss this possibility with his twelfth eldest uncle as early as 1925. In a letter, he wrote:

> Respectable Uncle:
> I have learned that you went back to the home village for half a year and did not return to Hong Kong. I wonder if there were important issues you must handle there, as this is really a chaotic period and very dangerous to stay in the home village. As for Yuan Brother's coming to America, the new rules still allow children of merchants to enter through the customs. But he should be familiar with the coaching paper and make a reservation of a ship ticket once he is ready. . . . According to the new rules, children of merchants should obtain the Chinese passport and the approval of the American Consul in Hong Kong. . . . A few days ago, there were about one hundred children of merchants arriving in San Francisco by the Lincoln ship. They did not have Chinese passports and were still waiting for interrogation, according to the new rules. There should not be problems since their documents have the signature of the America consul in Hong Kong. However, as the new rules were just issued, the immigration officers must be very harsh in interrogation. Brother Yuan's coaching paper is in great detail and, if he memorizes the detail, there should not be any problem. Once he makes reservation of a ship ticket, please let me know so that I can contact our attorney in San Francisco immediately.[49]

In another letter of August, Sam wrote directly to Ruyuan.

> Ruyuan Cousin:
>
> You should be very familiar with the coaching paper. Now the im-
> migration officers are very strict. Any mistake will prevent you from
> getting admitted. Yesterday a ship arrived in San Francisco. Six sons
> of merchants applied but only one of them was admitted. The other
> five were denied. I have enclosed this newspaper clipping for your
> reference.[50]

To get the approval of the Immigration Bureau, Sam and his wife Cen had
to appear in the INS office and go through testimony interviews again.

In a typical testimony interview, the INS officers did not ask questions
randomly. Their strategies included finding out the true identity of the interviewee and exploring all aspects of his/her family including the extended family, and then grilling the interviewee on minute details about family events
and residence floor plans. When they got answers, they would compare such
information with that given by other family members being interviewed. The
process was always overwhelming. Sam's interview transcript in 1923 is six
pages long with over 60 questions, and the transcript in 1926 is seven pages
long with 174 questions.[51] The longer Sam stayed in America and the more
family members he brought over, the more questions the INS officers would
have for him. The questioning officer was still Nardini, who interrogated Sam
in 1923 with the same interpreter, You Chung Hong. Nardini started with questions on the merchant status of Sam and his herbal business, then switched
to questions on family relationships. Sam again covered his son-and-father
relationship with Yitang and presented himself as a business partner. However, in responding to questions on his parents, Sam used "Choy Bing," the
name of Yitang's tenth elder brother, as the name of his alleged father.[52] The
character *Bing* clearly indicated this person was a member of the Chang family
and belonged to Yitang's generation, though little information was available
in Sam's writings about his life. In the interview, Sam stated that Choy Bing
passed away when he was fourteen and Choy Bing's wife died in 1908, which
could be true—and could also reduce questions from Nardini about those two
people. Using the life story of diseased family members as the alleged parents could be painful but did help Sam, his wife Cen, and other family members remained consistent in the interviews, as the basic facts were real except
for the twist in the relationships. Failing to find mistakes regarding Sam's
alleged parents, Nardini switched to questions on a diseased daughter of Sam

and challenged him as to why he did not mention this child and why his wife Cen denied her. Sam quickly replied that he wasn't asked about that girl, and that Chinese didn't want to talk about diseased family members. Then Nardini raised questions on the residential floor plan, including where the water well was, how deep it was, and whether water was drawn with a pump or a bucket. The officer would test Cen on similar questions.

If Nardini's questioning of Sam was tough, his interrogation of Cen was a torture. It was by no means easy for Cen, as any mistake would not prevent passing off this cousin as their alleged son. She had to be thoroughly familiar with Yitang's tenth brother's family history in the interview, because this tenth brother was used as her "paper father-in-law," and stand firm against all questions. Assuming that women were easier to get flustered, Nardini began with a very sexist and intrusive question on a physical feature of Cen, "When did you unbind your feet?" He could potentially test Cen's children on her answer. By replying that she could not remember, Cen closed this question and left no room for Nardini to verify this information with other family members. The most malicious part of the interview concerned the death of Cen's child. Attacking the vulnerability of a mother's memory of a diseased child, Nardini asked how many of her children had died. Cen replied, "I don't remember those things." Nardini pressed on: "Your husband answered this question and why can you not answer it?" Cen answered, "I don't want to say anything about it." Then Nardini threatened, "Do you refuse to answer that question?" Cen maintained her position: "I am not refusing but these things break my heart. I don't care to remember them." Nardini callously pursued: "Do you remember how many died?" Cen at this point complied: "one or two." Nardini went further, "Boys or girls?" Cen simply said, "Girls." When Nardini wanted to challenge her on this fact and asked,, "Two girls died, then?" Cen again refused the question: "I don't remember." In reality, Cen could not mention the boy who died in infancy, because Tingqu, son of Sam's second brother, had used the dead boy's name when he came to America with Cen in 1923.

Nardini, however, wanted Cen to acknowledge that the dead children were boys. As an INS officer, he did not want to leave any immigration slot for boys in a Chinese family profile, because he knew that, during the exclusion period, Chinese immigrant families were far more likely to bring boys than girls to America. While painfully responding to Nardini's inquiry, Cen did not neglect her obligation to protect the family secrets and insisted that the diseased children were girls. She boldly fought back when she felt Nardini's interrogation threatening her children and the family interest, and courageously resisted a psychological attack on her cultural sensibility as a Chinese immigrant woman. Her firm attitude somehow persuaded the officer to switch to another topic. Nardini's questions on the well in the house were offensive but funny. He did not seem to believe that Chinese people in Guangzhou (Canton) had already used running water, asking Cen, "Have you got running water in the house?" The reply was yes. He then ridiculously asked if the running water came from a well in the house, and the answer was, of course, no. He further asked if Cen had ever used the well. When Cen said no again, he was probably at a loss and demanded, "Why not?" Cen told the officer, "The old people used to use that well, but we never used it." At this point, it is not even clear if the officer was still questioning Cen for facts or merely pressuring her to give an inconsistent answer. Cen's calm attitude, firm position, and courage to refuse certain questions demonstrate how Chinese immigrant women confronted the unsympathetic INS officers, calmly handled interrogation, and courageously defended family interest. Surprisingly, Nardini's impression of Sam and Cen was very positive, as he wrote at the end of the interview record, "Demeanor of both witnesses very favorable."

In his separate report, Nardini also wrote:

> I visited the place on the 17th instant with Interpreter You Chung Hong of this office and found it to be free from objectionable features and an old-fashion[ed] residence building fast disappearing from the business section of the city. The families of the alleged father and the manager reside there. One of the rooms is devoted for the storage and curing of herbs and one for general consultation, it appearing that they cater quite extensively to the white trade. The words "Chinese Herb Company, Y. H. Chung, manager" appear in gold lettering on the front window. The alleged parents made a very favorable impression, answering all the questions readily and sincerely. They immediately recognized the photo of applicant (marked "No. 4") as appearing in the group of five furnished by the San Francisco office.

As a dutiful officer, Nardini observed not only that Caucasians were Yitang's major clients but also details such as the gold lettering of Yitang's store's name. This "big brother" type of inspection illustrates how closely Chinese American families and businesses were under surveillance by the INS.

Interestingly, Sam and Cen's interview transcripts have also left us with a detailed picture of their life in Guangzhou. They lived in a big brick house with two parlors, four bedrooms, a kitchen downstairs, and one bedroom and a parlor upstairs. They had two servants; one was Ah Ho, a "slave girl" or *mui tsai* whom they had purchased ten years before. *Mui tsai* means "little sister" in Chinese, and existed in Guangdong as a bond-maidservant system for a long time. Girls born to impoverished families were purchased by rich families as unpaid domestic servants until they reached marriage age. Then they would either be married off by the master family or become concubines in the family. Another servant was a middle-aged woman, Ah Som, who was already married and was paid monthly as wage help. They had running water but no electricity. They used kerosene lamps for light. Opposite the house was a temple, and a short distance away were a Baptist missionary school as well as a couple of regular public schools. The street they lived on also had a number of stores and the road was paved with white stone. The length of the street was about one block of an average Los Angeles street. When they traveled abroad, they used a rickshaw to go to the pier and then took a boat from Guangzhou to Hong Kong, from which they booked a ship to the United States.

Troubled Home

Although his wife and daughter joined him, Sam did not view the United States as his permanent home. Nor did he give up his intention to go back to China someday. In a letter to his second brother, he writes,

> If you come to America, you could come for a visit and then travel to see Europe. But you should return and find a government position in the North and stay away from Guangdong politics. . . . It is not wise for all of our four brothers to stay in this country. Someone should stay in China and take care of things there, so that we can go back when we need to develop our careers there. America is not our home, anyway. China has vast lands, though it is still backward in transportation and politics and has failed to be a strong country. In America, you can make a high salary, but everything is expensive here, too. Even if you can make one or two hundred dollars a month, it is still not enough for a large family. After I make enough money, I will go back to China and look for opportunities there.[53]

With his education and police officer's background, Sam probably still hoped to pursue a government position in China. If Yitang viewed his migration to America as a way to further expand his herbalist business and career, Sam regarded his stay in America as a way to assist his father and help the family business. He was a very educated person, but immigration often meant downward mobility for educated people. The more educated an immigrant was, the more disappointed he or she probably became, as professional jobs were usually not available for educated immigrants. Sam was not very enthusiastic about becoming a farmer in America after a promising police career in China, yet family interest obliged him to stay and assist his father in the family farming business. On the other hand, he may not have been too eager to go back to Guangdong at a time when his home village was experiencing bitter lineage politics and family feuds, and when China was witnessing increasing political chaos.

In Sam's correspondence with his relatives in China, we find several tragic episodes in his home village resulting from bandit attacks. In a 1922 poem, Sam Chang wrote:

> Chaotic is our hometown and rampant the bandits.
> Mention no Cattle Hill Village again,
> as looting and killing is always the news.
> To ransom the father, the folks sell the son.

In a supplementary note, he explained: "Our clan has recently been attacked four times by bandits. Five people were killed and eleven were kidnapped. One family had to sell their son in order to ransom the father."[54]

While Sam was in California, social order was deteriorating rapidly in rural Guangdong. Some local tyrant clans and evil gentry, acting like bandits, used violence to accumulate power and wealth. The situation reflected in the above poem is a case in point. Sam's home village, Niushan (Cattle Hill), was always on alert against the bandits from Hushan (Tiger Hill) Village. The Tiger Hill bandits were probably simply more powerful and tyrannical neighbors, who wanted to prey on weaker and smaller neighboring clans or villages during this chaotic period.

Since Sam had worked for the Police Bureau and his second brother worked for a local court, the Nine Families often requested they use their government connections to deal with bandit attack. In response to his relatives' request to use such connections, Sam wrote:

> I have learned that our home village has been attacked again. Twelve people were kidnapped, among whom were Dapei's wife and Nephew Chong. Uncle Libing's wife managed to escape from being kidnapped. The bandits were so rampant, and I really feel very angry

about it. Zhaopei wrote to me and requested Zhiqing to arrest the father and the son of the Tiger Hill clan. But I don't think Zhiqing has the power to do so. It will also give them an excuse to seek more revenge. In my opinion, you should submit a petition with the list of the kidnapped to the county magistrate and indicate where the bandits hide. This Magistrate Huang used to be a chief editor of a newspaper in San Francisco, and we have met each other once. If we turn to him for help, he may be able to do something.[55]

Sam Chang's letter indicates that his home village was far from being a safe place. Banditry was a problem beyond his control. His second brother was sometimes directly involved in fighting against the bandits. Several times, when assistance from local government troops was available, his brother Weizong guided the army to fight the bandits. In 1922, after reading a letter from his brother, Sam wrote:

I have read Brother Zhongping's [Weizong's] letter about the bandits and seen how thin and exhausted he looks in the photo. After guiding the army to fight against the bandits, my brother's hair all turned white. He also coughed blood. I could not fall asleep and have composed the following poems.

Tough is your double responsibility
Suppressing the bandits and protecting the kin.
In five years of fighting,
My brother has gone through fire and water.

In an explanatory note, he wrote: "My brother has led troops to search and fight bandits for several times. The battle was fierce."[56]

As Sam knew that neither military suppression nor legal punishment by the local authorities could completely remove the banditry problem, he advised Weizong to stay away from the village. Sam gave the following advice:

Yesterday, I received a letter from Lipei saying you would go back to the home village. . . . Whenever you go on a trip there, father and I are worried. It is too unstable to stay there. . . . You must always keep in mind that we are a weak family branch. Stay away from the lineage affairs as much as possible. Keep a low profile. It is a tragedy that strong sibling families bully the weak sibling families within the *wufu* [five mourning grades in a lineage]. . . . Remember how Dapei was killed, how a servant girl was kidnapped, how our property was looted, and how a hundred clan members had to flee before that criminal was sentenced to death.

Sam was pleased to hear that the local government had already executed the bandits who helped the Three Families. But other bandits were still around. He went on to write:

> But you still have to be careful. . . . In my observation, the decline and the final dissolve of our family cannot be helped. The longer you stay in the home village and Guangdong, the more deeply you will get yourself involved in family affairs. . . . That is not good. Don't worry too much about getting back the money we lent to others. Just try to get what you can. America lent millions of dollars to European countries in the European War and did not get back anything so far. Although our family is poor, we still have something to eat. The money will be paid back eventually. . . . We can use the money and land to build a school for the children of the poor families, such as Li, Qi, Chen, and Liang. We can help eight to ten children every year by paying their tuition with the rice rent, in the name of our father and grandfather, and make a record of it so that people will remember their names. . . . Father hopes that we brothers live away from the home village and keep ourselves safe from the murderous hands. At the moment, I am practicing shooting skills to protect myself. If you can get a license, you should buy a gun to protect yourself. You only need to go back to the home village on two occasions—to sweep the graves of Grandmother and Mother. Otherwise we brothers should never return to the Five Cattle Hill.[57]

As the letter indicates, Sam had no hopes of getting back the Chang family property owned in the home village. He did not even expect to get back the money that Yitang loaned the Nine Families. Faced with a precarious situation, Sam advised his second brother to bear arms on his visit to the home village if he intended to collect rent. However, Sam still cherished his home village at heart because it was his birthplace and his grandmother and mother's tombs were there.

In the same year, Sam also wrote to his son and described the suffering of the home village from the bandits' attack, and the hard job his second brother had in taking care of the family property there:

> In the last six years, our clan has been frequently attacked by bandits. More than a hundred of our folks fled to the city. Many were

killed; and many died of illness and poverty. Your uncle has a heavy
burden to handle everything by himself—dealing with the bandits,
taking care of those who have passed away, the land and housing
property.[58]

In explaining the situation in his hometown, Sam urged his son to go north
for his college education and not to get involved in family conflicts. Given
the chaotic situation in rural Guangdong at that time, neither Sam nor Yitang
wanted to go back and make use of their family properties in the home village. Both Yitang and Sam moved from the village, to live in Guangzhou City,
before traveling to America. After their own wives and children joined them
in America, and their herbal and farming business became an important income source, they gradually distanced themselves from the lineage affairs
back home. As Sam said, the only business they had to do with the home
village was to sweep their ancestor's tombs. Their attachment to the home
village gradually became more symbolic than real. When social instability
in China and a hostile racial environment in the United States prevented Yitang
and Sam, as first generation immigrants, from developing a sense of roots
on either side of the Pacific, family reunification, safety, and well-being, along
with the education of the second generation became a focal point of their
social existence.

CHAPTER 5

Asparagus Farming
as a Family Business

Sam began his farming career around 1918, when he took over the management of his father's farm, located at 4660 Whitsett Avenue in North Hollywood. Asparagus farming was a long-term investment and required fairly sophisticated skills. Usually an asparagus farm could not produce a yield until at least the third year. Although the Chang family did not use the entire farm to grow asparagus, still enough land was involved that it was a challenge for Sam to make sure the farm would yield asparagus on time under his management. This farm was the first land property the family owned in America, and the capital investment included money from relatives and friends. As a filially devoted son, Sam could not let his father down in this job.

As Sam had no farming experience, he began by experimenting, visiting other Chinese asparagus farms, making notes on his observations, and acquiring skills from other farmers. To learn and observe how to grow asparagus, Sam visited farms of other Chinese in Southern California and sometimes went as far as Stockton and the Sacramento Valley, where asparagus was grown on a large scale and had been a profitable commercial crop farmed by many Chinese since 1892.[1] Sam's farming career thus is part of the collective Chinese asparagus farmers' experience.

When Sam took over the responsibility for the family farm, he tasted the hardship of being a small, independent produce farmer. He wrote to a friend:

> I have been a farmer for three years. Life is boring and business is bad. My farm is losing money. Every day I have to get up at six in the morning and finish work late in the evening. I am terribly busy. I am sorry to write you back [only now,] after you have written me three letters. But I have no time to write. I can write to you today

100

because it has been raining continuously and I cannot work in the field.[2]

As the manager of the farm, Sam often worked in the field side by side with his workers from morning until sunset, because he felt that he needed to accumulate farming experience, supervise the workers, and, more important, save on labor costs. Working in the fields was a hardship he had never experienced in his police career in China.

During the first few years of his farming career, Sam on several occasions wanted to switch to another business. In 1922, he wrote to his second brother in China:

The soil is too poor and growing asparagus can hardly make any profit. Many friends and relatives advised me to give it up and try something else. If I switch to the warehouse business serving the Mexicans, I may have a more reliable job. But it will be difficult for Father to find someone to replace me. Father also found it difficult to hire more help for me. So someone from our family should come to help. We should try to get Cousin Wei and Yuan to come here, too.[3]

In his other letters, Sam frequently complained about the lack of profits and the need for capital, but also indicated his progress in farming. In November 1924, he wrote to his son Tennyson, still in China at that time:

In the last couple of years, the asparagus farm is getting better and finally beginning to make some profit. I plan to leave the farming career and find some other job so that I can make enough money for Yuhua's and your education and spare your grandfather from this tuition burden.[4]

The letter indicates again that Sam wanted to switch to another career and did not make much money, as Yitang helped him pay his children's tuition in China. However, he continued to work on the farm since his father wanted him to stay.

Like raising most vegetable crops, growing asparagus was an arduous and labor-intensive job. The harvest season usually lasted from March to September in Southern California, with April to July the busiest period. In his farming notes, Sam wrote:

If the soil is sandy, then the asparagus will not grow very well. I use a lot of fertilizer as my land is sandy. Each acre needs about a half pound of seed. Whether sowing by hand or by machine, planting should not be too dense. Water the field every two weeks, with some fertilizer. If the weather is warm, the asparagus will mature in mid-February. If it is cold, the crop will be about twenty days late. When the asparagus has grown to seven or eight inches, it is ready for cutting. If it is longer than that, it will not sell very well on the market.[5]

The cutting of asparagus was a delicate and arduous job, as the farmer had to be very selective about size. Asparagus spears that were too short would be sorted into a lower grade, while spears that were too long would be considered too old for sale on the market.

Harvesting first-grade asparagus, a good laborer could cut only one acre per day. For the second grade, one laborer could do two acres a day. And for the third grade, one laborer could handle three acres. Although the Chang family invested in twenty-five acres of land, Sam only used nine acres to grow asparagus, in the beginning. For this acreage, he hired five to six laborers plus himself. Once his wife and daughter joined him in 1923, they helped with cutting and with sorting, as well. During a warm season, the harvesting had to be more intensive, because the crop would grow fast. On the other hand, frost and wind could hurt the harvesting. The most backbreaking work, though, was digging up the asparagus root when the yield declined: after a farm had produced a yield for ten to twelve years, the farmer had to completely dig up the asparagus roots and plant new seed (the new field would not produce, however, until after the third year).

Under Sam's careful management, the farm began to yield asparagus in the third year. He became a master asparagus farmer and could handle asparagus growing on both rich soil and sandy land. In addition, he planted many other agricultural crops, including potatoes, sweet corn, hay, alfalfa, sweet potatoes, squash, pumpkin, watermelon, cabbage, and cauliflower. In a more optimistic letter, he wrote to his son:

> Now the farm business is getting better. After the deduction of various costs, we have made a profit of about two to three thousand dollars. Moreover, the price of land is now six to seven times higher than before. This investment could allow your grandfather to rely on the farm for his retirement. He plans to visit China in the fall and stay there for several months. After he comes back from his trip to China, I will find my own way of making money to support you children and your education.[6]

When the farm began to be profitable and the value of the land went up considerably, it became a symbol of success for an immigrant Chinese family in "Gold Mountain" (the United States). Together with herbal medicine, asparagus farming enabled the Changs to sponsor many family members' immigration to America. Sam did not make much money for himself, but he placed the collective interest of the Chang family above his own. He farmed for more than fifty years after beginning to work for his father. He sometimes wanted to explore other career opportunities and often talked about returning to China, but his strong sense of family obligation made him a life-long asparagus grower in America. The two farms under his management became a reliable source of family income, provided job opportunities for immigrant relatives and friends, and turned the once-novice into an experienced member of the local agricultural community. Sam's farming career transformed him from a sojourner into a settler. It was his motivation to succeed in a new career, his commitment to family interest, and his sacrifice of his own dream that made him a permanent resident of America.

Second Farm

Following the success of the first farm, the Chang family had become confident in asparagus farming, and interested in real estate property as the value of land in Southern California increased rapidly, beginning in the early twentieth century. In January 1928, the family purchased its second asparagus farm, this one at Hayvenhurst Avenue in Northridge in the San Fernando Valley. Sam wrote to his children:

> Together with Mr. Zhang and Yan, both of whom are from Enping County, your grandfather has purchased Mr. Tan's asparagus farm. Grandfather and your third uncle had visited the farm. A Western broker highly recommended this property. Thirty-eight acres of the farm have already yielded asparagus for four years. The price of the farm is fifty-three thousand dollars. Zhang and Yan will pay a total of twenty thousand dollars. Our family will pay the rest in three years.[7]

Asparagus farming was profitable, but required substantial investment. The Chang family was able to purchase the new farm and expand their farming business because family members had shared risks and profits in the first farm, used underpaid family labor, and accumulated experience and capital. Although the family's own capital was still modest, Sam had become an experienced farmer and was thus able to invite investments from other Chinese families. A typical way for Chinese immigrants to build and develop their family business was to pool resources, work as both owner/manager and laborer, and form partnership with one another.

Sam and other Chinese asparagus farmers bought their farms during a period when Asians were not allowed to own land. California had passed the Alien Land Act in 1913, forbidding Asian immigrants from owning land or leasing it for over three years. Chinese farmers needed to bypass this racist policy with strategies such as using their native-born children's names or establishing a stock-dividend company. Yitang's second wife, and his children with her, were American-born Chinese. In an immigration interview, Sam indicated that the property of the Chang family in San Fernando Valley was registered under Yitang's daughter's name.[8] Their farms also involved minor partners who were American-born Chinese, for property registration purposes. However, some immigrant Chinese farmers, according to Sam's recollection, did run into trouble. A Chinese named Zhao Song was banned from farming after he leased twenty acres of land in Van Nuys. Through a lawyer's arrangement, Zhao managed to gain the exclusive rights to market the crop while having somebody else farm it. Another farmer, named Chew, had a similar experience. When his attempt to lease forty acres of land for growing potatoes was rejected, his attorney helped him obtain a contract to buy and market the farm's produce for three years. Thus Chew was still able to make a net income of forty thousand dollars, and later he managed to buy one hundred acres of land in Van Nuys.[9] As asparagus farming was a long-term investment, Chinese farmers preferred to buy or lease their land.

The opportunities for the Chinese to purchase land in the San Fernando Valley probably arose from speculative land swindles of the early twentieth century. Land profiteers quietly bought up 108,000 acres of previously unirrigated land in the San Fernando Valley at prices of five, ten, and twenty dollars per acre, and then, after Los Angeles built an aqueduct to transport irrigation water from the Owens Valley to irrigate the San Fernando Valley land, sold their holdings for five hundred to one thousand dollars per acre.[10] Regardless of the restrictive Alien Land Act, the Chinese asparagus farmers aptly grasped the opportunity to purchase property from the land syndicate eager to sell its holdings. Irrigation for the Changs' second farm became available in 1930, two years after the family brought it.

The second farm was about forty acres. Two blocks away was the farm owned by Hu Zhu, another Chinese asparagus farmer. Hu was probably one of the wealthiest Chinese farmers in Southern California. According to Sam, Hu's farm was worth between three hundred thousand and four hundred thousand dollars.[11] After Sam moved to the Hayvenhust Street farm, the two families became good neighbors. They often visited each other, shared farming experiences, and helped each other in business. When his own business was slack, Sam helped the Hu family with their asparagus sales, charging a modest service fee. In a letter to his son, he wrote: "The money I have sent you is my wage from Hu Zhu. Last month, I made some money when I helped him sell his asparagus. The wage is four cents a case, which is low. It should be five cents a case. After I sold my asparagus, I usually help Hu with his sales."[12] After the Chang family purchased the second farm, Sam became more involved in the operation of the Chinese Asparagus Association of Southern California. He wrote:

> I was elected as the president of the Asparagus Association. I don't want this job. But I was elected and have to do it. The office budget is seventy-five dollars a month, but I don't have a salary, and there is a lot of work to do. This year's asparagus market is better since the production in Sacramento is reduced.[13]

Although he complained about the workload as the association's president, he knew the association was an important organization for Chinese asparagus farmers in Southern California and that it promoted sales of members through its own marketing system. Sam served as its president for three terms.

During the harvest season, farmers were responsible for hiring their own hands to cut and pick up the asparagus from the fields and sort the crop into grades in the packinghouse. Every Chinese farmer's home had a packinghouse, and a stable for horses and wagons. To save on labor costs, family members often helped with the sorting. Sam's wife, though coming from a wealthy family, always worked in the packinghouse. When his daughters became teenagers, they helped Sam pack two hundred cases a day (though they usually worked only during weekends). Each family would, in the late evening, deliver the crop to an agriculture market in Los Angeles for the next day's sale. All sales went through the collective efforts of the Association, although each farmer could market produce under a different brand name. At this time, Sam grew the most widely marketed brand of asparagus: the Emerald Brand.

Sam built a new, spacious, and comfortable house on the second farm. It had modern furnishings and a tiled bathroom with a tub. Shortly afterward, the family also bought their first car in the United States—a Model-T Ford. Sam was especially happy about the car, as it could help him commute between farms. In a 1928 letter to his son, Sam referred to the new home with evident pride:

The house has electricity, a telephone, an electric stove, a bathroom with tub and tile floor, and so on. We have a beautiful front garden and a large back yard. It is very comfortable. We have also bought a car. When you come to the United States, I can drive you to school. It was so difficult for me to take care of everything on the two farms when we did not own a car. But we still need more capital. The labor cost us too much and the workers are lazy. Next year we should buy a car for the old farm.[14]

The second farm was a good investment and began to yield crops soon after the Chang family took over. Although Sam still worried about capital flow and labor costs, he became more confident about farming. The Chang family went on to lease several dozen acres of land to expand their asparagus business.[15]

The house Sam built on the new farm gave him a firm sense of home in the United States. When his youngest daughter, Joyce (Yuzai), was born in May 1928, he sounded happy in a letter to his son and daughter about the birth of the baby, and optimistic about his life.

I am now very busy with my work on two farms. Your mother gave birth to a new baby girl on May 27. As I need to take care of many things, I did not write to you for two-and-a-half months. We call the baby Yuzai, meaning "planting jade." She looks like Yuhua. Yuchu looks like Tingxun. Your mother is in good health. Yuzai is, too. We will send you her photo in one or two months. Your mother's previous labor was very difficult. It was smooth this time, because we hired a good Western doctor and two assistants for the delivery at home.[16]

In another letter, he explained that this daughter's name, "Yuzai," was close to the pronunciation of the English name "Joyce," which meant "happiness."[17] *Yu*, meaning jade in Chinese, was used as the middle character in the names of Sam's daughters. The *Zai* character, meaning "planting," was obviously linked to Sam's farming career. Both the Chinese and English meanings reveal Sam's happy mood. After ten years' of farming, he had begun to cherish asparagus as valuable as jade. The profit from the crop had given him a new house and allowed him to buy a new car and hire a good doctor for his wife's delivery. Although Sam did not mention the fact, he was feeling more settled in American society. Although he never gave up his wish to go back to China, his farming career rooted him deeply in the local agricultural community.

A Diverse Labor Pool

Sam Chang was a shrewd agribusiness manager, especially in hiring laborers. An efficient work force could help reduce labor costs. In hiring laborers, Sam dealt with people of varied ethnicities. Racial background influenced the wages of Sam's non-Chinese workers. Writing in 1933, Sam commented:

> It is also important to get to know your workers. In the Los Angeles area, my labor supply comes from the Chinese, Mexicans, Filipinos, Americans, Germans, and Italians. Their monthly wages range from sixty or seventy to a hundred dollars. White workers are usually good, though they get paid higher than any other group. The Chinese are the second-highest-paid group, followed by the Filipinos. The Mexicans receive the lowest wages, as they are lazier than other groups. They only work in the first half of the month, and rest in the second half until they have spent all their money. Then they will work again. In the first few days, they work well, yet in ten days they become lazy. Good workers are usually stiff in manner and quick-tempered. Those who are lazy tend to have some humor and a good temper. Out of a hundred workers I have used, only a few are good workers with nice personalities. Five are Chinese, two Mexican, two white, and one Japanese.[18]

In contrast to the stereotypical image of the Chinese as clannish, Sam's letter presents a colorful world of laborers he interacted with as a Chinese farmer. Although he listed their nationalities and ethnic backgrounds, what mattered to him was their work attitude and personality, rather than their citizenship or English-language ability. When he described the Mexicans as lazy, it is unclear to what extent either prejudice against Mexicans or his personal experience influenced his judgment, but his generalization is contradicted by his listing "two Mexicans" among the few "good workers." Crossing ethnic boundaries, he included laborers from all racial backgrounds in this list.

It is interesting that Sam listed Germans and Italians as separate from Americans. Although Sam did not specify whether these Germans and Italians were immigrants or native-born, he did emphasize that the white laborers were paid best. Sam understood racial differences within the labor market. On his payroll, Caucasian workers usually received the highest wage, and Filipinos and Mexicans the lowest, as seen in another letter, written in 1933. He wrote: "I usually pay forty dollars to those who are in charge of plowing and irrigation, and thirty dollars to those who cut the asparagus. For the Filipinos and Mexicans, I pay twenty-eight dollars."[19] As a farmer, Sam had to pay prevailing wages as determined by labor market conditions. In 1933, wages for farm workers were particularly low because of the Great Depression.

When the harvest season arrived, Sam would hire thirty to forty Mexican laborers. Mexican workers stayed on the farm until the harvest was over. One worker was supposed to cut eighteen cases of asparagus per day. Sam preferred to hire Mexicans because he found them more stable than Caucasian laborers: while Mexicans followed the harvest, Caucasian workers went to whoever paid the better wages. Also, as local laborers, Caucasian workers could leave whenever they chose; as foreign laborers, Mexicans were subject to many restrictions and tended to grab the first employment available. They also relied on the farm owners to provide lodging and even food. On his farm, Sam had a place for workers to sleep, and sometimes provided vegetables, but he did not provide cooks or meals.

Hiring Relatives as Laborers

In his farming business, most of Sam's full-time Chinese workers were relatives, or people recommended by his relatives and friends. Hiring relatives had advantages and disadvantages. Relative workers usually were more stable than other workers, as their arrival in the United States was a result of Yitang's sponsorship. Sam and his father brought more than forty relatives to America, most entering as merchant immigrants (or family members of merchants) since laborers were not allowed to enter.[20] After arriving, these relatives worked either in Yitang's herbal business or on the farms. Some also shared stocks in the farms. As laborers, they usually stayed on the farm until they had saved enough money to send for their wives and children and begin their own business. Kin relationship gave these laborers a sense of security and responsibility.

The Chang family, as farm owners, and their relative laborers did not share the same goals or interest in the farming business, however. Sam comments on such conflict of interest in a 1923 letter to his son:

> Asparagus is growing better this year than last year, and the price at the market is stable. But we need capital to expand the business. Several of our relatives in the Chang families have shares in this farm. Whenever the farm makes some profits, your uncle Tianpei is eager

to cash out his profits and return to China. One day, he got mad over a minor incident. He swore in front of me and told me that the farm did not only belong to me alone, and I should quit as the manager. People like Tianpei do not care that the farm needed capital to expand. They are only concerned with living comfortably on the farm, getting paid well, and then returning to China.[21]

Unlike other laborers, Tianpei, or his father, probably also invested some money as a minor partner. If he felt his share of profit too small or his wage too low, he could, as a relative, express his unhappiness. Although Sam's chief concerns were labor costs, the market situation, profit, capital accumulation, and expansion of the business, the relatives working for him were interested in more immediate benefits, such as food, living conditions, workload, and wages. As they were not major shareholders of the farm, they held economical perspectives differing from Yitang's and Sam's on the farm's future.

Although some were closely related, his relatives were not necessarily as reliable as Sam expected. When Ruyuan, the son of his twelfth uncle, immigrated to California in 1926, Sam hired him as a field supervisor. However, Sam soon had regrets. He wrote: "Ruyuan has arrived in Los Angeles and is now working as a labor boss on the farm, with a salary of seventy dollars a month. But he is lazy. Only a week after he started the job, he complained about the hardship of the labor and wanted to find some other job."[22] Still, though the cousin seemed less qualified than his other workers, Sam paid him ten dollars more per month. During that period, the normal wage of a Chinese laborer was fifty to sixty dollars per month; Sam himself made ninety per month as the farm's manager.[23] Because of the kinship obligation, Sam put a less qualified relative in a key position on his farm, sometimes, against his own will.

Hiring Ruyuan was actually not the result of a labor need, but to please Sam's twelfth uncle, who lived in China. On payday, Sam remitted a large portion of Ruyuan's wage to this twelfth uncle—directly and in spite of Ruyuan's opposition. In a 1933 letter, Sam wrote: "I only give him fifteen dollars every month. The rest of the money is either remitted back to his family or goes back to the loan for his ship ticket, because he spends money recklessly."[24] In another letter, Sam told his twelfth uncle how he handled Ruyuan's wage:

> After I figure out how much he should be paid, I deposit the money into the bank. When he demanded it, I asked him what it was for. He said it was not my business; it was his money and he wanted it. I

told him that it was his father's idea that we should not give him money unless it was absolutely necessary. We were not to give him more than fifteen or twenty dollars a month without his father's permission.[25]

Ruyuan rebelled against such payments and wanted his total pay. As he could not tolerate a farmer's hard life, he often left the farm to visit gambling houses or nightclubs. One day, he went to hide himself in a nightclub owned by a white woman, and refused to go back to the farm. Sam's wife asked their neighbor Hu Zhu for help, as Hu spoke fluent English. Hu went to the nightclub a couple of times, but the white woman would not let Hu take Ruyuan away.[26]

Eventually Ruyuan quit the job and left for New York. Ruyuan's decision made Sam and Yitang very unhappy, as it meant the waste of one Chang family immigration slot after all the risks and efforts made in the sponsorship process. But family solidarity did not always work to bind every Chinese immigrant to family interest. Individualism in American society could influence an immigrant's decision regarding his or her relations with family and relatives. Ruyuan's leaving is obviously a divergence from the collectivism of Chinese family culture.

Labor Relations

Although hiring Chinese often embodied ethnic solidarity, Sam was cautious in handling relationships with his Chinese laborers. Chinese cultural tradition did not encourage him to engage in open confrontation with them, but the major reason for avoiding confrontation was a shortage of labor. Under the Chinese Exclusion laws, Chinese labor was difficult to obtain; conflicts between labor and management could cause serious losses for the farmers, as Sam wrote in one letter:

> Since it is extremely difficult to get workers here, we have to tolerate complaints. Every week, we get a lot of scolding from the workers. If we talk back, they will quit the job, and the farming will be neglected. Several Chinese farmers were already in trouble this year. A minor quarrel could lead to three or four strikes. And the owners of the farm bear the hardships themselves. Of course, tolerance is not always a good alternative. But we will see if the workers are skilled laborers. If they are skilled and lose their temper because of exhaustion from work, we should be sincere in listening to their com-

plaints, and give them an ambiguous response. They will gradually calm down. Confucius says that if you cannot bear small complaints, you will suffer great failure. As for those who always scold others but never work hard, you just get rid of them as soon as possible. While we are sympathetic and polite, we should be firm in our decision. When the knowledgeable quarrels with the ignorant, he lowers his integrity.[27]

As the letter indicates, the racial environment in American society, the labor market, kinship relationships, and family interests were all considered in Sam's handling of labor relations. Although Sam never forgot that he belonged to the "knowledgeable" class, he had to cross class lines to approach his laborers. Maintaining a modest style in management, showing due respect to his workers, and tolerating certain behaviors were all necessary strategies. Navigating the nuances of ethnic solidarity seemed a more complicated job for Sam than learning how to plant asparagus.

To avoid potential feuds, Sam carefully observed the personalities of his workers, assigned jobs according to each person's ability and character, and exercised restraint when conflicts arose. He wrote:

We have six workers on our farm. One of them is named Cen, from En-ping. He has a nickname—"No.1 Cen"—because he wants to be number one in everything. He will not allow disagreement with anything he says. He is illiterate and stubborn. He does not like other people to comment on his work. He tries to work fast but often does a poor job, though he may work harder than others. There is also a Li, a housekeeper of the laborers, who is slow and has poor hearing. Li likes to take small advantages but he has a good temper. He does not get angry when people blame or tease him. He is happy as long as he has got some money for opium-smoking. Lu, another worker, is about sixty. He works a little bit slowly but he is very careful, meticulous, and thoughtful. I often ask him to finish the neglected part of Cen's work. When I am busy, I also use him as my assistant. He can read and write a little bit. As he is also addicted to opium smoking, he can hardly save enough money to go back to China, though he is already fifty-eight. This is why he needs a job here. He has poor health, does not talk much, and seldom jokes with other people. But he is a fine worker. Another worker, Yu, is nineteen and has been in America for only one year. He has been gambling in the last several months. His brother-in-law once bought him a new suit that is worth thirty dollars. Wearing it for a few days, he went to gamble. When he lost, he sold the suit for five dollars and lost again. He did not know what to do. At that time, our farm was hiring laborers. We hired him to do both cooking and farming. On the fourth day, his skin got a little tanned because of sunshine. He wanted to quit the job, but I asked him to stay for three more days. He quarreled with the other workers several times and finally left the farm. Of the workers, Cen is most diligent, Lu is meticulous, and Li is very patient. These are the three we need most on the farm, and each has played his own role in the work. We cannot trade their positions.[28]

This keen and interesting observation demonstrates Sam's patience, flexibility, and above all, familiarity with his workers. Sam's writing presented his laborers not as a faceless horde of laborers, but as real human beings. Their humorous nature, eccentric behavior, or personal character made them distinct and lively individuals. Each had his own pride, hobby, and personality, and was willing to defend his rights whenever necessary. Each also had his aspirations and problems. Some had unrealistic dreams of striking it rich quickly and returning home as successful Gold Mountain guests, though they never made it. Others had already lost hope as they grew old, and therefore indulged in opium smoking as their last human pleasure. Although Sam sometimes disagreed with them, and often had conflicts of interest with them, he treated them with respect and got along with them. This lively and realistic description is one of the rare, vivid, and valuable pieces of written documentation of Chinese immigrant laborers left by the Chinese themselves.

Surviving the Great Depression and World War II

The labor market situation changed drastically in the early 1930s. The Great Depression hit the Chinese community hard. Businesses in Chinatown were closed down and many Chinese laborers became unemployed. In a letter, Sam wrote:

The economic depression spreads throughout the world. My asparagus farm is not doing well. The business and life of the entire Chinese community here is experiencing hard times. Unemployed Chinese are everywhere. People cannot get jobs even if they offer to work for food. We are very upset to see Chinatown in Los Angeles filling with several hundred Chinese who entered secretly from Mexico. A relative introduced three men named Liang to work on my farm, but I have already quite a number of people living on the farm and could not afford to let more people stay on my farm. I have been in the United States for more than twenty years but don't have much savings in the bank. During the Depression, only the Soviet Union does not have an unemployment problem. I am not a Communist but I think that the world is probably moving towards that direction.[29]

Sam's letter reveals the frustration and pain of the Chinese community. Los Angeles Chinatown received hundreds of unemployed Chinese from Mexico at the same time the local Chinese were hit hard by the Depression. Being an immigrant himself, Sam did not blame those Chinese who entered illegally into America but worried about their slim employment opportunities during this period. Sam's appreciative attitude towards the Soviet Union indicates his pessimism about the capitalist social system, but he only expressed such an attitude in private correspondence. Although Sam was sympathetic with the immigrants from Mexico, his farm could not take too many Chinese laborers, even if they were recommended by a relative and willing to work for food. The letter illustrates how, in times of difficulty, Chinatown functioned as a global network and how overseas Chinese relied on kinship or other social relations to find employment. The letter also illustrates how the Great Depression impacted Sam's own farming life. Commenting on the market situation for asparagus, Sam wrote: "The asparagus price is lower than any year before this. In July, it was seven cents a pound. Now it is six. The crop of the old farm sold for less than six hundred dollars yet the labor and other costs are over twenty-five hundred dollars. We must sell that farm."[30] As the letter indicates, the difficult situation almost forced the Chang family to sell the old farm. In 1933, a local white merchant made an offer to buy it at six hundred dollars per acre. But, though the old farm continued to lose money, the Chang family determined to hold onto it until they could sell it for a better price; they did so, for twenty thousand dollars, in 1937. However, more than half of this money went to the bank to repay loans.

In 1939, shortly after they sold the old farm, Sam had another difficult year. He wrote to his son:

> All Chinese asparagus farmers have suffered losses this year since each case of asparagus sells five cents less than last year. I want to switch to herbal medicine, as asparagus farming cannot make a profit and family expenses are heavy. Your third uncle invited me to open a medical office with him in Long Beach. I have not promised him yet.[31]

Sam managed to stay in asparagus farming, as the situation improved in 1940. In 1941, he also took over the ownership of the Chang family house on the second farm, and five acres of land in front of the house. He registered the property under his third and fourth daughter's names, as they were American-born Chinese. The rest of the land, he still owned with his father and another person, in a business partnership.

During World War II, labor shortages became a problem again, as Chinese could find employment in the military services and the defense industry. In a 1941 letter, Sam mentioned that four of his relatives went to serve in the U.S. armed forces. When they visited their families, coming in from military camps in other parts of the country, they looked healthy and high-spirited to Sam.[32] In May 1943, Sam claimed: "I have never been so busy in my life. Since April, I have had less than five hours of sleep every day. The harvest started one month earlier than usual and wages have risen so high that we can hardly afford them. Half of our crops remained uncut in the field."[33]

To solve labor shortages, the American government invited workers from Mexico. In 1944, Sam wrote to tell his son"

> The asparagus business is better than before. But agricultural products are subjected to many restrictions and cannot sell at a high price. Meanwhile, the American government helped us get about twenty Mexican workers and solved the labor shortage problem. The rumor is that the government may consider using German P.O.W. laborers rather than recruit workers from Mexico.[34]

However, German prisoners-of-war never arrived. When the war came to an end, many Chinese returned to China. Sam's last two Chinese workers left, too.

In 1947, Sam Chang entered into a sharecropping agreement with a Japanese farmer. Sam described him as a man with a family and farming experience.

> I have hired a Japanese man to run the farm. I provide the capital while he offers his labor. We will divide the profit of the harvest evenly. His family, which includes his parents, his wife, daughter and himself, lives on the farm. I will not charge him for rent, electricity, gas, or furniture. I think he is an experienced farmer and hardworking. If he can work until next summer, and everything is fine by then, I will renew another year's contract with him. . . . Both your mother and I are getting old. Next summer, your mother will

visit the East Coast with Yuzai. In another two years, we will return to China.[35]

This was probably a Japanese American family newly released from an internment camp. Although Sam was bitter about the Japanese invasion of China, he did not try to take advantage of the anti-Japanese sentiment of the times. As a veteran farmer in Southern California, Sam was certainly aware of the long farming history of Japanese immigrants before they were sent to the internment camps. With respect to the sharecropping Japanese man's farming skill, Sam not only hired him but let his whole family stay on the farm. Also interesting in this letter is that Sam expressed his wish to retire in China after almost thirty years' stay in America.

Sam's Perceptions of Chinese Life in America

While learning about farming operations, Sam observed other aspects of Chinese farming life in California, including gambling addiction and what he saw as poor morality at work. In his farming notes, he wrote the following comments on the pervasiveness of gambling among farm laborers:

> But, among the Chinese farm laborers, gambling is so common. In the Stockton area, there are always little boats on the rivers close to farms. These are gambling boats. Some laborers would spend all their savings on gambling and prostitution on these boats. In Los Angeles there are no such boats, but laborers would go to the gambling house located downtown even though my farm is pretty far away from the downtown. I hope our government will work with the American government to eliminate these bad habits among the Chinese farmers. And then we will be able to make the same kind of progress as the Japanese farmers here.[36]

Sam viewed the gambling addiction as a symptom of low morality. He was not able to see it as a problem deeply embedded in the racial environment surrounding the Chinese. Due to the limited job options, low wages, long working hours, and lack of family life, gambling became, for a long time, one of the few entertainments Chinese laborers could enjoy. Sam's laborers, for example, would go all the way from his North Hollywood farm to downtown Los Angeles to gamble.

In his letters, Sam also discussed the lack of family life among the Chinese. Writing to a friend, he commented:

Do not ever think that all overseas Chinese could marry more wives and concubines because they have money. The situation is just the opposite. I have found that there are about sixty-five thousand Chinese in America [the 1919 estimate], with about sixty-one thousand men and only four thousand women, including old people or young kids. There are not many marriageable women. And few of them know traditional Chinese values. . . . It could cost seven thousand to eight thousand Chinese dollars to marry a wife abroad. I hear [that] in London and Paris some Chinese married Western wives because Chinese women are few. But many have to leave for elsewhere to make more money due to the cost. Many marriages have ended in separation.[37]

Sam had probably done some research on this issue, as he provided a fairly accurate figure about the skewed sex ratio among the Chinese during that period. His letter tells us that Chinese immigrants were keenly aware of the negative impact of the exclusion laws on their family life. Under exclusion policies, the unbalanced ratio between Chinese men and women made marriage costs too high for average working-class Chinese immigrants. Viewing all overseas Chinese as a globally connected community, Sam's observation included the Chinese community in Europe.

Another social problem Sam was concerned about was the increasing concentration of Chinese immigrants in the service sector. He wrote: "I have noticed that most of the Chinese farmers are over fifty years old, or even seventy. Younger Chinese are engaged in gambling, restaurants, or laundries. They could not tolerate the hard life of a farmer who works on the scorching field from dawn to sunset." In comparing the Chinese immigrants with the Japanese, Sam continued:

The Japanese immigrants are mainly engaged in farming or the grocery business. They work very hard and have made good profits. Every year they will remit hundreds of thousand of dollars to Japan. That is why Americans started the anti-Japanese movement, to protect the interest of their own farmers. The Japanese cannot buy or lease land in California. They have to turn in one-third of their profits to the white landowners.[38]

In another letter, Sam wrote: "The old generation Chinese immigrants who came to the United States several decades ago are also hardworking people who have tasted all kinds of hardships here in building railways, working in the mines and forests, and reclaiming land."[39] While criticizing the newly arrived Chinese immigrants for pursuing gambling and service businesses, Sam saw social values associated with the occupations the Chinese had become involved in, in America, before the majority were driven into menial service jobs. He considered gold mining, railroad construction, or farming to be meaningful jobs that represented the significant contributions of the Chinese to American society. Laundry, restaurant, and gambling businesses, he considered a disgrace.

Although his writing was not a direct criticism of racism, Sam saw the Japanese following in the footsteps of the Chinese in their American experience. Like the Chinese, they worked extremely hard, engaged in farming and grocery businesses, and remitted money to support families back home. A hardworking spirit similar to that of the Chinese only earned the Japanese similar prejudice and hatred from American society. Sam's farming notes here reflect how the Alien Land Act of California, passed in 1913, prevented Japanese from leasing or purchasing land. His writing shows his sympathy for Japanese immigrants who had "to turn in one-third of their profits to the white landowners" as a result of the racist Alien Land Act.

Sam noticed that workers' morale was becoming lower and lower among the Chinese immigrants:

> While the Japanese have made much progress, the Chinese have achieved downward rather than upward mobility. They have received no education and have little knowledge. There are about seventy thousand to eighty thousand Chinese in America. If they work hard, each could make an income of one thousand dollars a year and could collectively remit hundreds of thousands dollars home. But my observation is that only two-thirds of the Chinese have money to send home to remedy the poverty there. The loss seems to outweigh the gain. Most of the Chinese farmers here are over fifty years old. They are different from those "parasites" who came to San Francisco as "lazy bones" with two or three hundred dollars [to start small businesses].[40]

Sam's perception of the Chinese experience in America as a downward social mobility reflects a deeply pessimistic view shared by many of his contemporary Chinese. Even though Sam's estimate about the average income a Chinese could make may not be accurate, his comment on the low morale of the Chinese was a realistic description. He again expressed his contempt toward those Chinese who worked in service businesses, such as laundries or restaurants. His class background may not have enabled him to attribute racial discrimination as the major factor that drove many Chinese into service sectors of labor, but his writing demonstrates a sense of humiliation as he watched laundry or gambling becoming a trademark Chinese American occupation.

Sam's Farming Notes

In the 1920s, Sam, while acquiring farming skills, kept a detailed record of his farming experience in a student notebook. His notes read like an unpublished paper on farming in America as compared with farming in China, and on the life of Chinese immigrant farmers in the Los Angeles area. (Being an educated immigrant, Sam also wrote many poems and reflections about life in America. When he passed away in 1988, he left a huge collection of his writings, including many family letters.[41] Like the diary of the legendary Ah Quin in San Diego, Sam's collection is one of the few written documents left by pioneer Chinese immigrants.[42]) Rather than offering us figures on the acreage, stock shares, or net profit of Chinese farmers, Sam's writing reflects aspirations, frustrations and motivations of early Chinese immigrant farmers. When placed into a larger historical context, his career and writing enable us to see important roles played by Chinese in asparagus farming in Southern California. While covering many aspects of the Chinese American experience, a significant portion of Sam's writing is about his farming as a family business, and his writing helps us understand how Chinese entered asparagus farming and operated it as family business, what their concerns and worries were, how they felt about farm life in America for immigrants, and how a Chinese farmer viewed his Chinese and non-Chinese laborers and handled labor relations. Sam's life and writing thus offer illuminating insight into the subjective meaning of Chinese life in America.

Originally Sam began to write his farming notes as a way to accumulate experience. Later, he intended to write a book on Chinese farming in Southern California. On the front page of his farming notebook, he listed six topics that he intended to write about: the importance of agriculture versus the importance of commerce, the incompetence of agriculture schools in China, the "backward" farming techniques in China, the lack of agricultural shows in China, government subsidy of farming, and lack of professional agricultural markets in China. Although he did not finish the book, Sam believed these were the crucial issues in China's agricultural development.

Sam's intention to write on these topics reflects his deep feelings for

China. As a former government official, he often received Chinese officials in his home and made friends with them. Most of these officials were concerned about the life of the overseas Chinese. In fact, his acquaintance with Fan Yuanlian, a famous educator and reformist in China, was what motivated him to write his book about Chinese immigrant farmers in America.[43] In July 1922, after he resigned from his third term as China's minister of education, Fan came to inspect rural education in the United States. When he visited Southern California, he stayed at Sam's home.

While Fan stayed with Sam, he made a careful inspection of the farm, and discussed many social and agricultural issues with Sam. Showing great interest in Sam's farming activities, Fan also requested a written description of Chinese farmers in Southern California. As Sam appreciated Fan's concern about overseas Chinese farmers, he was happy to turn in a book-length research report to him. Sam aborted the project in 1927 when, at the age of fifty-two, Fan died in Beijing. But Sam's farming notes have demonstrated his concerns about modernization and social reform in China. In commenting on the Chinese agricultural schools, he wrote:

> Although our country has established agricultural schools for a dozen years, these schools are not well managed. The teaching methodology is poor, and information about new developments in agriculture is not up to date. The language of the textbooks is difficult to understand and the new terms from Western countries have been translated mechanically without explanation. The teachers are probably good professors but not capable farmers. In America, things are different. I have had visitors from Los Angeles farming schools. The teachers take the students to the farm, let them inspect how to farm in the field, and allow them to learn the skill by doing. Our Chinese teachers will never conduct a class like that. Meanwhile the bandits and social disorder in the countryside are so rampant that it is difficult to arrange fieldwork for students.[44]

Sam was an educated man. Although he came from a rural landlord family, he received a modern education at a Guangdong police academy. Widely read in Chinese classics like Confucian or Tang poetry, and writing classic poems himself, he also had strong interests in the writings and ideas of turn-of-the-century reformists like Kang Youwei and Liang Qichao, and of later notables like Sun Yatsen, Hu Shi, Chen Duxiu, and Cai Yuanpei, and in translations of Western political and literary writings.[45] It was against this cultural background that he made critical comparisons between China and the United States in agricultural education, and intended to write his book on farming. Although busy with farming, Sam was not a socially isolated farmer: he received teachers and students from local farming schools and obviously conversed with them. The hands-on learning method in American farming schools impressed him and enabled him to understand that mechanical translation of Western textbooks was not enough to reform the Chinese education system. As an immigrant, he was still concerned about China.

Chinese Dominance in Asparagus Farming

According to Sam Chang, many Chinese entered asparagus farming in the Sepulveda area during the 1920s, and gradually their farms stretched from Chatsworth to North Hollywood.[46] Although he did not provide a reliable figure of total acreage in the Los Angeles area, Sam estimated that the Chinese grew about eighty percent of the local asparagus. In the farming notes, he also wrote:

> The Chinese have a good method for growing potatoes, and there are about six hundred Chinese farmers and their workers who used to grow potatoes before. In the last ten years, many of them have turned to asparagus. Our own farm grew potatoes for three years before we started growing asparagus.[47]

In his 1975 interview, Sam could still recall the names of his fellow Chinese asparagus farmers. He listed seven Zhang families, four Hu families, two Zhao families, four Guan families, and one Situ family, whose farming career was the longest among the Chinese. Sam estimated that many Chinese farms made net profits of two thousand to three thousand dollars per year. Some of the larger farms could make ten thousand dollars.[48]

Based on Sam's records, the golden era of Chinese asparagus farming in Southern California was from 1915 to 1930. He continued:

> Asparagus production in the Los Angeles area is not enough to meet the local demand, and therefore the local daily fresh products from Chinese-owned farms usually supply the local market. The Chinese farmers determine the price of fresh asparagus in consideration of the price of asparagus samples imported from other places. The local asparagus price will be two to three cents per pound higher than the asparagus price supplied from other places. The price is not necessarily determined before the sale is made, since the payment is on

a weekly rather than on a daily basis. Growing asparagus is a very hard work and it is difficult to find laborers. There are few Western asparagus farmers. So the Chinese grow eighty per cent of the asparagus in Los Angeles. As Chinese farmers are hardworking, they can handle it. Four acres of my farm began to produce asparagus and we would sell the product at fourteen cents per pound in the four years from 1919 to 1922. Based on this price range, we can make a little profit if we can keep the cost under ten cents per pound.

According to Sam's note, that most asparagus farmers in the Los Angeles area were Chinese was because asparagus farming was an arduous job. The Chinese dominated the local market as they were able to provide fresh products. As an experienced farmer, Sam also noted that Los Angeles was an important agricultural distribution center. Many products including asparagus were delivered there before they were distributed to other parts of the country. But Sam's notes did not record any prominent Chinese produce merchant competing with the white produce merchants for the national and international market. In the notes, Sam usually referred to Chinese as "farmers" and referred to white Americans as "merchants." This indicates that most Chinese farmers handled both farming and sales, while their white American counterparts were merely wholesale produce merchants. While Chinese supplied their products to the local market, white merchants controlled the more profitable national and international markets.

However, Sam knew well that asparagus farming in the Los Angeles area had a great potential for Chinese immigrants as real estate values in the area were rapidly rising due to the farming's importance in commerce and trade. He continued:

I really hope more Chinese will come to buy land and grow asparagus so that such profits will not go to the pockets of other people. Los Angeles is now among the five top metropolitan areas in America and will become the most famous city in the world. Land prices will rise drastically. Our farm was worth three hundred dollars per acre six years ago. Now the price is six hundred dollars per acre. In the south of the city, the Weilong Farm was bought at six hundred per acre. Now it is worth two thousand dollars per acre. And the Hu family farm, the Situ, Zhao, and Guan family farms, are all worth three times as much as when the families bought the land a few years ago.[49]

Although Sam saw farming as a good opportunity for the Chinese, he was different from Japanese farming community leaders like Abiko Kyutaro who viewed farming as a path for Japanese immigrants to move from being "settlers" to being "sojourners," and to transform themselves from Japanese into Americans.[50] Chinese immigrants mainly referred to themselves as *jinshanke* or "Gold Mountain guests," which did not specify whether they would return to home or stay in America; if some stayed, they would not forget their roots in China and would often view America as home away from home. Sam still wanted to return to China after several decades in America. For many Chinese, the purpose of migration was to explore opportunities overseas, rather than to look for another place to reside. When his farming notes described Los Angeles as an important metropolitan area and a famous city in the world, Sam viewed America as a meeting ground where the Chinese would intermingle with all kinds of people as they came to participate in the local economy. With hopes to see more Chinese in Los Angeles, Sam essentially perceived migration as an economic endeavor for social mobility. Although living over sixty years in America, he never intentionally tried to embrace American nationalistic ideology to guide his life and identity. Like those of his fellow Chinese asparagus farmers, his service to the Los Angeles area as a hardworking immigrant farmer, and his lifelong farming career made him a valued member of the local agricultural community.

The City Market of the Asians

Although Sam's farming notes were intended for a book project to be published in China, a considerable portion of the notes actually focus on the farming and agribusiness activities of Chinese immigrants in Southern California.[51] On professional agricultural markets, Sam wrote:

There is no professional agricultural market in China. In a developed country, there is always a stable market between the rural area and the city, which can determine the price of agricultural products. City people cannot fool farmers. Being a farmer in Los Angeles, I am familiar with the situation here. Los Angeles agricultural markets are big and famous in the American West. There are three big markets: one on Sixth Street, one on Eighth Street, and one on Ninth Street. The one on Eighth Street is the largest, where much of the import and export trade is done. The one on Sixth Street is smaller. And the one on Ninth Street is the smallest, operated by the Chinese and Japanese. As the white merchants often discriminated against the yellow race in the last ten years, the yellow race could not tolerate it anymore, so they opened their own market. The Ninth

Street market opens at 2 a.m., three to four hours earlier than the markets on Eighth and Sixth Streets, so that the peddlers or truckers are able to deliver produce to restaurants for use before the breakfast hour. The markets on Eighth and Sixth Streets have more wholesale businesses and need to deliver their goods to the railroad station. They open at 5 or 6 a.m. Chinese asparagus farmers mainly sell their products to the Ninth Street market.[52]

The market on Ninth Street is also referred to as the City Market, dominated by Asians.[53] According to Sam's farming notes, this market became the smallest of the three because Caucasian partners took out their shares from the City Market and set up the third market on Eighth Street when they failed to squeeze out the Asian partners. Sam wrote:

> At one time, the white merchants tried to oust Chinese from the produce area on San Pedro Avenue. They decided to sell shares for the buildings and land, and declared that the Chinese must contribute a hundred thousand dollars or be forced to leave. Chinese merchants raised some money but still lacked about thirty thousand dollars. The Asparagus Association decided in a meeting to make up the difference.[54]

Although Sam's intention was to discuss how a professional agricultural market was operated in America, he could not help making comments on the racial relations between Asians and whites. As a racial minority, Asian farmers and produce peddlers began their work two to three hours earlier than their white counterparts, partly because they wanted to be more competitive in their supply service and partly because many clients were local restaurants and needed their supply before breakfast. With more stable and larger clients from the national and international markets, white produce merchants did not have to work as hard as did Asians.

The usage of "yellow race" in Sam's writing is significant. In Chinese vocabulary, there is no difference between "race" and "ethnicity." When Chinese disliked national or racial groups, they used negative terms based on physical features, such as "white devil" for Caucasians or "dwarf devil" for Japanese. Sam used this term several times, in other letters, when he mentioned Japan's historical infringements on China's territorial sovereignty and the more recent Japanese military invasion. However, there had been no widespread racial discourse in Chinese society until the beginning of the twentieth century, when many Chinese intellectuals realized that China was subjected to Western domination not only as a nation but also as a race. The turn from the nineteenth to the twentieth century was a period not only of Western military and economic invasion but also of enormous influx of foreign culture, and, in translating and introducing foreign cultures, Chinese intellectuals paid special attention to the weak and oppressed nations and racial/ethnic groups. For example, Harriet Beecher Stowe's *Uncle Tom's Cabin* was one of the earliest and most popular novels translated into Chinese. In a preface and an afterword, translator Lin Shu discussed the parallels between Stowe's story of black slaves and the racism directed against the Chinese in America and domination of China by Western nations.[55] A few years after *Uncle Tom's Cabin* was translated into Chinese, "[T]he new nationalism produced in 1905 China's first modern boycott against the United States' discriminatory treatment of Chinese, particularly the total exclusion of laborers."[56] After this, "yellow race" had become an important term in Chinese nationalist discourse.

As mentioned earlier, Sam had read many Western literary works translated into Chinese. However, in his writing, Sam did not view Japanese immigrants as a separate race. When Sam used the term in his discussion on the farm market in Los Angeles, he actually referred to both Chinese and Japanese farmers in their alliance against white merchants. Such an alliance enabled the Chinese to stay in farming for a long time. Regarding the continuous Chinese influence in local agriculture, historian William Mason notes: "Refrigerated railroad cars brought tons of vegetables fresh from the Imperial Valley in mid-winter, threatening the Chinese vegetable-grower. He met the challenge well, however, for the vegetable-peddler turned produce broker. In 1900, only three out of forty-three produce companies were Chinese, but by 1910, there were seventeen Chinese produce companies out of one hundred fifty-five, and the Chinese have continued to be influential in Los Angeles' wholesale produce industry to this day."[57] Sam's writing reflects how white wholesale produce merchants, with more capital, tried to squeeze out their Asian counterparts, and how Chinese collaborated with Japanese farmers to keep control of their own market, well into the 1920s. The City Market, with its Asian farmers, has been the topic of a number of scholarly publications;[58] however, Sam's writing is a valuable piece of documentation left by one of the Chinese farmers themselves about their operation of the Market and their relations with white American farmers.

Although Sam wanted to retire in China, his busy farming life did not give him an opportunity even to visit his home country, once he left in 1915. When he finally retired from farming, in 1965, the United States and China were bitter enemies, and by 1979, when the two countries resumed relations, he was too old to return. Until his death in 1988, he spoke Cantonese at home, read Chinese language newspapers for information, and followed political events in China. When, in 1985, he was honored as a pioneer farmer in Southern California, at his one-hundredth-birthday dinner, sponsored by the Cultural Foundation of Orange Country, he delivered his speech in Cantonese.[59]

Sam, though he did not intend to stay when he first arrived, eventually settled in America because, among other reasons, he was commited to the collective interest of the Chang family. Such a tale is probably true of many Chinese immigrants of his time. Even though a China-oriented immigrant, Sam lived the majority of his life in America—a life deeply ingrained in the Los Angeles agricultural community. How, then, do we define him, in his role as a valuable and memorable member of the local American community—sojourner or settler? His life story poses a challenging question for Asian American historians.

CHAPTER 6

Education as a
Family Agenda

*W*hile Sam Chang was busy with asparagus farming in Southern California, he kept a close eye on family affairs in China. He remitted money to his wife and children, as well as to his second brother and twelfth uncle on behalf of his father, contributed suggestions and opinions regarding the management of lineage property, sponsored relatives' immigration to the United States, and above all, monitored his children's education in China. Sam and his father, Yitang, worked hard, in their herb and asparagus businesses, to provide a financial base for the younger generation to receive good educations. Self-sacrifice of the parents, in return, obliged the younger generation to compete vigorously at school that they might pursue good careers and achieve social mobility. The young Changs' accomplishments, in return, lived up to their parents' expectations and brought honor to the family.

Educational success, for a Chinese family, is not only an individual merit but represents a shared interest. Instead of family collectivism giving way to individualism, in the Chang's case, there is compromise between personal goals and the greater good of the family as a collective. When Yitang and Sam retired, they did not, as immigrants, accumulate much wealth for themselves, but they made sure that every child of theirs had accomplished a college education. The content of Chinese family culture is not just economic survival, filial piety, ancestry worship, or gender preference; children's education, too, is an important agenda in Chinese family life.

In Chinese society, education often means family separation. As mentioned in chapter 2, Chinese children in the rural areas could attend village schools for basic literacy training but, would have to leave home for more advanced schooling in towns or cities. Boys over ten lodged in schools away from home for years, if they hoped to pass the civil service examinations and if their parents could afford the tuition and food.[1] Following this tradition, Sam sent his children to appropriate schools regardless of location. His son Tennyson attended schools first in Guangzhou and then in North China, while his daughter Constance left the family's rural village to attend modern schools in the city, then immigrated to the United States. Education, for the younger generation in the Chang family, much like migration for the parent generation, has often meant pursuit of opportunities away from home. In this family history, we have seen how education could function as a pipeline for Chinese youth to leave their home regions for a metropolitan area, embrace national and international culture, and develop new identities.

While Sam's children were attending schools away from home, letters were the family's major communication channel. Family members wrote to one another and exchanged information on regular basis. As mentioned in this book's introduction, in the Sam Chang's collection of family documents, there are numerous lengthy letters between parents and children. These letters show how Sam and his wife constantly worried about their children in China and how these parents and children communicated their thoughts and emotions. In his letters, Sam frequently asked his children about their grades, discussed school curriculum and academic subjects, and meticulously advised the children on school and social life. When letters from the children revealed that they missed home and felt lonely, Sam and his wife responded promptly with encouragement and support and helped the children gradually become independent and mature. Family correspondence allowed Sam to closely monitor the children's education at a distance. In the trans-Pacific experience of the Chang family, the bond between parents and children became strengthened rather than weakened. Mutual expectations and commitment made this transnational family strong.

Adapting to Changes in Education

The early twentieth century witnessed many changes in China, including reforms in the educational system. After China abolished the traditional civil service examination system in 1905, it made a serious commitment to reform the national school system along the lines of Western models. A new system ranging from kindergarten to university gradually replaced the *shuyuan* or *sishu* (private school). New schools offered modern curricula and established new pedagogical principles. However, as a result of a shortage of qualified teachers, suitable course materials, and adequate equipment or funding, traditional schools coexisted with modern schools until 1930s. By 1935, traditional schools still constituted 40 percent of the elementary schools in the national system.[2] Tuition was also much cheaper at traditional schools. In his research on Phoenix Village, Guangdong, D. H. Kulp has indicated that a student's fee was about three-and-one-half Chinese dollars per semester at the traditional school, in contrast to eight dollars at a modern school.[3]

Such circumstances had to be considered by the parents and students in deciding on which school system to attend. To advise his children on attending new schools, Sam followed closely the social trends in Chinese society. Reform in education took a more radical turn after the May Fourth movement began. On 4 May 1919, a mass student demonstration broke out in Beijing, protesting the transfer of Shandong Province from German to Japanese control, a decision made at the Versailles Peace Conference of the same year. After that, a radical social reform movement, called the May Fourth or New Culture Movement, started to fervently attack Confucianism, traditional values like the patriarchal family and arranged marriage, and the old educational system. The movement also promoted the use of vernacular style to replace classical style in Chinese writing.

Even while busy with his farm work, Sam was keenly interested in these political and cultural developments unfolding in China. In his letters, he frequently asked for books and periodicals. In several letters in 1921, he requested his son mail him such magazines as *Nanfeng* (*South Wind*) and *Xin Qingnian* (*New Youth*). *Nanfeng* was a liberal magazine in Guangdong Province that often carried translations of Western literature; *Xin Qingnian* was a radical intellectual journal edited by Chen Duxiu, a leading figure in the May Fourth movement and later the first General Secretary of the Chinese Communist Party. These readings kept Sam updated about new ideas and social reforms in China and also helped him understand the challenge his children might find in their pursuit of education. Sam constantly wrote back to his children to advise them which schools they should attend. Some of his letters were ten to fifteen pages long. Coming from a rural landlord family, Sam was familiar with the old school system and was heavily influenced by traditional ideas, though he had received a modern education. As an informed parent, Sam had to carefully think how to advise his children to adapt to the radical changes in Chinese society and education.

During the early 1920s, Sam's son Tennyson (Tingxun) studied at the Tongzhi School in Guangzhou, a modern school (though classical texts were still used there). In one letter, Sam noted the influence of *Zuozhuan*, an ancient history text written in good prose style, on Tennyson's writing style. Even though encouraging his son to pursue a modern education, Sam was

FIGURE 1. A recent photo of the Chang family's reading house in Guangdong, China

FIGURE 2. Yitang's photograph on his immigration files,
upon entering America, 1904

房藥華中之業創美在原翅祖先

73

FIGURE 3. Yitang and his white partner in front of his herbal office on 917 South Hill Street, Los Angeles, around 1911

FIGURE 4. Yitang in the 1920s

Figure 5. Sam Chang in his police uniform in 1912

Figure 6. Sam Chang in 1915, entering America

FIGURE 7. Sam Chang, Yitang Chung, Yitang's wife (Nellie), and the Chungs' daughter Lillian (on the right) and son Arthur (in the middle), in front of the family herb store, ca. 1917–18

FIGURE 8. Sam Chang in 1986 celebrating his one hundredth birthday

FIGURE 9. Sam Chang tutoring Lillian and Arthur in the Chinese language, at home ca. 1918

FIGURE 10. Sam's wife Cen in 1923, entering the United States

FIGURE 11. Sam's daughter Constance in 1923, entering the United States

FIGURE 12. A family portrait taken around 1926

FIGURE 13. Sam Chang working at the asparagus farm, ca. 1928

FIGURE 14. Tennyson and Constance performing in a student drama at Nankai

FIGURE 15. Sam and his wife, Cen, behind Tennyson, Constance, Estelle, and Joyce in 1938

FIGURE 16. Wedding photo of Tang Mingzhao and Constance in 1938

happy to see his son learning some basic classic Chinese literature, which would balance the modern curriculum with traditional Chinese culture. Sam wrote:

> Young people should study very hard because you can hardly accomplish anything once you are over twenty to thirty years old. Your essay on commerce written at your twelfth uncle's home in Hong Kong is very good. I have sent it to Mr. Liang Ruhuai in San Francisco, who works at *Chung Sat Yat Po* [*China-West Daily*], and see if he could publish your essay in the newspaper. I could see that *Zuozhuan* influenced your writing style. With a good teacher, you will make great progress in one or two years if you study hard at this age. The British poet Browning could write good poetry because he was a good student when he was a child. Modern scholars emphasize the use of the vernacular instead of the classical writing style. However, you still need to practice classical writing for another two or three years before you turn to the use of the vernacular. As a student, you will not be able to write good vernacular essays unless you have a good classical writing foundation. Hu Shi is a pioneer vernacular scholar. But he received a good classical training and also studied in the United States. So did Cai Yuanpei, who was actually a *jinshi* [the highest academic degree in feudal China] in the Qing Dynasty. I know that 70 to 80 per cent of the students now study the vernacular, as it will replace the classical language as the main language in the future. As a student of the new China, you should study the vernacular. To practice your vernacular skills, you can write a few essays in your spare time and send them out to newspapers or journals for publication. However, most of our Chinese scholars are good at writing but not speaking. That is a great pity. Oration training is very important in modern education. A young scholar should bear three things in mind: determination, conscientiousness, and persistence. With determination, you always want to be the best. Being conscientious, you will never stop your study. And finally, if you believe there is a will, then there will be a way. You should always keep these three things in mind.[4]

This letter tells us how closely Sam followed the progress of his son's education, and the societal events that could impact that education. Although education reformists advocated the use of vernacular style to replace classical style, model school texts were still rare and many modern schools still used classical texts and teaching methods; moreover, many teachers were not adequately trained to teach the vernacular writing technique. This is probably why Tennyson's writing was still influenced by classical Chinese literature. Sam was not too worried about this, as he wanted his son to receive training in classical Chinese writing.

It is interesting that Sam submitted his son's essay to *Chung Sat Yat Po* for publication. This leading Chinese American newspaper in California was popular among Chinese immigrants, and many of their families in Guangdong were familiar with its name. Getting published in the newspaper could certainly enhance Tennyson's confidence in his education. As an overseas parent, Sam was quite resourceful in his involvement in his children's education.

Although living in America, Sam fully understood that the new trends in Chinese education were going to prevail, pointing out in the letter that 70 to 80 percent of Chinese students began to learn the vernacular at school. He wanted to make sure that his son would join the mainstream in education, become a "student of the new China," and master the vernacular that was going to replace classical writing as the dominant discourse at most schools. On the other hand, he urged his son not to ignore the classical Chinese: during this transitional period in Chinese education, Sam was not sure if the modern curriculum was a mature system and would lay a solid foundation for his son's Chinese language ability. In the letter, when Sam mentioned a number of well-known leading intellectuals, like Hu Shi and Cai Yuanpei in the May Fourth movement, who advocated radical reforms and modernization, he pointed out that these people had a good command of classical Chinese. Most intellectual leaders in the May Fourth movement totally denied Chinese traditional values, pushed for radical social reforms, and advocated rapid Westernization of Chinese society, but, as a parent, Sam did not blindly follow these extreme ideas but carefully balanced his advice to his children.

Having lived in America, and being exposed to Western culture, Sam felt that he should discuss with his children the differences between Western culture and education and the Chinese educational system. In some letters, Sam described the coeducational school system in America, the importance of mathematics and science subjects in the American school curriculum, and extracurricular activities such as sports, public speaking, and debate training. He encouraged his son to pick up public speaking ability, and told him that oration was an important part of the Western school curriculum and that many famous intellectuals benefited from this training. Sam reminded his son that such training was not offered in traditional Chinese schools and was not available in every modern Chinese school. Yet if Tennyson planned to pursue more advanced study in America in the future, he needed that skill.

In traditional Chinese education, memorization was important. Many Chinese parents believed that a child's success in education depended mainly on a hardworking spirit and long hours of study. It was "strength of mind" or "conscientiousness" rather than talent that really mattered in educational accomplishment. As long as a child worked hard, he/she could make a good student. "Where there is a will, there will be a way" is a typical Chinese proverb that most parents have used to encourage children to study hard; Sam quoted this proverb several times in his letters. Although Sam was not against educational reform modeled after Western education, he urged his son to cling to study habits always valued by Chinese. Sam believed that human memory was good at an early age and his son's major responsibility when young was to study. Although the content of education in China was drastically changed, the attitude of his children towards study should, Sam believed, remain the same: study hard when young. As a transnational parent, Sam was very observant of the strengths and weaknesses in both the Chinese and the American educational systems.

Sam's involvement was helpful. Tennyson was making good progress and becoming an all-round student. In another letter, Sam wrote,

> I am happy to learn that you are the president of the student association and the general editor of the school newspaper *Tongsheng Bao*, and have won an award in public speech at the school. But do not feel self-conceited for what you have achieved. You should know that it is not difficult to possess talent, but difficult to have integrity. Great people have both. The Chinese run the country with morality, Europeans and Americans govern a nation with law, but this does not mean that Westerners ignore ethics. Most American presidents have been people with high integrity. Washington, Lincoln, and others were all people with both talent and integrity. Lincoln could emancipate black slaves because he was, first of all, a man of great integrity.[5]

Sam's discussion of famous American politicians in the letter indicates that many Chinese students were familiar with these names, from the influx of Western culture into China during the period. These politicians were probably held up as role models for young people like his son. But, though respecting these people, Sam did not want to deny Chinese traditional values as a cultural influence on his son's character development. His letter implies that, though China was run by morality and the West by law, ethics is important in any society and therefore integrity was more valuable than talent for a person anywhere. With regard to his son's accomplishment at school, Sam sounded like a typical Chinese parent when he told Tennyson not to be self-conceited after winning an award.

From Reading House to Modern School

When Constance (Yuhua) was nine years old, Sam decided to switch her from a shuguan (reading house) in the village to a xuetang (modern school) in Guangzhou. Sam asked Tennyson to send him detailed information about prospective schools that Constance might attend. As the quality of the modern schools was uneven, he was very careful in selecting one for his daughter, and tried to find as much information as possible before he made his decision. In a letter, Sam wrote:

> Next year, your sister Yuhua has no *shuguan* to go to in the village. She should go to a *xuetang* in the provincial capital city. But many *xuetang* in Guangzhou are poor in quality. The grades of students at these *xuetang* are too low. I am afraid she cannot learn much there. It is necessary for Yuhua to have some solid basic training in Chinese language before going to those schools. I wonder how many words Yuhua has learned to write so far. The alphabet system is a new thing. It is simple and can help the Chinese language develop a standard pronunciation. Comparing Shuzheng and Rouhuai School, I think Shuzheng is better. Send Yuhua to Shuzheng next year. The total cost of annual tuition, books, food, and boarding is about sixty dollars, which is not very high. You can borrow money from your second uncle. If he does not have it, ask your mother to borrow it from someone else. We will pay it back soon. After your sister Yuhua learns some basic Chinese at the school, I will try to get her and your mother to come to America in a couple of years. School tuition costs too much money in China. Tuition is free in American elementary, middle, and high schools.[6]

As the letter indicates, Sam had read the curriculum and brochure of two elementary schools and made a careful comparison before selecting one for Constance. Under his arrangement, she left the rural village and attended modern schools in Guangzhou before joining him in America.

As an overseas Chinese parent, Sam cared about his daughter's as well as his son's education. Although footbinding for women had been banned, and modern schools had been established available to girls as well as boys, this was still a period when many rural Chinese families could not afford to send daughters to school. Girls' schools in cities were few and expensive. As an immigrant parent, Sam used the money he made in American to send his daughter to school.

After Constance began at the Shuzheng School, Sam followed up on her life and study there. Soon he discovered that the campus culture of the Shuzheng School did not live up to his expectations. In another letter, he wrote, "I am very upset to know that Yuhua learned to smoke at school. I hear that many girls in her school are smoking. It is clear that the teachers are not morally responsible for the students. Ask your mother to switch Yuhua to another school."[7] During this period, many modern schools in China were newly established and did not have codes of student behavior. Young people were exposed to many sorts of ideas. Biographical tales of rebellious Western women, like Joan of Arc, were translated and often were held up as role models in girl's schools. New thoughts and Western fads flooded China's larger cities. Smoking cigarettes, especially Western brands, was probably such a fad, imitated as a Western lifestyle by many Chinese female students, female as well as male. Although Sam intended his daughter to receive a modern education, he did not want to see her smoking, or tarnished with an undesirable lifestyle. Sam held the school teachers responsible for this behavior, because he felt that teachers should make students focus on studies rather than follow a social vogue. Sam was so disturbed that he wrote directly to Constance to stop her smoking:

I have received your letter and Tingxun's letter of November 16. You should not stay in that school too long. Next year, you should switch to Zhenguang School, which has an elementary girls' section and is a good school. I hear you started to smoke, which has made me very upset. You are only thirteen and should know that this is a bad habit. You should really change to a different school. Very few countries allow women to smoke in public. In America, you could hardly find one woman out of ten thousand who could smoke. If there is one, she must be a low-class woman. Decent women never smoke. In a train or ship, there is usually a smoking room. People are allowed to smoke only there. In our family history, several decades ago, the third and sixth aunt and the fifth grandma smoked. But at that time, it

was just a social habit like foot-binding for women. Now society for-
bids this habit. Smoking is as bad as binding feet for women. You
should give up smoking immediately. Otherwise, the whole family
including your grandparents, parents, uncles and aunts, and all decent people will not forgive you. If you smoke on the ship to America,
Westerners will look down on you as a low-class woman.[8]

Being a transnational parent enabled Sam to more convincingly persuade
Constance to quit smoking, by dubbing it a habit disdained in both Chinese
and Western society, and by labeling smoking among women a lower-class
practice in America. Being in America, he could discuss lifestyle and social
vogues in a Western society in an authoritative tone. He obviously thought
that students at his daughter's school regarded smoking as a Western fashion
and pursued it as a modern lifestyle. His daughter, he seemed to feel, probably learned smoking along with many of her schoolmates. It is interesting
that Sam treated women's smoking as old-fashioned, like the footbinding tradition in Chinese society. In the nineteenth century, some women of the
wealthy families in rural Guangdong did smoke tobacco or opium. But it was
not a prevailing custom and had nothing to do with the smoking trend in a
girl school. Since the influence of Western culture was overwhelmingly strong
over the young people in China during this period, Sam was only labeling
such smoking an old-fashioned habit to stop his daughter.

Ironically, Sam's letter reflects how a traditional Chinese family approached problematic behavior in its children. According to Sam, his
daughter's smoking was not solely an issue about her own lifestyle. The ill
reputation of her smoking could bring embarrassment to the whole extended
family. The letter indicates that watching over one's children's education was
a very demanding responsibility as China underwent tremendous social reforms. Even while working in America, Sam had to keep a close eye on China.

Sam's decision to switch Constance to Zhenguang School was based
on his careful observation of modern schools in Guangzhou. Zhenguang
started as a school for women, established by American missionaries in 1868.
At the beginning, it provided a Bible class for religious purposes, and a girl's
class and an adult women's class for educational purposes. Sam was initially
concerned about the school's Christian culture and tuition cost, and therefore first selected Shuzheng School for Constance. As its educational curriculum and teaching quality became more established, the Zhenguang School
was, in 1912, transformed into a formal girl's middle school with an elementary division.[9] By the 1920s, Zhenguang became one of the best schools in

Guangzhou. Sam quickly switched Constance to Zhenguang when campus culture at Shuzheng disappointed him. Tuition cost and Christian cultural background became secondary considerations; as a parent, Sam cared mainly about the quality of education, and felt that Constance should stay away from the bad influences at Shuzheng. Many missionary schools like Zhenguang were initially established for religious purposes but quickly converted into more comprehensive educational institutions when the civil service examination system was abolished and modernization created a large demand for modern schools. Improvement of educational quality was how such schools attracted an educated Chinese parent like Sam, heavily influenced by Confucianism. From Sam's careful analysis of the vernacular prose style in his son's essay, and from his stern warning of his daughter to quit smoking, we see this effect, as well as how meticulously he watched over his children's education in China, as a father and overseas parent.

The Family Letter as a Channel of Moral Education

Sam's daughter Constance once wrote in her student notebook the following paragraph about the importance of letter writing:

> Letter-writing is a kind of Chinese literature. It has always been the most natural and emotional writing. There are two kinds of letter-writing: one is to family; and another is to friends. As for family letter-writing, the best is by Mr. Zeng Wenzheng [Zeng Guofan's courtesy name] and Zheng Banqiao.[10]

Zeng was a senior government official in the late Qing government, while Zheng was a famous Chinese poet and painter. The paragraph is just one of Constance's numerous Chinese writing exercises, required by Sam after she arrived in America. However, this short paragraph also illustrates how letter writing functioned as an important communication channel, a vehicle of moral education in Chinese family culture, and was used as a composition writing exercise for children. After Constance spent a couple of years at Zhenguang School, Sam brought her over to the United States, where public schools cost no tuition. Shortly after Constance arrived in Los Angeles in 1923, with her mother, Cen, she started to write letters to Tennyson and other relatives in China.

Letter writing for Constance was both an exercise of her Chinese writing ability and a training in communication skills in the family culture. She usually drafted the letters in her student notebook first, then copied them down on letter paper before mailing them. Sam also drafted his letters first and then formally copied them on letter paper, sometimes in Chinese calligraphy and sometimes in pen. This is how he came to leave the huge collection of his personal letters.

Letter writing is important in Chinese culture. Family members, relatives, and friends, it is felt, should properly address each other, and articulate thoughts and ideas, in their writing. Parents and children used this channel to exchange both information and emotion, since many Chinese did not like to orally express affection, anger, or other emotions to one another. Emotional opinions and sensitive subjects, when too difficult to be verbalized aloud, could be conveyed in writing. More important, parents could use family letters to teach their children family values and traditions, and to influence their moral character with ethical examples in family history or famous quotations from established scholars. Thus letter-writing could be a vehicle to exchange intimate feeling between family members, or a channel for parents to deliver moral preachings.

Following this tradition, education was not the only topic in Sam's letters to his children. Filial piety, reverence to elders, family history, children's obligations and responsibility to the family were also important topics. Split family life could impact family relations. Parents might neglect their responsibilities to their children and lose control of their children's character formation when a family was split apart. In return, children could ignore their obligations to family and the expectations of parents about their education. Sam was keenly aware of such possibilities and in his letters often discussed what family obligation meant. He viewed letter-writing as a major channel of communication with his children about their lives, and as a way to influence their identity formation. In the correspondence, Sam's children sometimes frankly expressed their emotions and differing opinions, to challenge their parents' views. Social problems in China were also discussed and debated between the parents and children. The Chang family letters show how intimately, in a Chinese family, children and parents could exchange ideas, opinions, and feelings. In the Changs' correspondence, we see how Sam and his children, though separated, lived in a culturally *linked* transnational social landscape.

Among the many books Sam discussed with his children in the correspondence, he particularly recommended *Zengguo Fan's Family Letters* to his son. Zeng was a highly respected senior official and a scholar of the late Qing Dynasty, and many of his writings, especially his letters to family members and friends, were edited into books and widely circulated in Chinese society. Sam wrote in one letter:

You must have received my no.1 letter of January 29. How is your study recently? What about Yuhua, Yuan, Qu, and Wei? Do they study hard at school? I wonder if your second uncle has received *Ciyuan* (*Lexical Dictionary*), *Selection of Wang Yang-ming,* and other books that I had my friend mail to him from Shanghai. After all of you read them, send them to me and I will read them myself. I wonder if you have read *Zeng Guofan's Family Letters*. If you are very busy with your study, you can just read the first three volumes of Wang's books, beginning with *The Chronicle of His Life,* and two volumes of *Family Discipline* and *Chronology* in Zeng's writings. It will not take long if you read those books first. To finish other volumes may cost a lot of time; you can read them later. I have planned to read all the classics on Chinese culture beginning with books on Yao and Shun to Xuantong *Emperor*, and all the writings of ancient scholars. But I am too busy with farming and only have time to read from seven to nine in the evening. In our Confucian system, education was divided into two parts, general education and specialized education. In the German and French educational systems, they emphasize intellectual development, while British education focuses on character development. In the United States, they emphasize practical training.[11]

Sam probably heard of a new edition of Zeng's writings in Shanghai and had his friend there send the books to his brother and son to read. Although Zeng did not intentionally write letters for publication, many of his letters to family members contained ideas and principles on how a government official or elite wealthy family should train and discipline children to continuously maintain the high social status of the family. Zeng's descendants took his words as *jiaxun* (family guidelines). Thus, when Zeng's family letters were edited and published as a book, it became highly influential on family-ethics education during the late Qing and early Republic periods, in the 1910s and 1920s. In Zeng's discussion, a hardworking spirit, thrifty lifestyle, respect toward elders, modesty in public life, and obligation to family (by both men and women) were regarded as essential qualities that children of an elite family needed to learn to assure that the prosperity and social status of the family would continue. Zeng's writing was widely read as a guide to familial moral upbringing in Chinese society. Sam probably had his own family history in mind when he recommended Zeng's writings to his son. The Chang family had already declined by Sam's father's generation, due to intense family feuds.

Sam wanted his son to understand the ethical teachings in Zeng's writing, to learn to live a simple life and study hard. Through accomplishment in education, Tennyson was expected to dutifully fulfill his obligation to the Chang family. Not only did Sam urge his son to read Zeng Guofan's family correspondence; his own letters were often filled with ethnical and moral advice. He believed that a sense of obligation to family and a good character would inspire Tennyson to study hard at school even away from home.

Constance's comments on Zeng Guofan and Zheng Banqiao's letters, in her Chinese writing exercise, shows that letter writing was an important genre of literature in Chinese society. Selected letters of famous scholars or social elites were no longer private documents but published texts for general readers. Ethical teachings in such letters provided guidelines on family relations and on behavior in family culture. Ordinary Chinese used such letters as models in their own letter writing. Parents like Sam asked their children to develop letter writing, based on those texts, as a communication skill. When Constance arrived in America, Sam asked her to write letters on a regular basis for the family. Sometimes she wrote letters on behalf of her parents, sometimes for herself; within the first two months, she wrote a dozen letters to relatives and friends. Family correspondence in Chinese culture is not necessarily a communication between one individual and another, but rather a vehicle networking the entire family. The Chang family letters show us how closely Chinese immigrants and relatives communicated when apart. In her first letter to Tennyson, Constance wrote: "The Steamship Wilson arrived in the United States at eight clock p.m. on October 5th. The next day, we went to Angel Island. On the 15th, we had our interrogation. On the 16th, we went to Dabu [San Francisco]. A few days later, we arrived in Los Angeles."[12] Constance used the Chinese lunar year calendar. Had she not, she would have indicated that they arrived in November 1923. According to this letter, the trip took them about a month, including several overnight stops in Shanghai, Japan, and Hawaii. They left Hong Kong in September and arrived in San Francisco in October. It was a relatively comfortable trip. The most difficult part of their travel was to prepare for the immigration interrogation, as we saw in chapter 5. Constance called San Francisco *Dabu,* which means "big port city"; Chinese immigrants created and used this name for San Francisco beginning in the 1850s. Constance's letter indicates that many Chinese, including children, in Guangdong had learned about San Francisco by the 1920s.

Under Sam's guidance, Constance continued her study of the Chinese language after arriving in the United States, as evidenced by several dozen copied articles in her student notebooks. Copying was an important writing exercise in traditional Chinese education; it helped children practice handwriting and remember the content of texts. Very likely, Constance brought some textbooks from China and simply copied articles assigned by Sam from those books. Whatever the case, the articles she copied in her notebook were usually about famous people in China or the West, such as Hai Rei, Zeng Guofan, Sun Yatsen, Columbus, and Bismarck.[13] Obviously, knowledge about other countries had already been part of her schooling in China.

In a letter to Tennyson, Sam expressed his satisfaction over Constance's progress in the Chinese language: "Your sister studies very hard. In her spare time, I teach her Chinese and she makes progress in Chinese every day."[14] To maintain and improve Constance's Chinese language ability, Sam attempted to hire a Chinese student as a tutor. In 1924, Constance wrote to a potential teacher on behalf of her mother:

> Mr. Ruo Yao, we are pleased to receive your letter. In regard to your tutoring position, my mother has a woman friend who came from Shunde County. Her husband is a Chinese doctor and they have two sons who also need tutoring. They like to pay twenty dollars a month including food and boarding. You can go to your school during the daytime, and come back home to teach the children from 6 to 8 p.m. They would appreciate your help in the kitchen when you have time. You can also take more students for extra money if they are available. My mother said there are another two or three students who want this position. Please inform us if you would like to come.[15]

The offer to the tutor was a fairly good one at that time, and only a merchant Chinese family could afford to pay for such tutoring. As the letter indicates, Sam and another Chinese herbalist family would share the cost. Both families demonstrated commitment to procuring a Chinese education for their children. However, it is not clear if Sam and the other Chinese family sought someone to teach only the vernacular Chinese, or both vernacular and classical Chinese.

Upon arriving in Los Angeles, Constance and her mother stayed in Yitang's herbal residence, as it was close to school. As an immigrant student, Constance studied hard; in two years, she finished elementary school and went into junior high. In a letter to her maternal grandmother, she wrote that, in addition to following the regular school schedule, she attended summer classes and was able to skip a grade. She also made rapid progress in English. In another letter to her brother, she wrote:

> Dear Brother: I received your letter a long time ago, yet have been too busy to reply sooner due to my heavy school work. Did you receive my English letter that I wrote you last time? I have moved up another grade—the sixth grade. Next year I will enter junior high. Mother said today is your birthday. Cousin Qu and Wei work hard on the farm. Baby Sister Chu is learning to speak. My English name is called Constance and Sister Chu is Estelle.[16]

In another letter to a cousin on the same day, Constance wrote that English was easier than Chinese because English only had twenty-six letters while Chinese had many characters and did not have a spelling system. As Constance wrote English letters and introduced her English name to her brother, bilingual and bicultural lifestyle began to take roots in their life.

To maintain his daughter's bilingual ability, Sam also required Constance to read Chinese language newspapers. Many news items from China, however, seemed depressing to Constance. In a letter to a relative, she wrote:

> What is the situation in Guangzhou now? Yesterday, I learned from a Chinese newspaper that the British policemen used machine guns to shoot students to death in our country without proper reasons. Alas, our country is too weak and often bullied by others! As Chinese nationals, we have our responsibility to save China. Please let me know if any woman's movement occurs in Guangdong. Recently I hear that the Western powers are willing to return tariff authority to China. So our country is still hopeful.[17]

The patriotic tone in the letter seems too mature for the voice of a junior high student. But the tyrannical behavior of foreigners in China, Chinese resistance against colonialism, and the women's liberation movement was indeed the concern of young Constance in her letter. The letter also indicates how closely an average Chinese immigrant family followed events in China, using Chinese-language newspapers.

Tennyson at Lingnan School

In making arrangements for his family to immigrate, Sam first sent for his wife, Cen, and his daughter, Constance. Although Tennyson was his only son, and a teenager at the time, Sam asked him to stay behind. While Cen was very upset at leaving Tennyson alone in China, Sam believed this was the sacrifice the boy had to make in order to get a good and marketable education. Tennyson had been studying in Tongzhi School for three years and was a very conscientious student. He was the school newspaper editor, had won an award for public speaking, and could write smooth expository essays. In a letter of 1922, Sam explained to Tennyson why he sent for Cen and Constance but left him behind:

> We are planning to bring your mother and sister to America first. But your mother does not want to leave you alone in China. You are still very young. Her concern reflects true affection from a mother to a son, which I understand. But U.S. immigration laws are becoming tougher and tougher. Some people have recently proposed bills to totally ban Asian immigration to America. So Asian people should come as soon as possible. Schools are free for children here, while English is also a popular language in the world. It is a disadvantage to be in the United States without knowing some English. English training, however, is not popular in girl's schools in China yet. Although the attached elementary school of Lingnan College does offer good English classes, it costs too much money. Since Yuhua has already studied a few years of Chinese in Guangzhou, she should come to America and study English for a few years. Upon graduating from an American high school, she could go to Beijing University without taking an examination and her college education there would cost much less money. That is why I want them to come to America now.[18]

As Sam explained in the letter, his arrangement was to balance Constance's educational needs with the financial capacities of the family. He probably had done some research on admission policies of Chinese universities toward students from overseas. Although Constance could attend Lingnan School in Guangzhou, American schools were free and her high school education in the United States would then help her gain entry into a good Chinese university. Tennyson, however, would soon need to go to high school. If Sam brought him to California for this, language and cultural differences might hinder his chances to get into a good American college, but if he went to a good high school in China, one where competent English language training was offered, and then enrolled in a good Chinese university, Tennyson would stand a strong chance of transferring into an American college or being admitted into a graduate program at an American university.

At that time, a number of prestigious Chinese universities sent qualified students to study overseas every year, and Sam hoped Tennyson might enter such a university. In leaving Tennyson behind, he actually had a higher expectation for his son than for his daughter, and was prepared to invest more money in the son's education.

Sam continuously encouraged Tennyson to know Chinese well before coming to the United States. He wrote: "You are now sixteen and should study hard to have a good command of Chinese before you come here to study English, which is not so difficult. No great scholar can write a good article in English if his written Chinese is poor."[19] Then Sam reminded his son that the United States was only a place where people came for economic reasons: "If you want to achieve eminence and status, America is not necessarily the right place. But if you want to make money to help your family out of temporary difficulties, no other country's money is worth more than the American dollar."[20] Sam's letter demonstrates his perception of immigration as downward mobility for educated and professional Chinese. He believed that few educated Chinese could find a fine career in the United States and achieve prominence there, and advised his son to think of his future in China.

Living in the Los Angeles area, Sam sometimes invited University of Southern California scholars or students from China for tea or dinner at his house, and used them as role models for his children. Most planned to return to China. Several, including sociologist Lei Jieqiong and physical scientist Wu Daqiu, became prominent intellectual leaders or scientists when they returned to China after their graduate studies. From Sam's perspective, young people with high inspirations should think of China as their future. In his advice to his siblings and children, Sam always encouraged them to return there.

However, Sam believed that the most marketable education for his children would be gained by their attending schools in both China and the United States. English language ability was also an important skill; Sam urged his son to study where English training was competent. His first choice for the youth was Qinghua College in Beijing, an excellent university that sent hundreds of Chinese students to study abroad every year:

> If you cannot apply to Qinghua in Beijing this July, try it next year. Now you have been at Tongzhi School for three years. You will graduate in one more year. You can apply to Qinghua after graduation. If you cannot get into Qinghua, apply to Lingnan. After graduation from Lingnan, try to get into Beijing University. Then you can apply to an American university. But this plan costs a lot of money and takes too much time.[21]

Later he wrote: "Lingnan is a good school for English language training. You should be able to pick up enough English there, before you apply to Qinghua or Beijing University. Then you could apply to come to America."[22] At that time, English ability was not only useful in applying to an American university, but was also helpful for Chinese youth in good Chinese universities like Qinghua where, because of Western influences, many courses were taught in English. Admission into a prestigious school like Lingnan in Guangdong, Qinghua in Beijing, or Nankai in Tianjin would enable Tennyson to get a student visa when applying to an American university. Entering the United States on a student visa was a lot easier than entering as an immigrant. Chinese Exclusion laws did not ban the entry of students, and immigration officers sometimes were more lenient when questioning student applicants. Sam wrote:

> After studying in Lingnan School for one or two years, you won't need "coaching papers" to come to the United States. You could apply for a visa directly from the American Counsel and be spared the complicated paperwork and rough interrogation. You should apply to Qinghua College or study in Lingnan. If you cannot get into Qinghua, you should try to get into Nankai in Tianjin. Then you can come to America for a college education. This is the best arrangement.[23]

Here Sam did not just plan an immigration scheme, but actually mapped out an ideal educational route for his son. The ultimate goal was to get a good education in the United States through obtaining an exchange student status, which also meant much less hassle in the admission process. Although prestigious schools like Qinghua or Nankai could provide Tennyson an excellent modern education, a diploma from an American university was a necessary steppingstone for a college graduate to attain a good career in China. As Rose Hum Lee notes, a more calculated plan of a Chinese family for its children's education in the early twentieth century included studying at missionary schools at an early age, and later at institutions of higher learning that emphasized Western curricula. A good command of English from these schools paved the way for study abroad. The degree obtained in a foreign institution became the criterion for upward mobility and an established place in the Chinese social hierarchy.[24]

Tennyson went to study in Lingnan in 1923, following Sam's plan. Even though Sam was impressed by the school's quality, he still had reservations about its religious aspect:

The newspaper began to carry news about Qinghua College's entrance examination information. I do not know the exact date but I hear it is held only every three years. You should really plan to take it. Unless you fail to get into Qinghua, you can try Lingnan, which is known as a school of New Culture in Guangzhou. Although Lingnan is an excellent school, its curriculum contains religious elements. I hear that the school will force you to be a Christian when you enter the third grade. That is really not good.[25]

Established by American missionaries in 1888 through the merger of several small missionary schools, Lingnan was called Canton Christian College before 1916. It began to attract Chinese students after it offered English courses. Then it gradually developed into a university with a high school section, after receiving donations from overseas Chinese, especially Chinese merchants from Southeast Asia.[26] As one of the best colleges and high schools in Guangzhou, Lingnan attracted many talented local students, and did not force them to convert to Christianity. With strong ties to the overseas Chinese community, Lingnan also had special curricula for overseas Chinese students.

Going North for Education

Sam's dream school for his son was Qinghua College in Beijing. He repeatedly urged his son to apply for Qinghua, which was established in 1911 from Boxer Indemnity Funds and functioned to prepare Chinese students to study abroad, mainly in Europe and the United States. As one of the most prestigious universities in China, it had a faculty consisting of some of the most distinguished scholars in China, and its admission policy was highly selective. Only the brightest Chinese youth had a chance of being admitted. Once admitted, many of the students would have an opportunity to study in universities in America or Europe with financial aid. According to Rose Lum Lee, Qinghua sent over two thousand Chinese students to American universities in the first half of the twentieth century.[27]

Sam's third brother, Elbert, received a Qinghua fellowship, as a Chinese student, while studying at Georgetown University. This fellowship provided him, for three years, with an annual stipend of 480 dollars. Without the fellowship, according to Sam, Elbert could not have finished his medical degree.[28] Although it is not clear how Elbert got this fellowship, as he attended high school in the United States, here is another example of how the Chang family used resources on both sides of the Pacific.

Like many Chinese parents, Sam regarded Qinghua as a dream university for his son. He hoped that Tennyson was competitive enough to get admitted there so that he could have an excellent education and also a scholarship to study in America. But Sam had a second choice for his son—Nankai School, in Tianjin. In a letter, he wrote:

> Next year, if you fail to get into Qinghua College, you should try Nankai. After graduation, you can still apply to American universities. You can make friends there, and you will know both Southern and Northern culture in China and become a real Chinese. One year is enough for you to study in Lingnan. Next July, you should go to Beijing and take the examination. Should you fail, go back to Lingnan and wait for your next opportunity.[29]

Sam also commented on the difference between Lingnan and these schools in the North:

> I don't find many graduates from Lingnan getting admitted into American universities directly. They usually take pre-college courses for six months or a year if they want to attend universities in the southwestern part of America, and two or three years if they want to study at Yale or Columbia University. On the East Coast, universities are better than those in the West or Southwest. But graduates from Beijing University, Nankai, or Qinghua College can go directly to the East Coast universities.[30]

To urge his son to study in the North, Sam told Tennyson that his friend Fan Yuanlian, president of Beijing Normal University, had spoken highly of Nankai, and mentioned that Liang Qichao was a history professor there. Sam also mentioned that the school was founded and headed by two famous intellectuals, Yan Xiu and Zhang Boling. Sam emphasized their names several times in his letters, in encouraging his son to study at Nankai. Obviously Sam was familiar with the names of leading intellectuals in China.

To encourage Tennyson to study in the North, Sam informed him that other family members would join him in China for education in the near future.

> You should not come to the United States in a hurry and miss this important opportunity in your life. Even Aunt Xin and sister Yuhua will go back to China to join you when we have enough money for the tuition. After their graduation from American elementary and high school, we plan to send them back to study for two or three

years in Yanjing (Yenching) Woman's University, Beijing University, or the Advanced Woman's Normal University in Beijing so that they will know Chinese language and society.[31]

Meanwhile, Sam's third brother Elbert, with a medical degree from an American university, received an offer to work in Beijing Union Medical College as an intern, in August 1924.

> Your third uncle might teach and work as a doctor at Beijing Rockefeller College [Beijing Union Medical College]. Rockefeller is the wealthiest person in America and the world, and has established universities in many other countries. If your uncle gets this job, you would not be lonely studying there and could also learn a lot of Western culture from your uncle. By the way, most Chinese named Zhang spell their surname as "Chang." Students from the North all use this spelling on their passports when they come to America. But people in Guangdong use all kinds of spelling, such as "Chung," "Jung," or "Cheung." When you go to the North, use "Chang" so that people will not laugh at you.[32]

Arranging for his son to go to the North tells us how a Chinese parent like Sam would not hesitate to send his children from home for education, especially for a better quality of education. Schools such as Nankai would provide Tennyson not only with a good Chinese education but also with the culture of another metropolitan city of China. As a city in the North, Tianjin was very close to Beijing, the dynastic capital as well as a cultural center for hundreds of years. Educated Cantonese like Sam regarded Beijing and Northern culture as a more original and authentic Chinese culture. As Sam's letter indicates, he told Tennyson that the more correct way to spell his last name was "Chang" (rather than "Chung"). Studying, working, and living in North China would enable Tennyson and other Chang family children to learn and absorb Northern dialects, customs, and traditions. They would develop new identities and view themselves more as Chinese than as Cantonese. Education was a socialization process. To attend schools or work in the North gave children an opportunity to learn other parts of China and participate in a national rather than a local culture.

While studying in Nankai might eventually help Tennyson gain opportunities to come to America, Sam still planned his son's future in China. But Sam encouraged him to think about a career in China outside Guangdong Province. In a letter, Sam noted:

If you can get into Qinghua, its scholarship will cover both your tuition and travel to study in America. You will save a lot of money for your grandpa. Otherwise I hear that one of the most successful professional schools in Beijing is a school of taxation, where all except one of the professors are Westerners. If you can't get into Qinghua or Beijing University, you can try this school. After graduation, you can work and see other places, and your salary will be about seventy dollars a month in the first year. There will be a raise every year. If you don't want to work in China anymore, you will have a chance to study abroad, though you may have to pay your own tuition as your grandpa is getting old. In the recent several decades in America, tax policy has been the focus of political debates between Republicans and Democrats. If the Republicans come to power, there will be a raise in import tariff and a drop in export tariff in order to benefit the capitalist class. If the Democrats come to power, the policy will be the reverse to benefit the working class. In our country, a great deal can be accomplished in this field when we take back sovereignty of our tariff control.[33]

Sam tried to convince his son that he could have an excellent career and a quick avenue to social prominence in China through a college education in America: as a developing country, China needed Western-trained professionals.

While he was encouraging his son to leave Guangdong for North China, Sam probably did some research on North China. In another letter, he provided Tennyson with specific instructions on how to travel from Guangdong to Tianjin:

You should reserve your ship ticket through Hongfa or Tai-an Hotel. When your departure time is due, the hotel will contact you, instruct you where to board, and take you to the ship. It will be three days from Guangdong to Shanghai. Then you stay for one or two days in Shanghai at the Hongfa Hotel, where there will always be Cantonese at your service. But there are many swindlers in Shanghai. Most of the rickshaw men are thieves. You must be very careful. It will take four days from Shanghai to Tianjin. Taida Company offers a reasonable ship ticket. It will probably take about twelve dollars to get to Tianjin. The Chang clan has a relative who is a doctor in Tianjin. But we don't have his address. You will stay in Tianjin for one day and take the train to Beijing the following day. You will arrive in Beijing at three o'clock in the afternoon. At the train station, there are many hotel agents. Choose Fuzhao Hotel and ask them to get you a rickshaw. The hotel is owned by Mr. Zhu of Qingyuan County of Guangdong and is located on Mule and Horse Market Avenues in Beijing. It will cost you sixty to seventy cents a day. After one or two weeks, you will be familiar with Beijing. Streets in Beijing, Tianjin, and Shanghai are much wider than those in Guangzhou and easier to locate. You can also buy a train ticket to Tianjin and then buy the transfer ticket to Beijing. A second-class ticket will cost about thirty to forty dollars. In Shanghai, British money is more popular. In Beijing and Tianjin, French and Japanese money are popular.[34]

Family documents do not tell us whether Sam had ever visited North and East China. By 1924, he had been away from China for nine years. But his description of metropolitan cities like Shanghai or Beijing shows an intimate knowledge about life in China even though he was in the United States. The most fascinating part of the letter is his description of Cantonese networks that could assist Tennyson to travel all the way from Guangzhou through Shanghai to Tianjin and Beijing. Amazingly, Sam even knew the name of a Cantonese hotel owner in Beijing, and the owner's home district. Such knowledge again tells us the importance of social networks in Cantonese culture. It demonstrates how the social networks of Guangdong extended everywhere in China, and how such networks were available for a traveling Cantonese. In a way, such networks paralleled the ethnic networks of the Chinese immigrants in the United States and elsewhere.

Sam's comment on Shanghai, Beijing, and Tianjin also gives us a glimpse of the colonial traits of these cities. Shanghai was known as the paradise of foreign adventurers in the early twentieth century, and was a very chaotic city. "Shanghai," when used as a verb, could literaly mean "kidnap." This was why Sam asked his son to be very cautious there. Further, though a domestic traveler, Tennyson needed to know how to use foreign currency, as all these cities belonged to the spheres of influence of foreign powers.

Nankai as a Modern School

In the fall of 1924, Tennyson became a student in Nankai. Different social customs, weather, and dialect than he was used to made his initial stay uncomfortable. Shortly after he arrived in Tianjin, he wrote to his father, indicating he wanted to go back to Lingnan in Guangdong. Sam disagreed.

When you arrive in a new place, don't be too excited or too upset. Calm down and think of your future. You have arrived in Nankai only for a couple of months and don't know it well yet. Lingnan can only produce some fluent English-speaking students. But your Chinese is not good enough yet. Only recently have you demonstrated some progress in Chinese. Don't be upset. Stay there for a while and then apply to Qinghua.[35]

As an immigrant, Sam certainly understood the cultural shocks his son might be going through in the North. As a parent, however, he was firm in his decision, as he knew what his son needed was a good foundation of Chinese and a better education than he had been getting. He told his son that the United States had begun to adopt a new education system: students there in the past had spent eight years in elementary school, but now they spent six, followed by six years in high school. In China, Nankai was one of the few schools that had adopted a similar system.

Unlike Lingnan, Nankai was not a missionary school, though it was also under heavy Western influence. Two reformers, Yan Xiu and Zhang Boling, had founded Nankai in Tianjin in 1904 as a private boarding school for boys. The school became Nankai University in 1909.[36] Originally the school developed a curriculum based on Japan's educational system (at the turn of the century, Japan and the West were competing with each other for dominance in China). However, Zhang Boling, the president of Nankai, made a visit to the United States in 1908 and was deeply impressed by the American education system. He particularly admired the Phillips Academy at Andover, Massachusetts. After the visit, Nankai explicitly adopted Phillips as its model. Soon the school grew into a coeducational institution and developed into two campuses—a middle/high school and a university. Many of the students were children of middle-class or wealthy families. Nankai especially welcomed children from overseas Chinese families, as they were patrons with foreign currency.

As a student in the North, Sam knew, Tennyson would have a better chance of getting his visa approved—from the American consular office in Beijing—than would someone from Guangdong, where too many people applied to go to the United States.

Further, and more important to Tennyson's education and learning of Chinese culture, Nankai used the vernacular in instruction. Sam wanted his son to learn how to speak and write the vernacular. During the May Fourth movement, radical intellectuals like Hu Shi strongly advocated that the vernacular replace classical Chinese, as a mechanism to modernize China, but the adoption of teaching in the vernacular was still slow in Guangzhou. At Nankai, in Tianjin, Tennyson would be able to learn the northern dialect, the verbal basis for the vernacular. Sam told his son:

> You will have a good opportunity to learn vernacular Chinese in the North. Guangzhou is not a proper place to study the vernacular because of the strong influence of the local dialect. To study the vernacular, you must read books by Hu Shi, who is the champion advocate of the vernacular. His writing is a good model. Hu recommends translation of Western fiction, especially the translations of French author A. Dumas by Jun Shu. I do not know who Jun Shu is. But he uses the vernacular rather than classical Chinese in his translation. It reads more creatively and can better convey the flavor of the original novel. It is much better than Lin Shu's classical translation.[37]

Like his previous writing, this letter reveals Sam's keen interest and up-to-date knowledge of literary trends in China. As one of the pioneer translators of Western literary works in late Qing China, Lin Shu had translated Alexandre Dumas's *La dame aux camellias* and published it in 1899.[38] Sam had probably read Lin Shu's translations before he left China; he would read Jun Shu's translations from the magazines Tennyson mailed to him in Los Angeles. By citing the example of a famous translation of Western literature, he could point out the importance of learning the vernacular for an educated modern Chinese youth. It seemed to be a different educational emphasis than what Tennyson had received in Guangzhou. But the most important consideration in Sam's decision was that Nankai was a better school than Lingnan. As a Chinese parent, he would not hesitate to relocate his child from home to the North for a better education.

Tennyson's adaptation to life at Nankai was actually quite smooth. He met with many students from a similar background, and could identify with two specific groups of students—those from Guangdong and those from an overseas Chinese family. He wrote his father that there were about 150 Guangdong students in Nankai School and they formed a Guangdong Student Association. He joined the organization and made some friends there; he also mixed well with students from overseas. When Yuhua arrived in 1927, Tennyson had been elected as the president of the Overseas Chinese Student Association. Although he had never been to a foreign country, his immigrant family background enabled him to understand the cultural sensibilities of overseas Chinese students.

Nationalist Influence on Tennyson's Life at Nankai

Staying at Nankai, Tennyson was also able to visit Beijing and to see more of Tianjin, a cosmopolitan city in the North. He wrote to Sam:

I traveled to Beijing during the winter vacation and stayed in a friend's home about twenty days. I have no money left. Living expenses have gone up a lot. When I first arrived at Nankai, it only cost me five dollars a month for food. Now it cost nine dollars. Please mail me seventy American dollars. I like to see movies, though the tickets are expensive. There will be a new movie about American President Lincoln next weekend. We are going to see it. There is also a movie show every Saturday in Nankai, though students here have no manners and often scream during the show. I think American movies are the best. Have you met any movie stars on the street? Tianjin is a good business city. Unfortunately it is tortured by continuous wars that have greatly affected its business. The best area in the city is the foreign settlement area. The Chinese area is shabby and poor, much worse than Canton. I have great sympathy for socialists and have changed many of my previous opinions. I feel very sad about contemporary China. I sympathize with socialists because they speak for the poor people and disdain the rich. I want to be a diplomat in the future. But what future do I have as a diplomat with today's corrupt government. I have read a novel in English called *The Citizen* by James Francis Duyer, which is about a Russian who migrated to the New Continent—the United States—for happiness and freedom because of the political oppression in Russia. I was deeply moved by the novel. But when I think of the bitter experience of the millions of overseas Chinese, I am at a loss what to believe.[39]

The letter shows that American cultural influence was strong at Nankai, as students could regularly see American movies and read English novels. Tuition was also expensive at such a school: Tennyson worried about the rising cost of school life. Although Tennyson liked American movies, he would not so easily accept Hollywood's depiction of America as a free and happy society for immigrants as would some of his Nankai schoolmates. Coming from Guangdong and an immigrant family, he had certainly heard a lot of sad stories of Chinese immigrants in America, and the image of this country as a land of freedom precisely contradicted the experience of Chinese immigrants.

Tennyson was studying in Nankai during a period when China was experiencing serious political instability. A corrupt government, social chaos, fighting between warlords, and foreign domination characterized Chinese society of the time. This dark social reality troubled Tennyson and probably many of his schoolmates, though they did not belong to the bottom of society but, rather, enjoyed a fairly comfortable life in this boarding school. Sam and his wife often worried when Tennyson did not write them frequently enough: "From your letter, we know that Tianjin is now tortured again by war. Since Tianjin is in a strategic location in the North, the military forces always fight for it. Your mother is very concerned about your safety as the city is often suffering from military violence."[40] Military battles between warlords over Tianjin often disrupted classes at Nankai and other universities. The only safe place was a foreign settlement where Western countries had judicial and administrative authority. The warlords' troops would usually not enter, as the settlement was considered an enclave of foreigners and was protected by extraterritorial privileges. Such a place was left untouched, too, because the warlords needed financial and arms aid from foreign banks. Sam often asked Tennyson if he was able to escape to the foreign settlement when conflicts occurred.

Although Tennyson, and later Constance, often went to the foreign settlement area for safety when local wars erupted, both children resented Western colonialism in China. After a visit to Qingdao, a city in Shangdong Province, Tennyson told Sam that the city looked like a Japanese territory, as there were so many Japanese houses and stores and the city was full of Japanese. Like many contemporary Chinese youth at that time, Tennyson was frustrated when he saw foreigners everywhere, who enjoyed all kinds of privileges in China. In contrast, he as a Chinese had to hide in a foreign enclave when warlords, often supported and financed by foreign powers, were fighting each other. While Sam often expressed concern over his son's safety in his letters, Tennyson wrote about his frustration over China's social problems. His anger is best revealed in a letter of 1927 in which he wrote:

> Father: how come China has become a country like this? Isn't it true that our motherland needs revolutionaries more than the quiet middle-class professionals like bank clerks or railway station managers?! I think Nankai is a product of a feudal education system and that is why it advocates salvation of our motherland through education. But people should open their eyes wide and see how many families have gone bankrupt and cannot afford school for their children. Our society only creates elite students and trains young people to work for

the comprador and landlord class. . . . Father, I am disappointed in this kind of education. I have a request for you. I want to study in Japan. I have many friends and schoolmates there. I want to enroll into the Japanese Army Academy. Father, I know you do not want me to go. You want me to get a diploma from Nankai as I am your only son. But have you not heard the continuous gun fighting and crying of our people who are suffering from cold and hunger? Please pray for your son and the liberty of a new Republic China. You should be proud of me if your son is willing to die for the country.[41]

This was a period when Chinese youth were exposed to and influenced by all kinds of ideologies—social Darwinism, socialism, communism, anarchism, Japanese militarism. Tennyson's emotional request reflects not only his own bitterness but also the deep frustration and disappointment in China's political situation then felt by many Chinese youth. They felt that their country was faced with a national crisis, and that to study abroad must be to find a new solution to save China, rather than to pursue personal interest.

Sam was very upset about this letter and he wrote back to scold his son for his "crazy" ideas:

After reading your letter, I could not sleep. Your mother cried. We are all worried about you. We thought you were either sick or expelled from the school for violating school codes. Your mother asked me to get you over to America as soon as possible. Grandpa is very angry, calling you a useless grandson. You have greatly disappointed me. Grandpa and your mother blamed me for having placed too much hope in you when I sent you to the North for education. You have made bad friends and come up with this crazy idea of going to the Japanese Army Academy. That school is not easy to get into, and Japan always has territorial ambition over our motherland. A man from Siyi called Zhang Ronghai applied to the Japanese Army Academy after graduation from Nankai. He is still at a Japanese sergeant school, as the Academy refused to admit him because of his inadequate Japanese language ability. A grandson of a Siyi man has also applied to the Academy but was rejected with a similar excuse. A son of Mr. Huang in Los Angeles left for Japan to enter the Academy, after graduation from high school here. Failing to get admitted, he returned to China and now studies at Lingnan.

Sam's response reveals a large generation gap between the parent and child in their attitudes toward the national crisis, their sensitivity to social issues, and their understanding of educational goals. In Sam's opinion, Tennyson's patriotic emotion was stupid and a senseless daydream, and Tennyson's anger at foreign domination in China became a mental sickness. Obviously, Tennyson's letter was read to family members, as the whole family was upset about his intention to go to Japan. Yitang and all other extended family members were involved in the discussion of how to change Tennyson's mind about going to the Japanese Army Academy. Sam further wrote:

> Forget the crazy idea completely. Education is the only way to save China. The entire world understands the importance of education. No matter what a noble ideology or good policy you have, without a high degree of education, you cannot put them into practice. American politics is not perfect. But compulsory education is an unchanged policy. After World War One, Japan and Germany could rebuild their commerce and industry rapidly because they had advanced educational systems. Russia and Turkey are still suffering from chaos because they had poor educational systems.

Although interested in and supportive of social reforms in China, Sam became suspicious of those leading intellectuals who advocated radical social changes, when he saw how Tennyson had been influenced by their ideas. However, he did not totally reject his son's nationalist sentiment. In the rest of the letter, he emphasized that only education could save China, and also warned his son that politics was a dangerous thing:

> There are all kinds of ideologies proposed by all kinds of people. Chen Duxiu recommended communism, Cai Yuanpei advocated socialism, and Sun Yatsen was the first one to introduce socialism into China. Chen declared that communism would be realized in fifty years in every country. And it would be realized in China in a few years through education: young people with high inspiration should devote their lives to it. After reading Hu Shi's works, I find Chen a radical. Young people should not be led astray by Chen Duxiu and devoted to politics. Ten years ago, a Chinese named Huang in Los Angeles advocated anarchism. As a vegetarian, he diligently studied English by day and taught Chinese children in the evening. His father owned a laundry store. He advocated anarchism and communism to whomever he met. He was well known in Chinatown. Then he was arrested by the American government, when political pamphlets were found in his home.[42]

Interestingly, Sam's letter indicates how some overseas Chinese were influenced by radical ideologies such as anarchism or communism. At the turn of the century, increasingly modernized Japan drew a great exodus of students from China. As Jonathan Spence points out, "Japanese law and medical schools, military academies, departments of political science and economics—all seemed to offer Chinese new hope at a time when that traditional Chinese 'essence' seemed every year more fragile in the face of the West's overwhelming practical power."[43] For many Chinese youth at that time, a sense of urgency before national crisis and a passion to build China into a strong nation constituted the essential meaning of being a patriotic Chinese. As Sam and his son's letters indicate, students from elite boarding schools like Nankai, children of immigrant families in Guangdong, and Chinese American youth in Los Angeles all desired to enter Japanese military academies. Sam must have heard numerous cases of such youth eager to go to Japan, for he handily cited several examples of Cantonese youth interested in Japanese military schools in his letter to Tennyson. That Tennyson could hate Japanese colonialism in China but feel attracted to Japanese military school seems contradictory, but clearly shows how Chinese youth in the early twentieth century viewed Japan (and the West) as both enemy and teacher. When placed in historical context, Sam's debate with his son illustrates how the study-abroad movement and nationalism were intricately intertwined in shaping the identity of Chinese youth both at home and abroad. These youth were eager to go overseas to study modern technology, science, and social science, but at the same were deeply upset about colonialism in China.

Tennyson eventually gave up his idea of going to Japan and became more attentive to his studies. In his next letter, dated 25 February 1928, he promised that he would concentrate on his studies and get less involved in extracurricular activities. To make sure that his children concentrated on their studies, Sam requested reports of their grades. Although Sam was against Tennyson's involvement in politics, he encouraged his son to take more social science classes at Nankai and choose political science or international studies rather than medicine for his college major. Tennyson himself hesitated for awhile between selecting medicine or social sciences. As several members of the family were doctors, the medical career was alluring. But Sam believed Tennyson's personality better fit the study of the social sciences. As he planned that his children's future be based in China, he did not have to pressure them to major in engineering or science, as most Chinese immigrant parents had to. The choice, however, was made by Tennyson himself.

In general, Tennyson's education at Nankai was rewarding and successful.

He received a good Chinese cultural foundation before leaving for the United States.

In 1929, Tennyson applied to the University of Southern California. His grades at Nankai were competitive enough to gain him admission, though he needed to change his Chinese name. Since Sam planned to bring him over on a student visa, the Chang family had already used his name "Tingxun" as a "paper son" slot for a cousin. In a letter of 1929, Tennyson wrote,

> I have read your letter of January 12. School has started for two days and everything is fine. Don't worry about us. I have already submitted the University of Southern California application form. I will use the name "Boxun" and the home address "De-an-chang, Hong Kong." Is that O.K.? Tell me soon and send me more money immediately. Could you ask Ms. Lei about the application procedure for me?[44]

Although immigration procedure forced Tennyson to use a different name, he made a careful choice of words in taking "Boxun" for his name change. In Chinese family culture, the words "bo, zhong, shu, ji" represent first, second, third, and forth in male sibling ranking. Since Tennyson was the eldest son of Sam and eldest grandson of Yitang, "Boxun" fit nicely as a Chang family name, though he lost his generation character "ting," for immigration purposes. Still, his English name, "Tennyson," sounded somewhat like his Chinese name "Tingxun." In his reply letter, Sam assured Tennyson that the application procedure was fairly easy but he should clearly indicate that he could read and speak English, and that he would not work outside of school. Otherwise, he would be taken as a laborer and denied entry.[45]

Joining the Family as a Foreign Student

Tennyson arrived in San Francisco on 15 August 1929 without being detained at Angel Island Immigration Station. On the ship from China, he met a fellow traveler, from Enping County, the hometown of Tennyson's mother, and helped him locate a relative in San Francisco. Tennyson called home from the relative's house, then joined his parents in Los Angeles the following day, by train, after fourteen years of separation. During these long years, Yitang and Sam had sponsored dozens of young people of the Chang clan to enter the United States to work in the family herbal business or on the asparagus farms. But Tennyson stayed behind, because Sam did not want him to come as a laborer nor intend for him to inherit the farming business.

An ideal career for his son was as a diplomat, or a scholar in China, rather than to be a second-class citizen in the United States. It is an ironic twist that Tennyson had to join his parents in America as a foreign student due to racist restrictions against the Chinese: such restrictions were undoubtedly what had convinced Sam that his son's future was in China after college graduation.

Even after Tennyson traveled to California, Constance stayed on in China to finish her high school and college education. Sam had detailed plans for his children's education. Sam wrote, in a letter to his daughter:

> Your mother and I plan to retire in China after all of you finish your college educations. Hopefully, we will fulfill our plan in about ten years. For Tennyson, he will get a B.A. degree in Los Angeles, an M.A. at Columbia University, and a Ph.D. at Georgetown University in Washington, D.C., where your third uncle studied. Then he will study in Europe for two years before I send him back to China, and work for the Foreign Ministry. If a position abroad is available, it should at least be a consul position. Otherwise, he will stay in China.[46]

Thus, Sam's plan for Tennyson's bacalaureate and advanced degrees is not only detailed but calculated, as it includes Columbia, one of the best American universities, and Georgetown University, known for its international studies program. Degrees from such institutions would make Tennyson a very marketable professional should he look for a diplomatic career. Sam had a clear vision of his children's educational needs during this period. He firmly believed that they should obtain education from both China and the West even though their future was in China. The educational goals he set for Tennyson would take perhaps ten years to fulfill, but a good education was a steppingstone for a promising career. Like many Chinese parents, Sam was willing to see his children's education through to the end, and regarded this as his obligation. His hard work and personal sacrifice as an immigrant farmer was mainly for his children's future.

Shortly after his arrival in the United States, Tennyson began his college education at the University of Southern California, using "Tennyson" as his English name. While attending college, he also worked part-time as a way to reduce the financial burden on his parents. Sam wrote, in a letter to Constance: "He also got a teaching job at the Los Angeles Chinese language school. Tennyson got an offer to teach Chinese at Zhonghua School for seventy-five dollars a month. It is pretty hard for him to go to college at eight in the morning and teach from four to seven at this school."[47] Although he still spoke English with an accent, Tennyson was able to actively participate in social activities. Nankai having provided him with good English training, he also won the first place in a public speech contest at the school. In March 1931, Sam wrote to Constance, "Recently, Tingxun is busy lecturing everywhere. On March 27, an Association of the International Studies invited him to speak on China. Later his speech was published in both Chinese and Western newspapers. Chinese community in Los Angeles was very impressed by his speech."[48] Sam was supportive of Tennyson's participation in extracurricular work because many such activities related to the current situation in China. The Japan invasion of China directly affected the education of Chang family members in the home country. In a letter to his daughter, in 1932, Sam wrote:

> The "dwarf devils" [the Japanese] are now attacking Shanghai after having occupied the Northeast. Fortunately the Nineteenth Route Army fought hard against them. But the enemy is strong and we are weak. It is hard to say who will win. Under such a situation, World War Two will last very long, unless America and Russia get involved. If the "dwarf devils" deepen their aggression against our homeland from the Northeast, they will pass through Tianjin. In that case, you should evacuate to Hong Kong with your third and fourth uncles. It is a remote place and also a colony of Britain. Tennyson is very busy with anti-Japanese campaigns here. Zhonghua Huiguan [Chinese Consolidated Benevolent Association] asked him to work as the director of the Public Communication Department. Last Wednesday, three Chinese community organizations invited him to talk on China, though he is too busy to go all of them. Our country now is in great danger. Tennyson often speaks to Western organizations, in spite of his busy schedule with school work.[49]

Tennyson's student leadership experience at Nankai prepared him well to be a student activist in an American university. Soon he came to know Chinese student organizations on other campuses and was often invited to talk about the Japanese invasion of China, speaking at a variety of colleges. He once also had a long and tough debate with the Japanese general consul in Los Angeles at an international conference.[50] Sam did not regard Tennyson's activities for China in the United States as radical or extreme. He was proud that Tennyson could readily participate in these social actions even though he grew up in China.

After he received his B.A. from the University of Southern California (in January 1933), Tennyson followed exactly the direction Sam had planned for him and went to the East Coast. He first attended Columbia University in New York for his master's degree, and then pursued his Ph.D. in Washington, D.C., at Georgetown University. Encouraged by Sam, Tennyson continued to participate in extracurricular activities. When Sam heard that the newly elected Franklin Delano Roosevelt would be inaugurated in March 1933, he wrote to Tennyson:

> Roosevelt's presidential inauguration will be held on March 4. There will be a parade and it seems very exciting. It is also on a Saturday. You should go if you have the time. It is not very easy for overseas Chinese students to see such an event. New York is not very far from Washington, D.C., and will not cost much money. As your major is diplomatic studies, you should not miss the event. I hear you plan to visit Chicago and to see the International Trade Exhibition and famous museums there. I like the idea very much. Chicago is an important city in midwest America. You should know this city.[51]

In another letter, Sam noted that Tennyson had become an officer of a Chinese student organization: "I am pleased to hear you are the president of the East Coast Chinese Student and Youth Association. Hopefully it will be not a tiring job."[52] As an officer of the Chinese student organization, Tennyson was able to travel to several other cities on the East Coast and to become involved in more China-related social actions. In a letter of 1933, Sam wrote:

> Tennyson gave a speech on China over the radio that was broadcast throughout the world. His speech was highly praised by many Americans. An army academy military teacher spoke highly of his speech. I went to the Hu Zhu's home to listen to the radio speech, but they did not know how to locate the international frequency band.[53]

In the fall of 1934, Cai Tingkai, a Chinese general, arrived in the United States. His Nineteenth Route Army troops had resisted the Japanese attack on Shanghai for thirty-four days in January and February, 1932. In contrast to appeasing Nationalist leaders, Cai brought honor to the Chinese as an anti-Japanese hero. Moreover, he was a Cantonese. He visited several cities in the United States; wherever he went, he was honored with spectacular receptions. As Henry Tsai notes, Cai's visit was a good barometer by which the linkage between the Chinese in America and their motherland could be measured.[54] When Cai visited Washington, D.C., Tennyson made a speech, in both English and Chinese, as a Chinese student representative at the reception. Sam wrote Tennyson that, "When the *Jinshan Shibao* [*Golden Mountain Times*] carried the news about Cai Tingkai's visit, it praised your speech as the best one at the reception."[55] Sam also described Cai's visit to Los Angeles:

> Cai's speech in L.A. was improper, as it condemns the Nanjing government. His talk attracted several thousand Chinese. Four of my workers and I went to hear his talk, too. However, Cai only gave a brief account of the Shanghai Battle and then began to attack the Nanjing government. Fortunately few Westerners went and there was no interpretation. Otherwise he could have harmed the government's reputation.[56]

Tennyson shared this perspective with his father and actually advised Cai not to openly attack the Nationalist government before an American audience. He believed that doing so could hurt the national interests of China. According to one letter of Sam's, Cai carefully considered Tennyson's advice.[57]

As a parent, Sam continued to watch Tennyson's academic performance even when the young man was a graduate student at Georgetown University. Sam wrote to Constance in 1935 that her brother got three As and four Bs.[58] In another letter, Sam suggested to Tennyson that he write his dissertation on China's diplomatic history from the Qing Dynasty to the present.[59]

In 1938, Tennyson married. His wife, Xisi, graduated from Jiling University in Nanjing, one of the most prestigious universities, converted from an American missionary school in China, and her father was a Chinese diplomat while her mother an American-born Chinese.[60] Tennyson's father-in-law also promised to help him obtain a job in the Chinese foreign ministry. The wedding was held in the Chinese embassy in Washington, D.C., and was hosted by the Chinese ambassador. While preparing for the marriage, Sam wrote to Tennyson that his mother wanted him to stay in the United States for awhile. The older couple probably want to see their first grandchild, preferably a boy, before Tennyson returned to China. Sam told Tennyson that his mother was willing to help take care of the baby.[61] Tennyson and his wife had a daughter the following year. In 1940, Tennyson got his first job offer, as an assistant consul in the General Consulate of the Chinese Nationalist government in Nicaragua. Because of his family background, he was assigned to be in charge of overseas Chinese affairs. Writing to his father in 1940, Tennyson mentioned that as a low-ranking government official, his monthly salary was less than 150 U.S. dollars. Such a salary was too meager to raise a family. But Sam encouraged him to accept the offer: "I know you will begin as an assistant consul. It is fine to begin with a low position. You will have promotions in the future."[62] After Tennyson married, Sam and his wife began to expect a grandson from him, as many other Chinese parents did when their children married. They were still influenced by traditional Chinese culture. However, Tennyson's three children were all daughters.

Equally to Sam's disappointment, Tennyson's diplomatic career was not so smooth or promising as he had hoped. While in Nicaragua, Tennyson's wife became ill with amoebic dysentery. She could not find proper care in Nicaragua and therefore had to be sent to Costa Rica for proper medical treatment. After his wife's recovery, Tennyson left his position in the Chinese foreign ministry. He did not inform his parents and other family members until he had found another job, at the University of Colorado in Boulder. Then he switched between several jobs, including a position with the New York–based China Institute in America, where his salary was 250 dollars per month. Sam still hoped his son could obtain a good position with the Chinese government. When Tennyson's father-in-law was promoted in 1945, while in Chongqing (Chungking), the Nationalist government's wartime capital, Sam urged Tennyson to solicit help from his father-in-law in obtaining a new position. In 1946, when the anti-Japanese war was over and the Nationalist government began to negotiate with the Communists for a coalition government, Sam brought up this issue again:

> The overseas Chinese have great hopes in the Political Consultation Conference after the war. Many of them, including our family members, are waiting to go back. When the situation becomes stable, you should go back and serve our own country. We should also raise money for rebuilding Nankai School, and also the school in our home village.[63]

In other letters, Sam mentioned that a distant relative planned to open a cigarette factory in China, and that his third brother Elbert wished to go back to carry on his medical practice, as well. He also observed that many Chinese American veterans could not find proper jobs in America.[64] Under this encouragement, Tennyson too was thinking about going back to China. Writing from New York, he informed Sam:

> Both Nankai and Beijing University were willing to offer me a faculty position. But the economic situation in China is really awful. Many universities were damaged in the war, including Nankai. In

> regard to faculty positions, it is best to get a teaching position in Beijing University. But it is so close to the battlefields during the civil war.[65]

Obviously, this was the moment when the People's Liberation Army under Mao Zedong (Mao Tse-tung) and his Communist Party were about to take over Beijing. Tennyson was never able to return to China. His pursuit of a promising diplomatic career in China through a transnational education did not come through, because of the political changes in that country. But Tennyson did become a full professor at Georgetown University, in the department of international relations. Following this, he was a professor of Asian studies at Saint Petersburg University in Tampa, Florida, until his retirement. Growing up in a merchant immigrant family, he was fortunate enough to avail himself of opportunities on both sides of the Pacific.

Through the Chang family history, we see how the value of education was deeply rooted in an average Chinese family. Children's education, as an important family agenda, was viewed by parents as their obligation, and they closely monitored and involved themselves in their children's education. The Chang's example tells us how Chinese family culture in general expects each younger generation's success to be accomplished through education and career merit rather than to be based on the wealth of ancestors. On the other hand, young people were supposed to climb the social ladder through their own educational achievement and to live up to their parents' expectations. As good schools and colleges were not necessarily located in the home region, educational pursuit often sent the children away from home, allowing them to explore new lifestyles in metropolitan cities or even overseas. In seeking education, the younger generation embarked on a path to maturity and independence and were exposed to new cultures and social environments. Letters between Sam and his children tell us how national and international events impacted identity formation of Chinese youth, and how letter writing functioned as an important communication channel in Chinese family culture.

CHAPTER 7

China as a Cultural Home

*A*ttachment to China is not merely an abstraction defining the ethnic identity of Chang family members as Chinese Americans. It has real and pragmatic meaning: the family's life was oriented toward both China and America. Although owning business and property, and living most of their lives in America, Yitang and Sam did not regard America as their home. As immigrants, both planned to go back to China when they retired. Meanwhile, they understood that American society did not provide a good cultural environment for Chinese children. As parents, they noticed that American-born Chinese often had low self-esteem as a result of racism against the Chinese. Moreover, college education could not guarantee upward social mobility for American-born Chinese in the United States.

The racial environment in U.S. society had two significant impacts on the cultural orientation of the Chang family. First, Chinese language and culture training became a necessary component in the after-school life of the second generation. Second, the parents encouraged their children to consider a future in China.

An ironical coincidence in the Chang's family history was that, while Tennyson in China tried to find a school where English language training was competent, other family members in the United States, especially those born there, worked hard on their Chinese language ability. Chinese language and culture functioned as a useful mechanism for social mobility, for the American-born or American-raised generation of the Chang family. Sam's children, Constance and Estelle, and Yitang's children—Elbert, Lillian, Arthur, and Marian—all went to China either for education or to pursue a career. The land of their ancestors not only provided them with such opportunities but also enabled them to live a meaningful social life. In spite of their U.S. background, they did become culturally Chinese during their stay in China.

Through this reverse-migration experience, they actually embarked on a road of de-Americanization. Although most of them eventually returned to the United States, China was in many ways their cultural home.

Locating Sam Chang's family history in a global context makes the significance of their transnational experience apparent. Orientation toward both China and the United States is not merely an individual choice by one family, but a collective strategy adopted by many Chinese immigrant families of the period. As the number of Chinese children increased, Chinese-language schools were established in every Chinese community across the country. Chinese children were expected to go to these schools for a few hours of class on Chinese culture after attending public school all day. Although many American-born Chinese youth disliked the arrangement, taking a Chinese-language class became part of their daily life. Bilingualism was necessary because Chinatown might be the only place where they could find employment in the United States. The functions of the earliest Chinese schools, as Sauling Wang has pointed out, were not linguistic and cultural in the sense of preserving an ethnic culture; rather, "at the turn of the century, under Exclusion, the Chinese in America had no chance for integration into American life and were therefore seen as logical candidates for contributing to the development of China. Moreover, with the often arbitrary enforcement of harsh immigration restrictions on the Chinese, the prospects of returning to China someday, by choice or by necessity, were very real. It would therefore be sensible to supplement an American education with a Chinese one."[1]

The Chang family members were, then, not alone in this reverse-migration experience. Many Chinese American youth, living under the shadow of racism, attended schools and sought, or considered seeking, jobs in China to avoid being trapped in a segregated labor market. This is especially true of the educated and professional Chinese and children of merchant family background, whose entry to or departure from the United States was not totally banned by the Chinese Exclusion laws. In 1933, San Francisco Chinese-language newspaper *Chung Sai Yat Po* strongly advised Chinese youth to return to China, where opportunities were unlimited and they would not be denied jobs because of their race.[2] In 1936, Ging Hawk Club, a New York–based community organization, sponsored a national essay contest with the title "Does My Future Lie in China or America?" The contest stimulated a heated debate among the Chinese youth about where their future was.[3] When young Chinese in America were sent back to China, they joined other overseas Chinese youth from Australia, Cuba, or Southeast Asia to learn the language and culture of their homeland.

Education and professional job opportunities in China were open to all overseas Chinese, because the country was in great need of technicians and scientists for modernization and race was not an issue for their social mobility there. But their stay in China was not necessarily permanent; although obstacles to meaningful integration into American society made going back a pragmatic consideration for many American-born Chinese during that period, the United States was still their home. As mentioned earlier, most of Sam Chang's American-born or -raised siblings and children eventually settled down in the United States. Lillian and Arthur, for example, returned to the United States for retirement after several decades in China. The racial environment and occupational status of the Chinese in the United States also improved considerably, beginning in the late 1940s or early 1950s.

The Chang family's attachment to China and reverse migration experience is highly significant in illuminating and explaining the Chinese transnational experience. The family's journey back and forth between the Pacific demonstrates how racism in the United States, as a "push" factor, and alternative opportunities in China, as "pull" factors, linked Chinese Americans to their home country and drew the American-raised and American-born family members back to the country of their ancestors. Members of the Chang family traveled back and forth across the Pacific and maintained involvement in both societies for decades, before the Cold War period eliminated such opportunities. With social, economic, and cultural activities transcending nation-state boundaries, the Changs and other Chinese Americans developed a transnational life and identity.

Yitang as a Gold Mountain Guest

In 1929, Yitang returned to China for a visit with his American-born wife Nellie, baby daughter Maria, and third son, Elbert. This was Yitang's second trip to China since he had arrived in America in 1900. He had planned this trip since his second son died of illness, in 1927, in China. He needed to clear up debts left by this son and settle some other financial affairs in his home village. The trip also had a strong symbolic meaning, as he had been away from home for twenty-three years. Yitang intended to visit his home as a *jinshan ke*—a successful Gold Mountain guest. The trip attracted great attention from his relatives and friends in Guangdong, and they made preparations for his return. Sam contacted local Chinese-language newspapers and publicized the news in the Chinese American community. For a return visit like this, many Chinese immigrants made donations for the construction of bridges, roads, railways, or schools as a way to express their emotional attachment to the home village. Such contributions brought pride to the family clan and demonstrated a Gold Mountain guest's love and generosity to his home village. In return, the relatives and villagers took a Gold Mountain guest's visit as an important social event, often provided a warm welcome, and made the visitor feel at home.

However, the annoying part of the event was the application process to the INS for their re-entry permits. The process included submission of various application forms and recent photos, and an interview, for every applicant. As usual, such an application needed careful preparation and was often arduous. From the perspective of INS officers, a Gold Mountain guest's return trip always resulted in more relatives and friends being brought over to America. As a gatekeeper, an officer must ask the most detailed questions on every aspect of the family, and record the answers, so that a potential imposter would be hard-pressed, even coached, to provide a matching story as a result of the trip. All departing family members—husband and wife, parents and small children, immigrant or American-born—went through such a process, so that discrepancies could be found in a family profile. Plural marriages, multiple names, and social networks were all focuses of attention in the interview. The process reflected INS officers' deep suspicion of the Chinese community as an effective immigrant network in the immigration process. The inquisitive style of the interrogation treated the entire family as suspects or criminals. For Chinese immigrants and their descendants, the return trip was a voyage through two sharply different social realities. In one reality, they were celebrated as homecoming heroes. In another, they were dehumanized as potential imposters.

Yitang was an experienced interviewee, as he had to appear as a witness for almost every family member regarding immigration matters. He would not let such an interview deter his plan to visit his home village. He handled all the questions well and emphasized that he was over sixty-four years and this might be his last trip to China.

Many changes had taken place to the Chang lineage during Yitang's twenty-three years of absence; though correspondence between Yitang and his relatives in China never ceased, he still had to prepare carefully for the trip. Sam helped work out a long and detailed schedule for him, including meeting relatives and villager leaders to discuss his donation for the construction of a road and school, re-building Yitang's mother's tomb, checking family property, and finding a husband for Constance and a wife for Elbert. In addition to family and lineage affairs, the schedule contained advice on whom among his relatives Yitang could trust and whom he should avoid. In a letter to his cousins, Sam wrote:

> Your eleventh granduncle [Yitang] has been away from home for twenty-nine years. Since he left, about fifty people of our clan have passed away. About eighty people were born and married. He now knows no more than a dozen people. I hope you will assist him in family affairs.[4]

To make Yitang feel comfortable during his stay in Guangdong, Sam arranged that former servants of the family be available upon his father's arrival. Interestingly, he also recommended that his own former babysitter help take care of Marie, who was less than three years old. Old social relationships were always useful in Chinese family culture.

Yitang left Los Angeles on 12 November 1928. Several dozen relatives and friends saw him off at the San Pedro Pier. By then, San Francisco was no longer the only port for Chinese departures and arrivals. In a letter to Tennyson and Constance in 1928, Sam wrote:

> Your grandparents, third uncle, and Aunt Zhuang left for China on November the 12th from the Los Angeles docks, on the *President Monroe*. They have booked a first-class cabin. About thirty people went in seven cars to see them off. They also had pictures taken on the pier. The news of their departure will appear in *Jinshan shibao* [*Golden Mountain Times*] and *Shaonian shibao* [*Youth Times*]. Your step-grandma originally planned to leave Aunt Zhuang to the care of Ms. Lin. But Zhuang is too young to be left to someone other than her mother, so they decided to take her with them. Grandpa must arrive in Guangdong before December 25, because he plans to attend the meeting of the board of trustees of Kaiping County High School that will hold a new election of trustee members. He also plans to make a donation to build a road for the home village and establish a new elementary school in the village.[5]

As they traveled to China, Yitang and his family stopped at San Francisco, Hawaii, Japan, Hong Kong, and Guangzhou. They planned to return to Los Angeles from Shanghai. Hong Kong was no longer the only port city in China for international departure and arrival of Chinese passengers.

After Yitang arrived in Guangzhou, he first attended the board of trustees meeting for Kaiping County High School. Then he made a brief visit to his home village, and donated money for a new road construction project and an elementary school. The road was to connect his village to Yangqiao, a nearby market town. For the name of this new road, Sam recommended Qiaoxin, as *xin* represented his village Xinshali (also called Niushan). He had warned against using *Qiaoniu*, as that would represent Wuniushan, a village that often sent bandits to attack the Chang family, though the road served that area as well.[6]

As for family affairs, ancestral worship was most important. Yitang built a new tomb for his mother, an act that was a key indication of his improved social and economic status in the Chang clan. Sam helped Yitang select a site for the tomb, and had asked relatives to see if the place had good *fengshui* (meaning in English roughly "the magic power of the environment on the family's fortune"). If his brothers did not oppose the idea, Yitang wanted to move his father's corpse to the new tomb, too. By doing so, he could enhance his mother's position in the clan, even though she was dead. As the situation in rural Guangdong was still unstable, Yitang also wanted to remove the deeds for all his housing and landed property, to keep in the United States.

Yitang did not want to stay in Guangdong very long, as family feuds continued. Meanwhile, the war between Jiang Jieshi (Chiang Kai-shek) and the Guangxi warlords broke out. Guangdong was not very safe. In a letter to Yitang, Sam asked his father to leave the village shortly after he settled family and lineage affairs, and advised him not to let Elbert open a medical practice in Guangzhou: "As for my third brother's future, Guangzhou is not a good place. He has no one to help him there. He should stay in Shanghai or work for a government hospital."[7] Leaving Guangdong, Yitang and his wife went to see some famous Chinese cities, such as Hangzhou, Shanghai, Nanjing in the East, and Tianjin and Beijing in the North. His home visit became a leisure tour. This was Yitang's last trip to his home village, as he did not plan to live there anymore. Niushan was no longer a *jia* (home) for him but a *laojia* (a native or birth place) in which to trace his ancestry root. On his tour, he was greatly impressed by the beauty of Hangzhou City and immediately considered it as a place where he might retire. In September 1929, Yitang and Nellie left China from Tianjin, and returning to Los Angeles in October. After that, Japanese invasion, civil war, and social instability in China never allowed Yitang to realize his dream of Hangzhou. He died a peaceful death on 13 July 1952. As a filial son, Sam held a traditional Chinese funeral procession for him, with all family members in white mourning apparel, and a band performing Chinese funeral music, marching through Chinatown.[8]

Longgang Association in the Los Angeles Chinese community helped Sam in arranging the funeral. For Yitang, a Gold Mountain guest, China had become, after his 1929 visit, only a symbolic home.

Nellie Returns as an American-born Chinese Woman

Nellie accompanied Yitang, with their three-year-old daughter, Marie. This was Nellie's first and only trip to China. As Yitang's American-born wife, she was a total stranger to the villagers, though she could speak some Cantonese. When they arrived, the villagers would look at her and say: "Oh, her eyes are still brown? They aren't blue? Her hands and feet are so white! So clean!" A stranger herself in the village, Nellie was equally curious about why her relatives let their pigs out of the pen to eat vegetable leaves in the kitchen. It was also uncomfortable for her to sleep in a fortress-like block-house at night.[9] But this was a necessity: in addition to fierce family feuds and clan wars in rural Guangdong, kidnapping overseas Chinese for ransom was common by those days. Many villagers built blockhouses; indeed, Kaiping City still preserves thousands of such blockhouses as an exhibition of immigration history.

Viewing Nellie as a stranger, the villagers probably did not know that she was one of them as far as the INS agency was concerned. Through marriage to Yitang, Nellie had been deprived of her U.S. citizenship. Moreover, she had also lost her birth certificate. An INS letter on her application for reentry after the trip clearly stated: "Birth in the United States was not an issue because she was alien by reason of her marriage to a Chinese alien prior to September 22, 1922."[10] Although an American-born Chinese, Nellie needed to apply for her reentry permit just as Yitang did, and if anything went wrong with the permit, she might not be able to return. The process was long and difficult; she had to fill out and submit forms and recent photos, go through the interview. One written question on the application bluntly asked: "Did you take any money, letters, or anything else from the United States to any one in China on this trip, and if so, to whom?" In treating such trips as immigration fraud, the INS agency assumed that the Chinese often exchanged information on each other's family situations to create possible "paper son" slots. Another question read, "Did you visit any resident of this country who happened to be at his home during your recent stay in China, or did you visit the home of such resident?" The language used in such questions clearly demonstrates how the INS agency perceived the Chinese as potential imposters. The question absurdly defined the Chinese, including American-born Chinese like Nellie, categorically as merely "residents of this country," and refers to China as their "home." The question even asked the returning Chinese whether they saw each other in China. Two other questions implied that the Chinese used their social networks and cultural events as immigration schemes, in asking: "Were you ever introduced to the son, daughter, or wife of any resident of this country? Did you attend the wedding of any resident of this country or of the son or daughter of any resident?"

Ironically, the interview pushed Nellie to recollect every detail of her own family history, as she had to answer all kinds of questions. She was born in Ventura on 24 September 1888. Her Chinese name was Yee Muey or Yee Cai Muey. Both of her parents were immigrants. Her mother, Chun, died in 1894 and her father Yee Ha (or Yee Kay Hung) died on 16 September 1916. She had one sister and two brothers. The eldest sibling was Emily Yee, who married Lum Joe and lived in San Diego. Emily was followed by George Yee, who passed away in 1908 when he was twenty-four years old. Nellie had a younger brother, William Yee (or Yee Gee), who was four years younger and married Ng Shee, and who lived in San Francisco at that time. Nellie and Yitang had five children; in addition to Lillian, Arthur, Marian, and Marie, they had a daughter named Freda (or Kow Shi), who died in February 1918.[11] The INS inspector's questions were often specific and coldhearted. As the above information shows, Nellie had to acknowledge the death of two family members—often a sensitive topic in Chinese family culture. Sometimes an inspector would press for an exact date of a family member's death. The inspector also asked Nellie the names, ages, and whereabouts of all four children by order of birth. Nellie provided the answer at one stroke, including her children's Chinese names. When asked for their home addresses, Nellie promptly replied that they had lived, in chronological order, at 917 South Hill, 126 West Fourteenth Place, 1322 South Hill Street, and 224 West Street since she and Yitang married in 1910.[12] She had had to memorize all these details by heart to pass the interview.

The interview let Nellie taste the grueling immigration process that numerous Chinese immigrants had to go through. Although this was her only trip to China, it was not the last testimony she had to make. When her children applied to go to China later, she and Yitang had to testify, again and again, both orally and in writing. However, such an arduous process did not prevent her from encouraging her American-born daughter Lillian and son Arthur to go to China for educational and career opportunities. Both stayed there for several decades. Ironically, Nellie's photo on the approved reentry permit, taken before the trip, is one in which she wears American dress and hairstyle. The photo attached to her admission form and taken by INS officers upon her return, however, shows her in traditional Chinese clothes and hairstyle—as if she left as an American but returned as a Chinese.[13]

Elbert's Family and Career in China

This was Elbert's second trip to China since arriving in America. Although born in China, he grew up and attended high school in Los Angeles and college on the East Coast, and in 1924 received a medical degree from Georgetown University. Upon his graduation from medical college, his first job offer came from Beijing Union Medical College, though he had lost much of his Chinese language ability. Sam was very pleased about this offer and regarded it as a prestigious position, since the Beijing Union Medical College was a medical institution affiliated with and sponsored by the Rockefeller Foundation. Elbert worked there from 1924 to 1925; however, he felt lonely and uncomfortable as he spoke limited Chinese, and he intended to come back. Sam was very disappointed when he heard Elbert's decision, and tried repeatedly to persuade his brother to stay. Sam conveyed his advice to Elbert through his letters to Tennyson, since Elbert did not read Chinese well and Sam did not write in English. On 16 November 1924, Sam wrote:

> Yesterday I received a letter from your uncle saying that the intern curriculum at Beijing Union Medical College was no good and that he wanted to come back to America. This is a naive idea that indicates that he is a naïve person. He should work there for three years and then go to Germany to study for a year. After that he could go back to China and open his own medical office or hospital in Tianjin, Shanghai, or Guangzhou, because he would have adequate experience, knowledge, and reputation by then. If he returns to America, his financial income would depend on his clients. In America, the racial difference is profound. The whites are regarded as the most superior race. Very few white people would go to a Chinese doctor. His patients would either be low-class people or have very difficult symptoms. He will not make much money. There is a Kaiping man called Zhu Zhonghui who practiced medicine in Tianjin for years and has made a great fortune there. We know a Chinese dentist called Li Xiuji who opened a practice in Los Angeles, but many people advised him to return to Guangzhou.[14]

Sam's words were blunt, since his advice was going to be forwarded to Elbert through his son. It would be awkward for Tennyson as a nephew to tell his uncle that his father called him naïve. But Sam was particularly concerned about Elbert's career in America, as he was the first from the Chang family to graduate from American university and hold a medical degree. His success could be a role model for other siblings and for Sam's own children. Based on his observation of the United States, Sam did not believe his brother could gain respect as an American medical professional, because of the racial hierarchy. As Asians considered to belong to an inferior race, in America, it was rare for middle- or upper-class Caucasian to use a Chinese physician's service. Sam had to be straightforward with his brother, as he regarded Elbert's career development as an important family issue. In another letter, Sam wrote to Tennyson:

> If your uncle comes back to America, he may make a bit more money now. But his reputation and social status is low, and his medical knowledge will be wasted. He will become a low-class citizen without high status. He will never become a respected man, since America is the most racist society and a very biased place against people of the yellow race.[15]

Sam's point is clear. As a Chinese medical professional, you could make a living in America but you would not live a great life. Western medicine in America had few Asian doctors. It could be a serious challenge for Elbert to break into this field. In fact, when Elbert returned to America from his second trip to China, in 1938, planning to open a medical office in Long Beach, he still invited Yitang and Sam to join him as herb doctors in order to attract more clients. Sam's advice to Elbert reveals how pessimistic and frustrated ordinary Chinese felt about their racial status in American society. Sam did not discuss racial issues very often in his letters, and seldom criticized American society and culture. If this letter had not been a discussion on Elbert's career opportunities, he would probably not have so explicitly expressed in it his opinion of the United States.

Elbert did not follow Sam's advice, but instead returned to America in 1924. Difficulty in adjusting to life in Beijing was part of the reason. But Beijing Union Medical College was an important experience in his life. A family document mentions that, though a junior doctor, he participated in Sun Yatsen's (Sun Zhongshan) surgery, the youngest doctor among the eight participating physicians.[16] After he returned to the United States, he worked briefly as an intern at a public hospital in Los Angeles, and left, on a research fellowship, for Austria, which was probably as foreign as Beijing to him if not worse. Before his 1929 trip, Elbert had just finished his research project in Austria and returned to the United States after visiting London, Paris, and Geneva. But it was again China that offered him a position as a doctor. In a letter to Tennyson, Sam mentioned that Elbert had received three job offers in China:

> Your uncle plans a long stay there after this trip with your grandpa. You should meet them at the Tianjin Railway Station. There are three job offers for your uncle: Beijing Union Medical College, Wuxing Gospel Hospital, and the Medical College of Shandong Qilu University. The salary is about two hundred dollars and there will be raises later. But they are all hospitals run by Westerners. If you work there, you are not allowed to open your own medical office. Grandpa and Elbert's preference is to work for the Nationalist government and open his own clinic at the same time.[17]

During this trip, Elbert had an opportunity to visit Niushan Village, where he was born and spent his childhood. Then, traveling to the North, he headed for his medical career in China. All the hospitals mentioned by Sam were established by American businessmen or missionaries. In contrast to the racial environment in the United States, China provided many middle-class jobs for Western-trained Chinese professionals in the 1920s and 1930s. Western enterprises and educational institutions in China were attractive not only to native Chinese but also to those born, raised, or educated overseas. From the late nineteenth century onwards, many Chinese worked in foreign businesses as interpreters, clerks, or salespersons. "The British-American Tobacco Company, for example, required that a large proportion of its Chinese workers be able to use English; its interpreters and most of its bookkeepers were Chinese."[18] In the medical field, Americans founded the Peking (Beijing) Union Medical College in 1906, and St. Luke's Hospital in Shanghai in 1914. The Germans founded Donaji Medical College in Shanghai in 1907. The French Doumer Hospital was opened in 1900 in Guangzhou.[19] The difference in social status and salary at these enterprises, compared with offerings at a Chinese establishment, certainly gave the Chinese employees a strong sense of self-esteem.

To Sam's great surprise, Elbert found a wife before he got a job, during his second trip to China. In Shanghai, Yitang and Elbert visited a rich Cantonese merchant family named Tan. Originally, the two families met to see if Tan's son would be a suitable match for Sam's daughter Constance. At the meeting, Yitang and Elbert declined the proposal, as they noticed a large age difference between Tan's son and Constance. However, the Tan family liked Elbert a great deal, and asked if Elbert wanted to marry their daughter Tan Zongren. Happily, this match became successful, as the two young people liked each other very much when they met. Although arranged by the parents, theirs was a marriage based on their own decision.

To hold a grand wedding ceremony for Elbert and his wife, Yitang requested Sam to send him four thousand Shanghai dollars and one thousand Hong Kong dollars while he was in China. Although Sam was a filial son, money was tight. When Yitang left for China, he borrowed three thousand dollars from a bank owned by an Italian American company and promised to pay it back after the asparagus harvest. While he was away, his herb business slackened. Sam informed him that, in the beginning of December, the store had three or four clients per day, but later hardly any came. The store assistant, a relative of Yitang, was often absent from duty.[20] While Sam worried about the future of the herbal business, the bank requested payment of the loan plus interest. Sam had already borrowed money from relatives to pay part of the loan. Now he had to borrow more money for Yitang's trip and Elbert's wedding, as this wedding was a big event for the Chang family. In April 1929, Sam wired the money to his father, and, on July 29, Elbert held his wedding ceremony in Xihu Lake Park, Hangzhou, a neighboring city to Shanghai.

Elbert married a beautiful wife, established a family, and found a good career. To adapt to Chinese society, he quickly improved his Chinese language, including his understanding of the local Shanghai dialect. He first prepared to open a medical office in Shanghai, but Sam advised him to begin either in a missionary or a government hospital in Nanjing, then the capital of China, as he still needed experience and connections, and did not know Chinese society well. Following Sam's advice, Elbert worked in an army hospital in Nanjing in 1931, then switched to the Central Hospital of the Chinese government, and later became the head of its ear, nose, and throat department. Sam was very happy to hear of Elbert's promotion; in America, such an opportunity could hardly come to an Asian during that period. Working in China also provided Elbert with opportunities to know many government officials and social elites. In a letter, Sam wrote him:

> You will know Chinese society better and get acquainted with important people in the capital city. It is good for your future career. I also hear that you, my sister-in-law, and her mother would like to make a tour to America and Europe. If you come, you'd better apply

for a passport as a government official from the Foreign Ministry
and bring with you an entourage of two staff associates and a maid.
You will make six to seven thousand dollars out of this.

The letter indicates another strategy of the Chinese to enter America during
the Exclusion period. As government officials were not restricted by immigration laws and were allowed to bring associates and servants, many Chinese immigrants bribed these officials when they traveled to America. In his
letter, Sam listed seven to eight examples of such cases to Elbert, and assured him that he could easily get such passports, as the Chang family had
recently hosted several visiting officials from the Chinese Foreign Ministry
and built necessary connections. He continued:

> Those people are staff associates in name. In reality, they are people
> who plan to stay and make a living in America. And the sponsor can
> at least make three thousand Chinese dollars per person. Many people
> in Hong Kong and Shanghai are willing to pay you this amount in
> order to get the passports of staff associates. According to the new
> rule, the visiting officials and their associates cannot stay in America
> very long. But these associates will find ways to stay after they arrive.[21]

Sam tried to explore possibilities to sponsor more friends and relatives to
America through Elbert, once Elbert had built a good career and established
himself as an upper-class Chinese in China. Yitang gave Elbert some family
responsibilities. He asked Elbert to keep all the family property deeds of
Guangzhou and the home village.[22] The following year, Elbert quit the job
in Nanjing and went to Shanghai again. While opening his own office, he
worked for another government hospital there. It seems that Elbert had so
many different opportunities and his income was so large that he purchased
a big house by Xihu Lake, the most prestigious neighborhood in Hangzhou,
a city close to Shanghai. When Arthur went to China and visited Elbert, he
was overwhelmed by the magnificence of the house, the upper-class life style
of Elbert's wife and mother-in-law, and the hierarchy relations between servants and masters in Hangzhou.[23] In 1933, Elbert invited Yitang to retire to
that house, and his invitation made Yitang and Sam very happy.[24] By then,
Yitang was already sixty-seven years old and planning to retire in China.
Elbert was the first American-raised and -educated child of the Chang family to find a successful career in China. The hard work of Yitang as an immigrant parent had begun to bear fruit. The transnational approach to education
and career had succeeded, in this case.

However, Yitang never realized this retirement plan. The Japanese deepened their invasion into the south and east of China. In August 1937, Japanese troops occupied Beijing and Tianjin, then began to attack Shanghai. When Chinese troops resisted the Japanese invasion, Elbert participated in Red Cross activities and worked in the Chinese army hospital to treat wounded soldiers. Sam was happy to see Elbert serve the country but urged him to evacuate his family and other relatives to Hong Kong. Fortunately, Shanghai was a city where many Western powers had "concessions," which were technically regarded as foreign enclaves rather than Chinese territory. Japanese troops finally agreed to let Shanghai become a neutral area and did not devastate the city as they did Nanjing.

In 1938, Elbert visited San Francisco as a Rotary Club member to attend an international conference. He brought along his wife and three daughters. After the conference, he and his family joined the rest of the Changs in Los Angeles and stayed. Back in China, the Japanese invasion spread to other parts of China. In 1939, Hong Kong and Guangdong both fell. As the situation worsened, Elbert changed his wife's and daughters' legal status (in 1941) and decided to open a medical office in the United States. The Japanese invasion destroyed his successful career in China and Yitang's dream to retire by beautiful Xihu Lake in Hangzhou City. Elbert became a naturalized U.S. citizen in 1945 and died a peaceful death in his Los Angeles home in 1986. China gave Elbert a happy family, a respected career, and a meaningful life during his formative years. If it had not been for the Japanese invasion and then the civil war in the 1940s, China could have been a permanent home for Elbert and his China-born wife and daughters.

An Alumni Family of Nankai

Elbert is not the only one in the Chang family who formed a family in China. Arthur, Tennyson, and Constance came to know their spouses in China, as well. Moreover, they were all attending Nankai School in Tianjin. The educational experience of Tennyson at Nankai created a family connection in North China and a bridge between other family members and the school.

When Tennyson left Guangzhou for Tianjin in 1924, his uncle Elbert had already started working in the Beijing Union Medical College. During the holidays, Tennyson often went to visit Elbert in Beijing, as Sam urged his son to learn English from his uncle and prepare himself for his future studies in America. It took Tennyson about two hours to travel from Tianjin to Beijing by train. With a relative in a neighboring city, he felt less lonely in the North. While Elbert provided a sense of home, Tennyson himself served as a link between the Chang family in America and family members in China, especially with regard to educational opportunities. During his stay at Nankai from 1924 to 1929, he assisted Constance first, then Arthur, when they applied to Nankai School. In 1926, when Constance finished her junior high education in America, Sam asked Tennyson to find out if Nankai would consider her application. Tennyson mailed school brochure application forms, provided advice and information, talked to the school president, and informed Sam that Nankai welcomed overseas Chinese students. In July 1927, Constance left California for Tianjin.

When Sam's half-brother Arthur was about to finish his high school in 1930, Sam asked Tennyson to find out if Nankai would accept him as an American-born Chinese student. Arthur recalled:

> During the Great Depression, father suggested that I go back to China to study Chinese. I felt excited and adventuresome. Lingnan was the best-known school in China. The other possibility was to enroll in Nankai University. I had a nephew there. Father got the information from him about Nankai University.[25]

After Tennyson left Nankai for America in 1929, Sam asked Constance to continue to assist with Arthur's application procedure. In 1931, Arthur, too, went to study in Nankai.

The Chang family did not necessarily plan this partial family reunion in China. But it indicated that they were always watching for educational opportunities in China, and prepared for going there. Yitang and Sam made sure that the younger generation in America did not lose its Chinese heritage; Chinese was the major language spoken at home and would be a useful tool for the young people's future career. Arthur recalls, "Father Yitang felt strongly about the importance of a Chinese language education. I did not feel it was important. I spoke Chinese with my parents and spoke English with my brothers and sisters."[26] After Constance arrived in the United States in 1923, Sam personally taught her Chinese and let her write family letters to relatives in China. He taught his other daughters, Estelle and Joyce, Chinese, as well. One of Sam's letters, in February 1937, indicates that he read aloud Wu Chengen's *Xiyou ji* (*The Monkey Story*) to his daughter Joyce. According to Joyce's own recollection, it was her mother who often read her this famous Chinese myth. In any case, such reading was a daily joy for all involved, the entire way through the book.[27] Through reading this work of classical mythology to Joyce, Sam was not only teaching this American-born child Chinese language and culture but also instilling a love of China.

However, sending Constance back to China was not an easy decision. Although she worked hard at her Chinese while attending American public school, Sam still decided he should send her back to China for senior high. He wrote:

> After your sister finishes her junior high, we will send her back to China for her senior high and college education. Then she can come back to America or go to Europe for awhile. In this way, she will know Chinese language and culture. Your mother disagrees with this plan, for she thinks Yuhua already knows Chinese and should attend her senior high and college here, as American high school is free and this would cost us less money.[28]

Economically, it would have been ideal for the second generation to complete their high school education in the United States the tuition was free. The decision to send Constance to China reflects Sam's strong reservation about American campus life. In a letter of 1926, Sam wrote to Tennyson:

> I want to send Yuhua to Nankai. She has no future in America. She will forget her Chinese. In America, girls can hardly finish their college education if they look beautiful. Even in high school, men harass and run after them as if they would marry them. Your third uncle has told us many such stories about his college. There are many scandals in the American coeducational system. Attending high school here is a perilous thing for Yuhua, but we do not have enough money to do otherwise. I feel guilty about this.[29]

Although campus cultures at American high schools varied, Sam seemed seriously upset about the campus environment at both high school and university for his daughter. He finally made up his mind to send Constance back to China even though it would cost the family more money. In a letter of March 1927, Sam asked his son to mail him all of Nankai's textbooks, so that Constance could begin to read them, and also told Tennyson to prepare to pick her up in July at Shanghai Pier. In Sam's decision about Constance, economic considerations gave way to cultural considerations.

Sam taught Chinese to his half-bother Arthur and half-sister Lillian, when he was not busy with the farming. In Lillian's family album, there is a photo that shows Sam teaching her and Arthur Chinese in the backyard of

Sam's house.[30] In an interview, Arthur recalls: "Sam had a profound influence on my life since early childhood. He instilled in me the love of China's language and culture that prompted me to go to China after graduating from high school."[31] Arthur here recalls Sam not only as a brother, but also as a teacher whose mentorship and knowledge helped shaped his ethnic identity.

In addition to benefiting from Sam's mentorship, Arthur went to a Chinese language class offered by Chinese exchange students. He recalled:

> Kit King Lei (Lei Jieqiong) was a sociology major and studied in Los Angeles for her master's degree. She offered to teach Chinese in the community. Father signed me up immediately. I was the only high school student. The class was held at the home of a friend, Mrs How Wing Tom. I got out from school at 3 p.m. and went to Mrs. Tom's house for Chinese class from 4 p.m. to 6 p.m. I took the class for two years.[32]

Two Chinese language schools were established in Los Angles around 1927, on the recommendation of Cai Yuanpei and Fan Yuanlian, two celebrated Chinese educators of the time. When such schools were not available or convenient, some Chinese parents would hire college students, such as Lei Jieqiong, from China to teach a language class in their homes. Lei Jieqiong, now a retired vice chairman in the People's Congress of the People's Republic of China, was a Cantonese and came from a "gentry" family. The Chang family liked her and treated her with great respect. Sam wrote: "She is from Taishan. Her father Lei Ziliu was a *juren* [provincial degree holder]. She is studying sociology and education at the University of Southern California. Your fourth uncle and others are attending her Chinese class at Tan's house. She seems to be a woman of vision."[33] After Lei received her master's degree from the University of Southern California, in 1931, she returned to China and became a professor at Yanjing University.

Arthur went to China in that year, too, on the same steamship with Lei. Yitang had planned to let Arthur stay in China for two to three years. As a family friend and a prospective professor in Beijing, Lei was the right person to offer advice and assistance to Arthur, who was on his first trip to China and would have difficulty in understanding the northern dialect and social customs. Sam informed Constance of their arrival:

> Your fourth uncle will take a Japanese ship from Los Angeles to Shanghai in June. He will go with Ms. Lei Jieqiong, who has an M.A. degree from the University of Southern California and has an offer

from Yanjing University to be a sociology professor. You should meet them when they come to Tianjin.[34]

Yitang and Sam learned through Tennyson and Constance that Nankai would have no problem admitting Arthur, because of its special policy toward overseas students.

In sending their children to China, Yitang and Sam hoped that they could find suitable prospective spouses there, as well. This expectation was based more on class than cultural considerations. As parents, they were not worried about cultural differences between American-born Chinese and those Chinese born and raised in China. After all, Yitang's second wife, Nellie, was an American-born Chinese woman who had no problem to quickly adapt to Yitang's China-oriented lifestyle and herbalist career. Being merchant-class Chinese, however, Sam and Yitang were sensitive to the low social status of Chinese in American society and the low self-esteem among many American-born Chinese. In their own social life, Yitang and Sam preferred to socialize with the educated or wealthy Chinese. They often hosted important visiting officials or intellectuals from China in their home. For example, Fan Yuanlian, a former minister of education, stayed in Sam's house when visiting Los Angeles in 1922. The Changs also received Zhang Fakui, a warlord in Guangdong, in 1934. When Yitang celebrated his seventieth birthday, the family received greetings from such social elites as Hu Shi. At Sam's eightieth birthday, in 1965, many top officials from the Nationalist government sent him their greetings from Taiwan. In the Changs' observation, many American-born Chinese belonged to the low social class, and they did not encourage their children to socialize with them.

When Elbert took the job with Beijing Union Medical College in China, Sam repeatedly advised him to find a girl friend there. In a 1925 letter, Sam asked Tennyson to tell Elbert, "It is a lot better for your third uncle to find a wife in Beijing, Tianjin or Guangzhou. The native-born children of Chinese in America are much less educated than those from good families in China."[35] In a 1926 letter, Sam offered the same advice to Tennyson:

> If you meet a nice-looking girl with a good personality at Nankai, get acquainted with her. After graduation, you can come to America with her and go to college together. Girls in China are better than American-born Chinese girls. I have been in America for ten years and have not found any suitable girl for you.[36]

Their children certainly noticed the sensitivity of their parents toward class status. Arthur recalled, "Father was very sensitive about prestige. When mother's sister married a Chinese janitor who worked for a movie studio, father always laughed at my uncle."[37] Yitang and Sam's contemptuous attitude toward American-born Chinese reflects their class prejudice. But on the other hand, such an attitude also shows their perception of Chinese life in the United States and their pessimism about the cultural environment and social upbringing for those Chinese born and raised there.

Sam and Yitang fully understood that the reason they could send their children to China for education was because they belonged to the merchant class. When Sam sent his daughter Constance back to China, she had a merchant's visa. In a 1928 letter to Tennyson, Sam remarked:

> Yuhua's visa is different from a native-born Chinese person's visa. Her status is child of the merchant class. A native-born Chinese cannot bring his wife and children to America, though he can stay in China as long as he likes during a visit. Merchant Chinese can bring family in, but if they or their families visit China, their visas are only valid for a year. Before coming back to America, they should apply to the local American consulate, two months ahead. But Yuhua does not have to do this, because she is under twenty-one. After she graduates from high school, she will not yet be twenty-one and we can reapply for her visa anytime in America. She can also try to get a Chinese passport from the Chinese Foreign Ministry as an exchange student.[38]

The economic situation in America also played a role in Yitang's decision to send Arthur to China. During the Great Depression, Yitang closed a branch office that his son helped operate because Yitang's herb business was slack. In his interview, Arthur explained:

> The Depression affected the family. Many patients could not afford to see a doctor. Everyone in the family was at school. Father had to support all the children and to support relatives in China. Father's idea was to send me to China for two years to study Chinese and hope that the situation would get better in America so that I could return for a college education. I liked the school and wrote to father for permission to study medicine at Nankai University. Tuition in China was cheaper than in America.[39]

By 1931, Arthur had already completed high school, and helped manage his father's herb business office in Ventura County. But, as we have noted, Yitang decided to close his branch office; soon, Arthur adjusted to school life in China and decided to stay longer.

Family networks played a key role in exploring educational opportunities in China when the three family members attended Nankai. Following a chain migration pattern, Tennyson arrived first and paved the way for Constance and Arthur. Family members provided information and support to one another. In Arthur's recollection, Constance helped him select a Mandarin-speaking roommate, found him a Chinese language tutor, arranged a meeting with the president, and advised him on his curriculum. As in Los Angeles, Arthur could easily communicate with her in a mixture of Cantonese and English for advice on his adaptation to life in Tianjin, China.[40]

Education in China enabled the younger generation of the Chang family to learn about their cultural roots, explore new opportunities, and develop a new identity.

Constance as a Feminist Daughter in China

In 1927, when Sam sent Constance to join Tennyson in Nankai School as an overseas Chinese student, she had to go through the application process for a reentry permit. After four years' stay in America, Constance could communicate with the INS officers in fluent English. Her interview was scheduled on June 2, and that day she answered some long and tough questions. One question asked, "How many teachers did you have at the 16th Street School from the first grade to the sixth grade?" Constance remembered at least six teachers, though she studied at that school only for two years and then went on to attend the Sentous Junior High School. There, taking subjects like cooking, drawing, gymnasium, music, mathematics, and English, she had more than ten teachers. In the following three days, Constance had three teachers showing up at the INS agency to testify as her white witnesses. One presented a certificate signed by the vice principal to prove she was an enrolled student. Another presented Constance's student card that listed all subjects she took. Her application was smoothly endorsed.[41]

Constance took a Japanese ship; the Chang family did not have to worry about Americans' sentiment against the Japanese, as they did when Sam arranged for Constance and her mother to come to the United States, in 1923. In her first letter home, Constance informed Sam that she had a good trip and did not get seasick. The steamship had 190 passengers, provided five meals a day, and showed a movie every other day. In the first and second class cabins, Constance found dozens of "Tangren" passengers—a term for

Chinese immigrants from Guangdong who believed that they were "descendents from the Tang Dynasty." One passenger told Constance that her husband often visited the Chang family in Los Angeles.[42]

Constance was admitted into Nankai without difficulty, though Tennyson accidentally forgot to pick her up in Shanghai, creating delay and confusion in her arrival on campus. The school waived the entrance exams since she was an overseas Chinese student.

Nankai in Tianjin, Lingnan in Guangdong, and a number of other schools had special admission policies toward overseas Chinese students. These schools were always interested in recruiting such students as a way to diversify their student population and to earn some foreign currency from their tuition. Although many overseas Chinese sent their children to these schools, some of the wealthy ones also donated money to such schools and colleges. Education at such institutions became an important channel networking overseas Chinese across the world and linking them to the home country.

This was the first time Constance was away from her parents. North China was different from Guangzhou and California. Tianjin was cold in winter. In a letter, Constance told her mother that it was much colder there than in America in September, and she was scared of winter in Tianjin. The city also looked shabby; Constance found its streets dirty and filthy-smelling. As for school codes, they were far more strict than those in California schools. The students were not allowed to wear fancy clothes. If they wanted to leave school, they needed permission from their teachers or counselors. On 23 August 1927, Constance wrote,

Mother, Your Excellency: I have been missing you every day since I left home. I arrived in Tianjin on August 18. Don't worry about me. I will write home every two weeks or at least every month. The school treats the overseas students very well. The school provides two meals: lunch and dinner. We buy breakfast ourselves, usually for thirty cents. A girl student usually spends five hundred dollars a year. However, my allowance is only four hundred dollars. So I should live a plain life, because I am not from a wealthy family, and grandfather and father work hard in order to provide us with education. Two overseas students named Chen and Li met me and showed me around. Chen is a vice president of the Overseas Student Association, and Brother Tennyson is the president. I share a bedroom with three other Guangdong students. They are all named Li and come from Portland, Oregon. They are also students far away from their parents.[43]

Constance began her school life in Tianjin by making friends with students from a similar background. Though she referred to them as Guangdong students, they were actually children of Chinese immigrants and came from Oregon. Apparently, Constance identified her native place of Guangdong as more important than her American experience, in her socializing with schoolmates. At Nankai, Constance began to use a new Chinese name, Xixian. Sam Chang asked Constance to use this name as her official name at school. This was also the name used on her visa and passport in 1938 when she returned to the United States. Similarly, Sam gave "Xining" to Estelle and "Ximeng" to Joyce for formal Chinese names at school. Constance studied hard and improved her Chinese language ability rapidly. She caught up with the others in a short time, and passed the examinations in every subject in her first semester.

Life at Nankai played a vital role in the identity formation of Constance as she grew from an innocent young teenager to an independent-minded older adolescent. Born in Guangdong, and having attended middle schools in Los Angeles, she was excited to see and live in a cosmopolitan city in northern China. However, the more of China she saw, the more disappointed and angry she became about the semicolonial reality of Chinese society. As Tennyson took her from Shanghai to Tianjin, they stopped in Qingdao, Shandong Province, for a visit. They found the city clean and quiet. But much to their dismay, they saw many Japanese houses, and upscale stores full of Japanese shoppers. They realized that the best part of the city belonged to Japan, and Japanese residents lived a much better life than did ordinary Chinese. In their eyes, Qingdao looked like a Japanese city. Qingdao's colonial history actually began as a German colony, beginning in the late nineteenth century. When Germany became a defeated country in World War One, control of the city was transferred to the Japanese. After Constance arrived in Nankai, she also discovered that there were also parts of Tianjin where foreigners lived and dominated as "foreign settlements." Differing from a Chinatown as an ethnic enclave, a "foreign settlement" protected foreigners from Chinese jurisdiction, and granted them many privileges. She wrote to her mother, on October 14:

> Dear Mother: As you have not been to the North, let me tell you something about it. In Tianjin, there are many "foreign settlements" separated from the Chinese area. Nankai School is in the Chinese area. But we need to buy almost everything in the "foreign settlements" because all the major foreign banks are there. Oh! How mis-

erable our China is and our people are! Foreigners are bullies in China. Many Chinese are afraid of them. Some Chinese make use of foreign power to boss around other Chinese. They don't care about our motherland, which is so weak now, but just want to be running dogs for the foreigners. They are the scum of our nation. I think China will become strong one day, because every Chinese youth is patriotic. Mother, if there is a war between China and a foreign country, I will join the army to save our miserable motherland. Mother, don't say I am naive. I mean it.[44]

Constance's letter indicates how rapidly she had changed herself after she arrived in China. In her first letter, we can still see the influence of her parents and Guangdong culture on her writing and the way she observed and understood the outside world. She had talked about the service on the ship and noticed a dozen "Tangren" among the passengers whom she could identify with. In this latest letter, however, foreign domination in China had become the focus of her attention. "Running dogs of foreigners," "scum of the nation," and "to save our country" were common phrases among patriotic and leftist Chinese youth during this period; she quickly absorbed them and used them in letters home.

Constance and Tennyson studied at Nankai during a period when warlords in the North and South were frequently fighting each other for strategic regions and metropolitan centers; Tianjin was an important city in the North and a primary arena for military actions. Constance's safety was a concern for Sam and his wife. When battles between warlords occurred, students of Nankai often hid in the "foreign settlements" where warlords would not bother them. In a letter of 1928, Tennyson told his parents that Tianjin was in chaos; the school was closed and most students stayed at home. But the school took care of the overseas students, and promptly sent them to the British settlement.[45] In a letter to her mother, Constance wrote:

> The war between the warlord in the South and the warlord in the North is going on fiercely. The school will be closed for another week. Many classmates have gone home. I miss home and am feeling very lonely. But I have nowhere to go. Seeing me so unhappy, my girlfriend Cai asked me to stay in her home, which had been relocated to the foreign settlements.[46]

As the letter indicates, the chaotic situation in China often scared Tennyson and Constance and made them homesick.

Her frustration about such a chaotic situation, and about the social instability and foreign domination in China made Constance even more radical in her views. She wrote, in another letter:

> Respectable Father: I have several purposes in seeking an education.
> You can accomplish nothing if you study without purpose. Do you
> want to know what I want to accomplish? First, I want to promote
> equal status between men and women in our society. It is not a fight
> against men, but to promote the interest of women and enable them
> to shoulder more responsibilities to help men. Second, I want to re-
> form Chinese education. At least, everyone should be able to receive
> a high school education. Third, I want to reform the political sys-
> tem. When people receive adequate education, the political system
> can easily be monitored and then there should be also an election
> system, in future. By that time, those financial monopolies cannot
> oppress and exploit the ordinary people at will. Our country will re-
> main stable. By then, we can get rid of all our national humiliations.
> Fourth, "national humiliation" become the two words printed in my
> mind. They will not go away. The wolf-like British and the dwarf,
> evil Japanese devils killed the innocent students in cold blood dur-
> ing the May 30th and other massacres. Though the students died, we
> will remember their names forever. They are our heroes. We will re-
> venge this hatred. When China becomes strong, we will help other
> small and weak nations like India and Korea, and help them get rid
> of imperialist domination.[47]

The May 30th Massacre referred to in this letter occurred in 1925, before
Constance's arrival in China. She had mentioned it when she wrote to a relative in Guangdong shortly after her arrival in America. In that letter, she simply felt sad about the dead students. But in this letter she seemed to have
embraced many nationalist ideas. The massacre occurred during a mass movement protesting the killing of a Chinese union leader in a strike against a
Japanese factory owner in a foreign settlement in Shanghai. About 250 thousand workers, students, and merchants participated in the protest and demanded abolition of the foreign settlement system and the elimination of
privileges for foreigners. To suppress the movement, the British police arrested hundreds of students, killed dozens of protesters, and wounded many
people. As Constance's letter indicated, the brutality of the Japanese and British imperialists were still fresh in the minds of Chinese students. Although

an overseas student coming from an immigrant family, Constance shared such nationalist sentiments.

Constance's letters also began to contain rebellious ideas and comments on traditional Chinese family culture. In one letter to her mother, she wrote: "My Dearest Mother: I have not seen you for a long time and miss you very much. But, mother, why do you want my brother to marry now? It is already the twentieth century. We don't follow the old idea of filial piety. Brother Tingxun is only a high school student."[48] After she learned about the Chang family conflicts beginning in Yitang's generation, through some of the long letters on family history sent by Sam, Constance expressed her anger at the polygamous tradition in feudal China. While Sam worried about family conflicts caused by this tradition, Constance resented the unequal social status between men and women in Chinese society. She believed that polygamy was a bad system because men could have multiple wives yet women could not have multiple husbands. She was also angry when she observed the many ways boys and girls were treated differently in the Chang family.

In a letter to her parents in 1930, she lamented the gossip among the Chang relatives about her education in China:

> People say that I should feel flattered to be able to return to China
> for an education. The Chang family could have sent Cousin Qu and
> Cousin Wei back to China; however, the family sent me instead. There-
> fore, I should not demand more. Such gossip shows the Chang family's
> biased attitude toward sons and daughters. They believe that sons are
> entitled to education but it is a waste that daughters go to school.[49]

Here she expressed the pressure she felt at being able to study in China, as a girl, while two sons of Sam's second brother were working on the family farms in Southern California. She complained that the Chang family was still influenced by the traditional attitude toward women's education. When away from home, she seemed far more independent and rebellious than Tennyson, with her frank attitude and the challenging tone of her letters.

As a student at Nankai, Constance accepted not only nationalist but also Marxist ideas. A few years after her arrival at Nankai, Sam's letters began to express his anxiety over the influence of radical ideologies, especially communism, on his daughter. Once, he wrote a long letter to Constance about the consequence of being a communist in American society:

> You should avoid unpopular subjects in your discussion with other
> people. In the United States, for example, the most prohibited

political parties now are the communists and anarchists. A few years ago, a Chinese called Jiang Xize spread anarchism in America. He had been arrested three times in one year before he was deported. He was beaten up in San Francisco when he spread his ideas to the Chinese there.

In commenting on Constance's claims that she hated rich people and respected American Indians, Sam continued to reprimand her:

> You said that you did not like rich people nor cared about the prestige. You admire the red people [American Indians] most. But the European and American countries are big powers now, and in these countries, every one admires money and wealth. Without our money to support you, you would be still living in the rural village as an illiterate woman. Look at your second uncle's daughter Yupei. She is fourteen but has no financial support to leave the countryside and pursue a modern education in the city. In a few years, she will marry an uneducated rural man and remain a housewife forever. You are now studying in Nankai. Very few girls from Enping and Kaiping area are lucky enough to have this opportunity. You are at school because your grandpa and I have some money to pay your education. You are so stupid not to realize this. To hate the rich is a bad influence from the Russians. That is wrong. You will regret holding such crazy ideas.

As in advising Tennyson, Sam pointed out the importance of education, and he asked Constance to accomplish her education before reaching radical conclusions.

> One should not go against the social trends. How could you talk about reform just after reading a few textbooks at high school? All great social reformists and revolutionaries and innovators have gained rich experiences before they succeeded in their careers. Sun Zhongshan (Sun Yatsen), the founding father of the Republic, advocated revolution after he had visited Japan, America, and Britain. He developed his ideology and ideas and wrote his political writings after he was forty. Whatever ideology you want to believe in, you should sit down and study it first.

Reminding Constance that he was not an old-fashioned father, Sam also emphasized the importance of traditional culture:

Don't take for granted that we, the older generation, are old-fashioned
people influenced by the Tang and Song Dynasty's culture and you
are the new youth of the twentieth century. You should know that a
good legal system is the key for any civilized nation. The better a
nation's legal system is; the fewer crimes there will occur. As for freedom and equality, they are concepts within the law. That is true in
America or France. Freedom does not mean you can disobey the law.
I read from the newspaper that young girls parade in the nude in
Hankou City. People both at home and abroad will look down upon
these modern girls. But Tang Dynasty's poetry, Li Ba and Tu Pu's
poems, will pass on not only to the twentieth but also to the twenty-
first century. You should not let new ideas affect your study and life,
and bring shame to the family. You should not go off campus your-
self and make boy friends. We are very worried about you. Whenever we receive our children's letters from Tianjin or Guangzhou or
other places, your mother can hardly eat for several days. We are so
worried about you children's lives away from home.[50]

Letters between Sam and his daughter indicate how receptive Constance
was to new ideas and social trends in Chinese society. She discussed foreign
aggression, gender equality, and even concepts of class struggle in her letters home and challenged many traditional Chinese ideas. Sam's writing reveals his surprise and frustration over these changes in his daughter, just as
he was upset about Tennyson's radical thoughts a couple of years earlier. He
did not realize that the school environment in China for his son and daughter was totally different from that in America. While China experienced war
and social disorder, the school environmen allowed them to pursue new ideas
and approaches, with the other students, to solve China's problems; though
from overseas, they were not treated as outsiders by their schoolmates.

Existing studies on Chinese Americans often assume that the Chinese
became more liberal and progressive after they immigrated to America because they were exposed to Western culture. In the reverse migration experience of Constance, however, we see a reverse picture. Her world outlook at
Nankai was probably far more liberal and progressive than that of contemporary Chinese youth in America, as she was not living under the shadow of
racism. Unlike those contemporaries' experience in an American school,
Constance and other overseas Chinese students found that their voice on social issues was respected. Their interest and participation in campus activities and cultural events would not be marginalized. They were equal partners
in student life.

Correspondence between Constance and Sam is highly informative in assisting us to understand Chinese transnational family life. The letters demonstrate how frankly and emotionally Chinese parents and children could communicate about their differing thoughts and viewpoints regarding social issues. Constance's discussion of imperialism, class struggle, and racial disparity gives us firsthand information about the identity crisis that a Chinese American young person could go through in her/his transnational experience. Sam's response is equally informative regarding the mentality, inner thoughts, and attitudes of the older generation toward key social issues. Sam was neither ignorant nor insensitive toward these issues. He was ready to discuss serious social issues with a daughter just as with a son. However, Sam had a more realistic family agenda to fulfill—he wanted to see all his children's education through, and did not want the children's progress disrupted by too much concern over social problems.

Soon Sam and Cen began to worry about their daughter's social life, as well. When Constance first arrived at Nankai, she was not used to her new school. In one letter, she complained about the cold weather in September; in another, she described the tough academic subjects she had to deal with. She wrote:

> Since I returned to our home country, I have been very busy with my studies. I am very skinny as I am too exhausted. The examination has been very tough for me because I have language difficulties. I have had to catch up with the rest of the class in just a few days. Fortunately, I passed every course. I was lucky to pass the math exam, because the math course in Nankai is more difficult than that in American schools.[51]

But Constance quickly adapted to the new environment in China and became involved in many school activities at Nankai. She took piano lessons, participated in student political debates, performed several times in student dramas, and played basketball. She participated several times in regional or national sports meets for Nankai and for the Tianjin city team. Musical and very athletic, she became a campus idol in a couple of years. Sam and his wife were not too worried about this part of her social life, and they probably understood that Constance would not have had an opportunity for such rich extracurricular activities in America. In a letter, Sam wrote:

> In the Qing period, a good woman was one without education. In modern times, women feel ashamed of themselves if they are not

educated. . . . At school, Yuhua has involved in many social activities. Last March she was the coach of the women's basketball team of Tianjin at the National Sport Meet in Hangzhou. Her name and photo has appeared in *National News Newspaper*, *Tianjin Dagoung Daily*, and *Liangyou Pictorial*. She has socialized with famous people like Mr. and Mrs. Jiang [Jiang Jieshi], Hu Hanmin, Dai Jitao, and Zhang Jingjiang. . . . Through this Sport Meet, Yuhua's name became known in many schools. That is the pleasure of school life.[52]

Constance was also active in political discussions and liked to travel with friends and schoolmates to see other parts of China. Beautiful, sociable, and English speaking, she attracted many male students at Nankai. Sam was gravely concerned that Constance attracted the attention of too many male students. Although she did not write about this part of her social life, Sam and his wife had their own channels out of information. There were many Cantonese or overseas Chinese students on campus who could pass on anecdotes to their parents; as mentioned before, educational institutions in China were part of the Chinese immigrant community network. In a letter of October 1929, Sam told Constance, "I have not heard from you for three months. But your grandpa has learned from his friends that many of your friends are men. You are at the most dangerous age. Your mother and I are very worried about you."[53] Sam believed that if any man wanted to pursue a serious relationship with Constance, he had to contact and get consent from Sam and his wife first. Acceptance of a woman's parents was an important step for men in asking for a girl's hand. In a 1931 letter, Sam told his brother Elbert that he had received letters from dozens of men asking to marry Constance. Four of them actively approached Tennyson for support.[54] Sam and his wife were very upset about Constance's popularity with male students. Whenever he heard gossip that she had visited a male student's family, or accepted gifts from male students, or joined a group trip with them, he would write to reprimand her for not being serious about her social life. He even threatened to come to Tianjin to drag her back to America.

The disagreement between Constance and her parents was not about whether or not she should have a boyfriend, but about how to make or choose one. Constance wanted to date whomever she liked, and a date, in her opinion, was not necessarily a boyfriend. But Sam and his wife did not want her to go out with any male unless he was her boyfriend, and they regarded every date as a boyfriend. They required Constance to inform them first about any man she intended to date. They would send Tennyson to make inquiries about the man.[55] In fact, they wanted to select a boyfriend for Constance themselves. As mentioned earlier, Yitang and Elbert met the Tan family in Shanghai so as to match Constance with the Tans' son. While criticizing his daughter for having too many boyfriends, Sam, in his letters to Tennyson and Elbert, often asked if they could recommend a nice young man who could be introduced to Constance. What he preferred was a young man of upper-class family from the Four Districts in Guangdong, who would be able to go to the United States for an advanced degree after a college education in China. In a letter of 1932, Sam wrote:

> Your mother is very concerned about your marriage. Hope you will find a suitable "lover" when you are at the university and then come to study in the United States together. And then, after marriage, you two could go back to China. It is better to find some one from "siyi." I hear Tingxun had a friend named Yu Reiyao who is smart and capable. All his three brothers are college graduates. He is now at Yanjing. Find out about this man. You may go to Lei Jieqiong for assistance. I am a little different from your mother about the marriage issue. I thought that the most important thing is that the two should get along. However, the man should have a good education, and should let us know about his family. When we find out all the information, you two can marry. Others should not impose their will on this matter. I don't want to control your marriage. You can make your own decision. But you should not do anything that may affect our family's reputation.[56]

Sam cared a great deal about the class background of the young man's family. When Sam learned that one of the male students Constance had socialized with was from a Kejia (Hakka) background, he objected to the relationship because there had been long bitter feuds between the Kejia and the native Guangdong people in the Four Districts.[57] Having learned of the family origin of another boyfriend, Sam told Constance that marrying that man would bring shame to the whole family, because an uncle of the boy was a village teacher in the Four Districts and had a low social status.[58]

It seems that Sam was not happy with any man Constance selected herself. In another letter, he wrote:

> I wonder you have received the candy I mailed to you. When you date, you should let us know in advance. That means you care about your parents' opinion. Since we received Tang's letter in early Janu-

ary, Grandpa is very upset. Your mother and I are also very worried. Originally I planned to let you stay in Beijing for two years of college and then have you back to America. Now your mother wanted you to return immediately; [then I told her] my opinion is that you should complete your high school, at least. Your mother said that, after you finish your high school at Nankai, I should go to Tianjin to fetch you back. I will follow your mother's advice and return to China and get you back to America for your college education. It is impossible for you to attend college in Beijing. First, you are so naïve and could be easily fooled by other people. You insisted that you should have some friends who are men because society was made of both women and men. And if you wanted to serve society well in future, you could not do it as a single, because you needed help from friends. Therefore you needed to make some friends with men, and this was not a big deal. What you have said shows how easily you could be fooled by other people. In my opinion, you are now a talkative and foolish girl and are not experienced enough to participate in social life. I hear that four men have fallen in love with you and every one of them wrote long letters. Now even the local newspaper has carried the news that Chang Xixian has many boyfriends. Did you know this? Your mother and I have tried our best to give you good advice. Since Tennyson came to America, you are our only worry in China.

Although Sam was well informed about the situation in China and very flexible in arranging his children's education, his attitude toward dating, friendship between men and women, and marriage remained traditional. Sam's letter not only tells us about the generation gap between parents and children in the Chang family, but also illustrates rapid social changes in China. While Constance quickly adapted herself to Chinese society in the North, Sam still belonged to the generation born and raised before the May Fourth Movement.

That gossip about Constance in the local newspapers that was passed to Sam also shows how closely the overseas Chinese community was linked to China. He continued to write:

In your letter to your brother, you said that you had something to say yet could not say it in your present situation. That shows that you are a stupid girl. After reading that letter, your mother said you had changed so rapidly and even regard your parents as strangers and are on guard against them from time to time. . . . I agree that a letter is a private thing and children's letters should not be opened. But Tennyson let me open every letter of his and there is nothing that we cannot talk about between father and son. So he let me open his letter. After reading your two letters to him, I will never open your letters to him any more. I will put your letter to Tennyson in a separate place. I will never talk about your school life. You do whatever you like. And you can tell your brother whatever you like and I will never open your letter. By the way, in your previous two letters, you have ten misspellings.[59]

The above letter indicates that Sam heard complaints from Constance about opening her letter to Tennyson. With some reluctance, Sam agreed to respect Constance's privacy in future; however, Sam's comment on this issue tells us how he, as a parent, viewed family correspondence mainly as a communication channel for the family as a collective, while Constance as a contemporary teenager regarded it as a space for private emotion. Just as Sam believed that there should be no secrecy between children and parents, his daughter felt her individuality should be respected.

Constance was now living in a very different world from Sam. Her schoolmates in Nankai came from all parts of the country, and had diverse family backgrounds. Among the four male students who actively sought Constance's friendship, one was from Hebei Province, another from Sichuan (and preparing to go to Belgium for further education).[60] No doubt, most students at Nankai came from middle-class or wealthy families, but some did come from working-class families and received scholarships because of their academic merits.

In spite of her parents' reservations, Constance made her own decision in choosing Tang Mingzhao as her boyfriend. Tang was born in 1910 in Enping County and arrived in San Francisco in 1920 when his immigrant father returned to China for a visit and brought him over to the United States. In 1927, his father got to know Zhang Boling, president of Nankai School, during Zhang's visit to America, and asked Zhang to take Tang with him and enroll him at Nankai. After graduation from Nankai, Tang was admitted into Qinghua, as he performed exceptionally well in his studies. He joined the Communist Party in 1931 and became an underground Party leader in Beijing. After studying in Qinghua for two years, Tang was admitted into the University of California, Berkeley, and later received his master's degree in history. He later went to New York and became the founding chief editor of the famous *Meizhou huaqiao ribao* (*China Daily News*).[61] However, Sam believed that the Tang family were low-class Chinese. Tang's father, according to Sam, had been a live-in cook for a Caucasian family, and then became a laundry owner—definitely a different class background from the Chang family's. Although Sam opposed Constance's choice, he was a fairly liberal-minded parent and sensitive to his daughter's feelings. In another letter to Elbert, he agreed that, as parents, he and his wife should not impose their will on Constance, and indicated that, in a modern society, a girl should at least have "half say" over her marriage.[62]

Beginning in the early 1930s, Japanese troops deepened their aggression from the northeast into the North. The conquest of Tianjin was a major military goal. In February 1933, Sam urged his children to evacuate either to the British settlement or to Shanghai, where Elbert could help them evacuate to Hong Kong in case of emergency. In August, Constance went to Shanghai. She went there not only to escape the war but also to see her sister Estelle and her aunt Lillian, who arrived in China together that year. Arthur came, too. This was the first, rare opportunity for the Chang family members to have a reunion since Constance's departure from Los Angeles in 1927.

Despite the unstable situation in China, Constance did well in her studies. In August 1933, she graduated from Nankai and was admitted into Yanjing University in Beijing. In the summer of 1936, she graduated and intended to return to America for a master's degree. Even though they had been separated for nine years, Sam asked her to stay a little longer:

> Your mother is eager to see you coming back home after graduation. But our financial situation is not very good. Since you lack teaching experience, it is difficult to find you a job in Los Angeles. The Chinese Language School in Chinatown will not hire a teacher this year. Even if they do, it is not an ideal job.[63]

At first, Sam urged Constance to get a teaching position in the North. Since the situation there was unstable, she went to Guangzhou; a relative of the Chang family promised to help her find a faculty position at Guangdong National University. Meanwhile this also enabled Constance to take care of Estelle, who arrived in Guangzhou in 1933 for her elementary school education. As Sam had property there, the two girls would have a place to live without worrying about rent. But Constance did not find a stable job in Guangzhou. She was working as a part-time lecturer, teaching Chinese, English, and sports classes for five schools that year.

In January 1937, Sam began preparing the immigration paperwork for Constance's return to the United States to obtain her master's degree.

I have consulted with attorney Ma. He told me it was better for you to enter on a student visa and passport. Students will not be detained by immigration officials upon arrival. And you will not need sponsorship money, as your parents are in the country. The application forms will be processed by the university. I have asked Tennyson to get you the forms from the University of Southern California. You should go to the Education Ministry for a passport and the American Consulate for a visa.[64]

Sam reminded her of some basic facts about the family, such as the birthdays and origins of her parents, advised her to purchase at least a second-class ticket, and enclosed coaching papers. After consulting an attorney, Sam also requested assistance from a friend who worked as a consul in the Los Angeles Chinese consulate. This friend promised to contact the immigration office in regard to Constance's entrance. After careful preparation, Constance arrived in Los Angeles on August 15 without experiencing any problems. It had been a ten years since she left home in 1927. She no longer looked like the innocent teenage girl of ten years before. As a college graduate, she was also culturally different from what Sam and his wife had expected. In a letter to Tennyson, who was now studying on the East Coast, Sam wrote that Constance's behavior and manner looked as if she was going to make a family revolution.[65]

In September, Constance left for New York to attend Columbia University. The following year, she married Tang Mingzhao, who was now teaching English to Chinese immigrant children in Brooklyn, New York, after graduating from the University of California, Berkeley. "In 1937, he joined the Chinese Hand Laundry Alliance and became an influential figure in the New York Chinese community, where he appeared as the representative of the CHLA at many community meetings."[66] In 1940, Tang and several other activists founded *Meizhou huaqiao ribao,* which became a powerful voice representing the interest of Chinese laundrymen and leftist elements in the Chinese community for a long time.

While Constance was studying at Columbia University, Sam did not have money to support her tuition. The salary from Tang's job as an editor for the newspaper was also modest. The couple rented a small apartment and lived a fairly frugal life, but Constance managed to complete her degree. After graduation, she needed to change her student visa, as it was no longer valid. Although Tang's status was an American-born Chinese, she was unable to stay in America, under the existing immigration laws. In a 1939 letter, Sam informed her: "I have consulted with Attorney Hong about your visa. According to the 1924 immigration rules, you cannot stay after graduation even if you are married to a native-born Chinese. Native-born Chinese cannot bring a Chinese citizen wife to America and let her stay."[67] Interestingly, this Attorney Hong was the very INS interpreter who had interviewed Sam in 1923. In his letter, Sam cited a similar case to his daughter's. A Chinese named Chen found a faculty position at Pomona College and married a native-born Chinese woman, but he could not change his visitor's status. Even with the help of the Chinese ambassador, Chen was only able to extend his stay for another year.

To continue her legal stay in the United States, Constance needed to claim herself as a merchant or as the child of a Chinese merchant, rather than as a Chinese exchange student. But changing immigration status was not an easy procedure. After Sam registered Constance as a shareholder and a bookkeeper in the Chang family's herbal business in 1941, the INS office only allowed her to stay on a temporary basis. From 1941 to 1945, the Immigration Service interviewed her and the Chang family several times about her role in the business. She had to travel to Los Angeles from New York for the interviews when requested by the INS.

After graduation, Constance also found it difficult to find a permanent job; she sometimes taught the Chinese language in New York's Chinatown and sometimes helped Tang with his editing work. In 1943, she gave birth to a daughter, who was named Nancy. Sam recommended "Wensheng" among several choices for his granddaughter's name. He wrote, "Both 'Meisun' and 'Wensheng' are fine but 'Wensheng' is better. As for 'Shenghua' and 'Meihua,' they both have a character similar to your name, which is against Chinese tradition."[68]

Although Constance eventually solved the problem of her legal status, she was forced to leave the United States again because of the political environment in the nation. In the Cold War period, many political activists in the Chinese American community, including Tang Mingzhao, became targets of persecution. Tang was a target even though he had served in the United States government in the Office of Strategic Services and in the Office of War Information during World War Two. On 11 October 1949, following the founding of the People's Republic of China on 1 October, J. Edgar Hoover, director of the Federal Bureau of Investigation (FBI), informed the Central Intelligence Agency (CIA) and the army and navy intelligence bureaus that the Chinese Hand Laundry Alliance was a "Communist infiltrated" organization.[69] Meanwhile, the Nationalist government in Taiwan also stepped up its anti-communist campaigns and tightened its control in the Chinese American communities. After serving as English secretary for the Laundry Alliance and as general manager for *Meizhou huaqiao ribao* for more than a decade, Tang returned to China in 1950. Constance and the couple's daughter, Nancy, left New York and stayed with Sam in Los Angeles. FBI agents made a couple of unexpected visits to Sam while Constance and Nancy stayed there. However, Sam did not let the FBI search his house. In 1953, Constance and Nancy returned to China through Europe.

Twenty-two years later, Tang Mingzhao and Constance returned to New York. This time they were neither immigrants nor exchange scholars. Tang arrived as an eminent official from China, and was later joined by his wife, Constance. After the United Nations abandoned Taiwan's representative, and transferred membership in the organization to the People's Republic, China sent a diplomatic mission to the U.N., and, as a member of the mission, Tang worked as an undersecretary-general for political affairs and decolonization in the U.N. from 1972 to 1979. The couple's Brooklyn-born daughter, Nancy Tang, also became a celebrated figure in China. She attended Beijing Foreign Language Institute in the 1960s; while majoring in English, she also worked hard on her Chinese, and, after graduation, she went to work for the Chinese foreign ministry. When Richard Nixon visited China in 1972, she was the interpreter for Mao Zedong (Tse-tung) and Zhou Enlai, and received a great deal of attention in the international press. When American media televised Nixon's meeting with Mao Zedong, the Chang family was excited to find Nancy Tang interpreting for the two world leaders. In fact, Nancy began to attract attention from the Chinese American community, when Mao received American journalist Edgar Snow in 1971. Sam Chang was extremely proud of Nancy and Tang Mingzhao. In 1972, he wrote:

> *Life* magazine on April 30, 1971, the Chinese *Pacific Weekly* in San Francisco on April 29, and *Meizhou huaqiao ribao* in New York on April 26 and 29 carried the news and photos of Mao's conversation with Snow, and they all noted that Wensheng was the interpreter for Chairman Mao. When President Nixon visited Beijing and met with Chairman Mao and Premier Zhou, my granddaughter Wensheng was their interpreter and participated in the meeting. The U.S. president was impressed by her American accent. My son-in-law also became undersecretary-in-general at the United Nations.[70]

Ironically, Sam, like many other overseas Chinese, had been supportive of the Nationalist government. As the People's Republic of China began to enjoy increasing respect in the international community, he began to change his attitudes. Meanwhile, his son-in-law and granddaughter's prestigious public service positions could hardly be matched by any Chinese Americans in the United States at that time. The migration journey of Constance thus did not begin or end in the United States; for Constance, Tang Mingzhao, and Nancy, China is the real home.

The Return of Lillian and Estelle

Two years after Arthur's departure, Sam's half-sister Lillian and her husband David Huang (Wong) left California to work as a schoolteacher and as an engineer, respectively, in Guangzhou, after graduating from the University of California. They brought with them Sam's third daughter, Estelle (Yuchu), so that she could attend an elementary school in China for her Chinese education. Thus, in a reverse chain-migration pattern, most of the American-born or American-raised members of the Chang family had returned to China by the mid-1930s.

Lillian's application was approved, though her testimony has a number of discrepancies with the testimonies of other Chang family members. In the interview, the officer routinely asked questions on dates, ages, and other detailed aspects of Chang family life. The questions included "Could you give me the names, ages, and whereabouts of your brother and sisters in the order of their birth?" Like her mother, Lillian provided both the English and Chinese names of her siblings for the officer to match with the Chang family files they possessed. The officer also asked her questions on the death of her baby sister and on what home addresses the family had had. Lillian provided four home addresses in the same sequence that Nellie had. However, Lillian's statements had discrepancies with the Chang family files at the INS. In her testimony, she indicated that only one of the sons born to Yitang and his first wife was in America, while the immigration files on Yitang clearly recorded that all three had come. When asked about Yitang's names, she provided three but could not determine which was the marriage name. When asked about her address in China, she replied she did not know, and provided Elbert's address in Shanghai; however, Sam's testimony for Estelle indicated that Lillian was going to stay in Lingnan University in Guangzhou. In the interview, Lillian told the officer that she was not married, though the INS files on her included a copy of her wedding photo with David Wong. Surprisingly, the applications were approved in spite of these discrepancies in Lillian's testimony. The INS inspector, Mr. Nardini, who had questioned Chang family members during the past ten years, did not find fault with Lillian's testimony.[71]

Sending Estelle back to China meant Sam and his wife had to go through the torture of an INS interview again, for the reentry certificate for their daughter. As was routine, the inspector checked the dates, names, and relevant locations of the Chang family. He asked, "When, where, whom were you married?" Sam replied: "In KS 30–10–20 (26 November 1904) to Sum (Qin) Shee in the Sun Sar Village, Hoy Ping District, China." "KS" here stands for the period of the Guangxu Emperor in the Qing Dynasty. In the 1930s and 1940s, immigrants like Sam still used the traditional Chinese calendar to refer to the significant dates in their life, during the INS testimony process. The officer also questioned why Sam lived in the San Fernando area while having an herbal office in Los Angeles. Sam replied that his "partner" Yick Hong Chung's (Yitang's) daughter owned a house there. Obviously, the Chang family had purchased a house in San Fernando in the name of Yitang's American-born daughter since the Alien Land Act in California did not allow Chinese to own property. Sam claimed to be an herb merchant rather than a farmer, to convince the INS that he was a merchant, though the monetary value of the farming property was higher than that of the herbal business. Sam and Yitang never mentioned that they were in farming, as it might indicate involvement in manual labor.

However, the most agonizing questions to Sam were those on the death of family members, a subject Chinese did not discuss outside the family circle. In one question, Nardini asked Sam: "When did your son, Chang Hing Way, die?" Sam responded: "About two years ago." Nardini pressed on, asking "Where?" Sam replied in detail: "In the Menlo Hospital, Los Angeles, California, from tuberculosis. 1931." Nardini was still not satisfied and demanded further, "Can you not be more specific as to the exact time of this death?" Sam provided the exact date this time, saying "December 7th." Chang Hing Way (Chang Ting Wei) was actually a son of Sam's second brother, and came to America with Sam's wife in 1923. His death was a painful event in the Chang family, as the boy died while his mother in China could not come to see him, since he had come in the name of Sam's son. Sam felt deeply sorry and guilty. Not able to find any loophole, the inspector switched to the death of another family member, as the following conversation indicates:

Question: Have you had any children born in this country who died?
Answer: Yes, one son. I do not remember his name.
Question: When did he die?

Answer: He was the second born; I did not know his name when he
   died; he died shortly after birth.
Question: How long did he live?
Answer: He died immediately after birth.
Question: Where was he buried?
Answer: In the Chinese Cemetery, Los Angeles, California.
Question: Did you get his birth certificate?
Answer: No.
Question: Never did get one for him?
Answer: No, I did not.
Question: How soon after the first born was he born?
Answer: About three years.

With these seven probing questions, the INS inspector obtained minute details on the death of an infant in the Chang family. Such details assured the
INS officers that Sam did not and could not use the birth certificate of this
family member for someone else. The officers had no concern for the feelings of a parent over the loss of a child, when they drilled Sam with such
heartless questions, or for the psychological impact on Sam's eight-year-old
daughter Estelle, who was present at the interview. Sam's reply about the cemetery where the dead son was buried also informs us that the Chinese were
buried in segregated graveyards according to another racist policy in
America.[72]
   Returning to China for school was an overwhelming experience for a
child like Estelle, only eight years old at the time. She had to go through the
interview and answer questions from the INS officer just as would an adult.
She experienced the same grueling process that the eight-year-old Tingwei
went through in 1923. When asked about her schoolteacher, Estelle offered
the names of five teachers to convince the officer that she was a genuine student, rather than an illegal immigrant working in America. She provided the
accurate street addresses of both school and home. She also had to remember that she could not call Lillian "aunt," because, on paper, her father Sam
and her grandfather Yitang were only business partners. Fortunately, the interview was short and she passed it.
   When he sent Estelle back, Sam believed that racial prejudice and the
low social position of the Chinese had inbred a sense of inferiority into
American-born Chinese children. They felt that they were different from white
American children and would have no opportunity to pursue good careers
and climb the social ladder. Attending school in China was not only for

learning the Chinese language and culture but also for building self-esteem and self-confidence. Separation, however, was painful for both father and daughter. The following letter reveals the deep pain of such family separation:

> My dearest daughter: I miss you and hope you study hard and be-
> come a person with great accomplishment. Make sure to get rid of
> the sense of inferiority of an American-born Chinese kid. I have re-
> ceived your letters from Shanghai and Guangdong. I am pleased to
> hear that now you are at Peizheng School and have played with the
> daughter of Principal Huang. I hope you will study hard and do not
> waste this opportunity. If you can write to me in Chinese, write in
> Chinese. Otherwise write in English. But you should write to me at
> least every month, so that we will not worry about you. You should
> listen to your uncle-in-law and aunt. You should take care of your-
> self in clothes and food, and be careful when you go out on the street.
> Your sister Yuhua wrote us a letter after she met you in Shanghai.
> That is what she said of you in the letter: "She is very independent,
> smart, and active. But she is not in good health and often had a bleed-
> ing nose. She has had to travel to a strange place when she is so
> young. I feel very sad. I cried as I sat on her bed during that night,
> before her departure the next day. She did not know why I was so
> sad." When your mother read this paragraph, she cried, too, and could
> not eat and sleep. Whenever I recalled how you said good-bye to your
> mother, I cannot help my tears. My dearest eight-year-old daughter,
> I hope you will cheer up, and that you will become somone who can
> make a contribution to the country, society, and the human world.
> You should get rid of the humbleness of the native-born Chinese in
> North America, who have no inspiration to advance. Our sad sepa-
> ration today is a sacrifice we have to make for a better future. Al-
> though you lost a suitcase of clothes, a bad thing can be turned into
> a good thing. You will be more careful in future having learned this
> lesson. As you don't know Chinese and I cannot write in English.
> In future, you should ask your aunt and uncle-in-law help read this
> long letter. After you are gone, your mother and I are very sad. When-
> ever we talk about you, your mother has cried.[73]

The letter reveals the emotional price that a transnational Chinese family had to pay when parents sent children away. Yet, although family separation was painful, Sam understood that going back to China was not only an educational investment but also an opportunity for the Chang family's American-born children to develop self-esteem and a sense of ethnic pride. Living in America did not give them a sense of belonging, but China could function as a cultural home for the second-generation Chinese Americans.

In Sam's opinion, then, racism produced tremendous negative impacts on the psychological development of Chinese American youth. He wrote, in 1931:

> Very few native-born Chinese youth in America have high aspirations, due to the racial environment here. From childhood to adulthood, they have been exposed to all kinds of prejudice against the Chinese. The bias of the Westerners against the Chinese is deep-rooted in America. College education is useless for the Chinese here. There are so many college-educated Chinese who cannot find suitable jobs. Chinese youth have to return to China, get to know the motherland, learn the ethical values, and pick up the language at college there. Then they can go to Europe and America for some intern opportunities, for a few years. They will get good positions when they return to China after that.[74]

No other letters of Sam so explicitly explain why he was so determined to send his children to China for their education. According to his observation, what the second-generation Chinese Americans faced was a hostile cultural environment, in addition to the limited career market. In a 1975 interview, Sam still remembered that a fellow Chinese farmer's son was the first Chinese person to graduate with a civil engineering major from the University of Southern California but could only work on his father's farm.[75] When Sam arranged for Tennyson and Constance to come to America, he made it clear that their future was still in China and that they were just in the United States to obtain a more advanced education as a stepping-stone for a better career in the home country.

The application procedure for a reentry permit was probably the most awakening moment for Lillian and Estelle as American-born Chinese. It was a painful experience to come to understand how difficult and complicated it was to get a permit simply for returning to their American home after a visit to the country of their parents. The procedure did not make sense at all, as China was their parents' home and the United States was theirs. The suspicious eyes of the INS officers and the inquisitive questions clearly reminded them of their race as Chinese; the hostile interview culturally denied their American identity. Both eventually came back to the United States, however.

Estelle returned sometime around 1938 and served in the U.S. military forces during World War Two. Lillian came back in 1975, after working and living in Hong Kong for several decades.

Arthur as a Student Rebel in China

Yitang often reminded his children of the prejudice against the Chinese in American society. Arthur recalled, "Father suggested that I become an engineer or doctor. He said that, for Chinese in America, it was very difficult to find a job unless one could work independently, like in some professional field."[76] By the turn of the twentieth century, violent anti-Chinese sentiment in California had gradually quieted down. But racist sentiment was still prevalent, though Japanese immigrants replaced the Chinese as the main target. Carey McWilliams called the 1910s "the Years of Yellow Peril" and pointed out that the campaign for the segregation of Japanese children in education was a major anti-Asian theme in California.[77] Under such circumstances, education was not always pleasant for Chinese children. At school, Arthur often felt ignored and was made fun of as a minority student. He recalled: "The classmates sometimes made fun of the Chinese students. They always looked down upon the Chinese. I was left out of many social activities. But the Chinese students were good students and the teachers liked them very much."[78] Arthur resented this prejudice against the Chinese. When he took a speech class and participated in oratorical contests, he talked about the xenophobia phenomenon in America. Yitang also encouraged him to discuss the subject of prejudice. During one contest, Arthur used Western domination in China as a topic, and won third place. In another contest, he used the topic of the relationship between stereotypes and truth to discuss how ordinary Americans often judged the Chinese by impressions rather than truth. Although he had never been to the land of his ancestors, his extracurricular activities were oriented toward China. His high school environment did not encourage him to develop a full American identity.

Arthur left for China in June 1931. Like Lillian and Estelle, he had to apply for a reentry permit through an INS interview. Nardini did not question him very long, as Arthur could answers all questions smoothly in English and had been interviewed two years before, as he had originally planned to leave America earlier. As was routine, Yitang and Nellie testified for him as parent witnesses.[79] The interview was short and travel arrangement easily made, and little did Arthur realize that this trip would keep him in China for more than ten years.

Arthur traveled with Lei Jieqiong, a returning sociology scholar and a Chang family friend, and was met and accommodated by his uncle Elbert when he arrived in Shanghai. Before his arrival, Arthur had already heard much about Nankai University and its middle and high school from Tennyson. When Arthur arrived in Tianjin, Constance, who had been studying at Nankai since 1927, picked him up and assisted him in settling in. Like Tennyson and Constance, Arthur met many Cantonese-speaking and overseas Chinese students as schoolmates. In his later life, he could still remember some of his Chinese American schoolmates, like Liu Yingchun, daughter of Gim Liu, a friend of Nellie's father in Los Angeles.[80] Assistance from the family network and the friendly school environment in Nankai made Arthur feel at home.

For an American-born Chinese youth like Arthur, school life in China was different but interesting. He adapted to the crowded dormitory room, began to eat more steamed buns than rice at school meals, as the buns were the main staple in North China, and he also learned to speak Mandarin. He was treated kindly. The day after his arrival, the university's president, Zhang Boling (Chang Po Ling), received him, spoke to him in English, and assigned the head of the Chinese literature department at Nankai High School to be his Chinese language tutor. Arthur could also select some science courses taught in English, though he soon found out that the mathematics and physics knowledge he had gained at Los Angeles High School was far from adequate.

Although Arthur liked Nankai very much, two years later he decided to transfer to Yanjing (Yenching) University in Beijing, which offered a better premedical program and could automatically lead to entry at Beijing Union Medical College. He wanted to be a doctor. The president of Yanjing was Leighton Stuart, a noted sinologist, and most faculty members were either Americans or Chinese trained in the West. On his registration day, Arthur ran into a Chinese American from Hawaii who spoke no Chinese and regarded Yanjing as an American university in China. Their similar background made the two youths roommates. As in Nankai, Arthur could easily find a group of overseas Chinese students who came from Hawaii, Indonesia, Malaya, or Burma. Educational opportunities in China drew students from overseas Chinese communities across the world.

Social life for Arthur was rich and diverse in China. He became a left fielder of a baseball team made up of overseas students. In the evening, a few Chinese American students from Hawaii played their instruments and sang as Arthur and other overseas students hung around listening. Arthur made bicycle trips with other Chinese students to the nearby Western Hills for hiking. He played the principal role in several student theater performances, including George Bernard Shaw's *The Devil's Disciple.* This play was so successful at the university that it was staged twice in a theater in downtown Beijing.[81] As an Asian, Arthur would probably never have had an opportunity to play a role in an English drama in America.

Arthur was very enthusiastic about life at Yanjing, and felt involved in student life even though his native language was English. He continuously worked hard on his Chinese language ability, and he took sociology and nineteenth-century Chinese history courses since he was concerned about current social issues in China. At a social gathering, he met a girl who shared his interest in social issues. She was Sylvia (Liang Siyi), daughter of the famous scholar Liang Qichao. Frequent discussions on political issues and participation in student movements bound them together and eventually made them husband and wife. Although a Christian college, Yanjing was one of the main universities to promote nationalist fervor, during the 1930s. Its affiliation with the West prevented the then-current Nationalist government from exercising tight control over its students. In fact, Leighton Stuart sometimes openly encouraged students to demonstrate their patriotism against the Japanese. Yanjing was instrumental in initiating the December Ninth movement, a national student movement protesting Japanese aggression and the compromising policy of the Chinese government. The movement ignited sixty-five demonstrations in thirty-two cities in 1935.[82] Arthur actively participated in the movement. He went to the planning meetings, joined the street protest marches, and distributed anti-Japanese pamphlets to the soldiers of the Nationalist army. He was so active that one night he was secretly recruited to be an underground Communist Party member, though he later lost contact with the organization.

Sylvia was also a student activist. While they were involved in student activities, she often asked Arthur if he genuinely hoped to transform himself from an overseas Chinese to a "real" Chinese. She pressured him to replace his Hawaiian Chinese American roommate with a local Chinese roommate to refine his Mandarin Chinese ability, and encouraged him to identity himself with China. Her attitude reflects the typical cultural expectations of ordinary Chinese toward overseas Chinese in China. The local Chinese expected the overseas Chinese to improve their Chinese ability, respect and mingle with the local people, and culturally identify as Chinese. In contrast to the mainstream American culture that persistently denied Asians were part of America, Chinese people viewed overseas Chinese as part of their country. This is why

Arthur and so many other overseas Chinese students could smoothly assimilate into Chinese culture. It was not the ancestral roots but the receptive and accommodating environment that made American-born Chinese like Arthur an integral part of the Nankai and Yanjing student community.

In 1936, Arthur graduated from Yanjing and was admitted into the National Medical College of Shanghai, a well-known public university with most faculty members trained in the West. During his second year there, the Japanese invasion forced the school to move into the French Settlement in Shanghai, as Chinese areas in the city was not safe. Arthur noticed how embarrassing and bitter the university president felt when he made this decision, because he had often criticized Western colonialism in China. Two years later, the school was evacuated, together with a number of other universities, to Kunming, a city in Yunan Province, Southwest China, as Japan intensified its military attack. In 1940, Arthur took an internship opportunity, facilitated by the Chinese Red Cross Medical Relief Corps, headed by Robert Lim. Lim was an overseas Chinese from Malaya and a renowned professor of physiology at the Beijing Union Medical College. The intern training was in an army hospital in a poor rural area in Guizhou Province. Arthur's intern supervisor was David Liu, a Chinese American from Hawaii and a graduate of Beijing Union Medical College. While working as an intern, Arthur also met many volunteer Western medical professionals and overseas Chinese physicians from Europe and Southeast Asia. The corps often received donations of medical supplies and equipment from overseas Chinese across the world. Arthur once saw donated supplies from Chinese Americans in Los Angeles, and happily wrote to his parents about his discovery. As the internship location was rough, some of his intern schoolmates wanted to return to the university, but Arthur felt obliged and proud to stay and complete his intern's work as an overseas Chinese.[83] His patriotism toward China grew continuously as he witnessed how overseas Chinese communities across the world supported their home country during World War Two.

In 1941, Arthur graduated from Shanghai Medical College, and decided to return to the United States for a more formal intern opportunity as a resident doctor. In a simple wedding in Shanghai, he married Sylvia, as they had known and been in love with each other since they were students at Yanjing University. In September, Arthur, with his wife, took a ship to the United States, after ten years' separation from his family. Although he possessed a U.S. passport, the INS officer still made a careful comparison between his photos in 1931 and his photo of 1941. On the Certificate of Identity form, the officer wrote, under the line of physical marks and peculiarities: "Cut

Scar base joint Rt Index Finger. Sml flesh mole back of neck."[84] None of the white fellow passengers had to go through this. Arthur immediately felt his second-class citizenship status as he went through the immigration paperwork.

Arthur had little difficulty in readjusting to American life, though Sylvia was shocked at how traditional and old-fashioned the life of the Chinese in Los Angeles was compared with the rapid social changes in China. She often felt lonely and useless as an educated Chinese woman in America, while Arthur worked first as an intern in the Los Angeles County Hospital, in 1942, and then took a postdoctoral fellowship at Harvard Medical School to study pathology. Later Arthur worked at White Memorial Hospital in Los Angeles for nine months and for five years in the pediatrics department at Bellevue Hospital in New York (from 1944 to 1949). During this period, Sylvia gave birth to a daughter, Evelyn and then a son, Alvin.[85]

As Sylvia insisted that their children needed an education in China, Arthur left the United States again with his wife and children in 1949, just as the People's Republic of China was about to be established. It was a difficult decision as Yitang was in poor health and getting old. The departure could mean a final good-bye to his aging father. It was Sam who encouraged Arthur to go to work for the new China, and promised to take the best care possible of their aging father. Shortly after Arthur's departure, his sister Marian also went to China. Graduating from the University of Southern California as a pianist, Marian went to work for novelist Pearl Buck's *Asian Magazine* in New York. Then she married Yang Keqian, a medical student from China. In 1949, the two returned to China.

In China, Arthur became a respectable doctor; he officially joined the Communist Party of China in 1958. Meanwhile, he experienced the turbulent political campaigns, and was persecuted, like many other intellectuals, during the Cultural Revolution of the 1960s.[86] In 1973, he was sent by the Chinese government to work at the World Health Organization in Geneva. Representing China, he became an assistant director general, a senior WHO executive. He could never, during that period, have reached such a level at a United Nation organization as a Chinese American. However, missing his aging mother in America, and frustrated by endless political movements in China, he quietly applied for a new U.S. passport at the American consulate office in Geneva, abandoned his WHO job, and came back to the United States. The Chinese government was furious about his departure, though his decision actually hurt his wife more than the government. They were divorced in 1977. His American-born children, Evelyn and Avin, did not forgive him for a long time, until they finally joined him in America in the late 1980s. As the Chinese saying goes, patriotism can hardly go hand-in-hand with filial piety. Giving up his pubic service for China, Arthur took good care of his aging mother in America until she died in her sleep in 1984, at the age of ninety-six. Arthur spent over forty years in China—the land of his ancestors and a country of his own—when he pursued his college education and medical profession. Although he eventually retired in the United States, China had been a home where he drew cultural inspiration, established a family, and found a prominent career. He made both his sacrifice and his contribution to China, and still loves it as an overseas child.

Conclusion

The family solidarity, ethnic resilience, and internationalism revealed in the transnational history of the Chang family strongly contest the existing paradigm of immigration studies. The family members' journey back and forth across the Pacific demonstrates how racism in America as a "push" factor and alternative opportunities in China as a "pull" factor linked Chinese Americans to their home country. But going to China meant more than education and career opportunities. When Tennyson, Elbert, Constance, Lillian, Estelle, Arthur, and Marian studied and worked in Tianjin, Beijing, Nanjing, Hangzhou, Shanghai, and Kunming, their new experiences made them a different type of Chinese American than their parents. The younger generation's stay in China coincided with the most chaotic period in Chinese modern history, but this was also a period of rising nationalism against foreign invasion. National crisis in China in a way deepened their understanding of racial oppression in the United States and greatly impacted their ethnic identity and consciousness. In contrast to the United States, where they and their parents constantly worried about their legal residency, citizenship rights, and acceptance by mainstream America, China gave them a strong sense of belonging. China drew these American-raised and American-born youth back as their cultural home.

Genealogical Chart: The Chang Family Tree

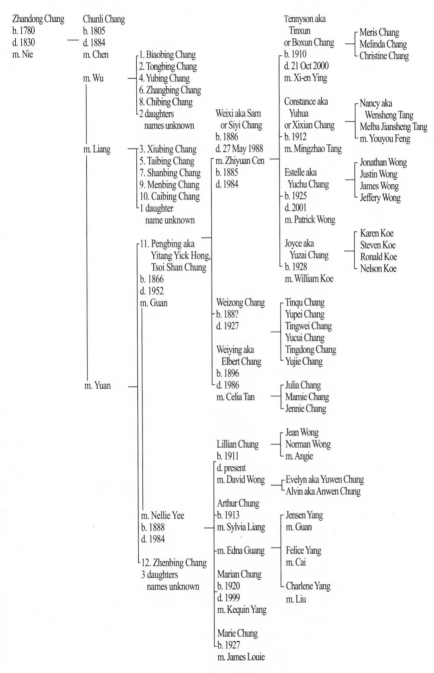

NOTES

Introduction

1. The Chang family members used both "Chang" and "Chung" as the spelling of their name.
2. I refer to Yitang and Sam as the "immigrant generation," and to their American-born, -raised, or -educated children as the "younger" or "second" generation, even though theirs is a three-generation immigrant family history.
3. Susan Mann, "The Male Bond in Chinese History and Culture," *American Historical Review* 105 (5) (December 2000): 1600–1614.
4. Madeline Hsu, *Dreaming of Gold, Dreaming of Home: Transnationalism and Migration between the United States and South China, 1882–1942* (Stanford: Stanford University Press, 2000), 9.
5. For an example of such scholarly works, see Gunther Barth, *Bitter Strength: A History of the Chinese in the United States, 1850–1870* (Cambridge, MA: Harvard University Press, 1964).
6. Carey McWilliams, *Brothers under the Skin* (Boston: Little, Brown, and Co., 1942), 111.
7. Lei Jieqiong (Kit King Louis), "Problems of Second Generation Chinese," *Sociology and Social Research* 16 (1932): 456.
8. John K. Fairbank and Edwin O. Reischauer, *China: Tradition and Transformation* (Boston: Houghton Mifflin, 1989), 393.
9. For comprehensive descriptions of these Christian colleges, see Jessie Gregory Lutz, *China and the Christian Colleges, 1850–1950* (Ithaca, NY: Cornell University Press, 1971), John K. Fairbank, ed., *The Missionary Enterprise in China and America* (Cambridge, MA: Harvard University Press, 1974), Shiliang Gao, ed. *Zhongguo jiaohui xuexiao shi* [*A History of Missionary Schools in China*] (Hunan, China: Hunan jiaoyu chubanshe, 1975), Philip West, *Yenching University and Sino-Western Relations, 1916–1952* (Cambridge, MA: Harvard University Press, 1976).
10. "INS" stands, to be sure, for Immigration and Naturalization Service.
11. Yong Chen, "In Their Own Words: The Significance of Chinese-Language Sources for Studying Chinese American History," *Journal of Asian American Studies* (October 2002): 243.

12. William I. Thomas and Florian Znaniecki, *The Polish Peasant in Europe and America* (Boston: Knopf and Co., 1927).

13. Theodore Blegen, ed., *Land of Their Choice: The Immigrants Write Home* (Minneapolis: University of Minnesota Press, 1955); Alan Conway, ed., *The Welsh in America: Letters from the Immigrants* (Minneapolis: University of Minnesota Press, 1961), Charlotte Erickson, ed., *Invisible Immigrants: The Adaptation of English and Scottish Immigrants in Nineteenth-Century America* (Coral Gables, FL: University of Miami Press, 1972); Arnold Barton, ed., *Letters from the Promised Land: Swedes in America, 1840–1912* (Minneapolis: University of Minnesota Press, 1975); Samuel Baily and Franco Ramella, eds., *One Family, Two Worlds: An Italian Family's Correspondence across the Atlantic, 1901–1922* (New Brunswick, NJ: Rutgers University Press, 1988); Walter Kamphoefner, Wolfgang Helbich, and Ulrike Sommer, ed., *News from the Land of Freedom: German Immigrants Write Home* (Ithaca, NY: Cornell University Press, 1991); and Josephine Wtulich, ed., *Writing Home: Immigrants in Brazil and the United States, 1890–1891* (New York: Columbia University Press, 1986).

CHAPTER 1   *Origins of the Chang Family*

1. Sany*i* (Sam Yup in Cantonese), translated as the "Three Districts," is located to the west of Guangzhou (Canton); Siy*i* (Sze Yup in Cantonese), translated as the "Four Districts," is located to the southwest of Sanyi; and Zhongshan (Heungsan in Cantonese) is a county located to the south of Sanyi. *Yi* means "county" or "district" in Chinese.

2. Records of the INS, Los Angeles District Segregated Chinese Case Files, 1893–1935: Files 4935/6 (Box108) at the National Archives and Records Administration at Laguna Niguel, California (NARALN).

3. Daniel Harrison Kulp II, *Country Life in South China: The Sociology of Familism—Phenix Village, Kwantung, China* (1925; repr., Taibei, Taiwan: Chengwen Publishing Co, 1966), 86ff.

4. Hugh D. R. Baker, *Chinese and Kinship* (London: The Macmillan Press, 1979), 133.

5. The account of the Chang family's origin in China is based on: a genealogy of the Chang family ("The Family Genealogy") composed by Lillian Wong, Yitang's daughter; "Yitang's Seventieth Birthday Celebration Announcement," by Sam Chang; *A Special Booklet of Sam Chang and His Wife's Eightieth Birthday Anniversary*, n.d., by Tennyson; transcripts of the Nellie Chung interview and Arthur Chung interview; and Sam's letter to Tennyson and Constance on 3 January 1928. I possess copies of these documents.

6. Sam to Tennyson and Constance on 3 January 1928.

7. E. H. Parker, *John Chinaman and a Few Others* (London: John Murray, 1901), 70.

8. One *dan* is equal to 2.94 U.S. bushels, and 1 hectoliter equals approximately 185 pounds. See David Faure, *The Rural Economy of Pre-Liberation China: Trade Expansion and Peasant Livelihood in Jiangsu and Guangdong, 1870–1937* (Hong Kong: Oxford University Press, 1989), 215.

9. For the average yield of paddy rice per *mu* in the Zhujiang Delta, see Faure, *The Rural Economy*, 48.

10. Sucheta Mazumda, *Sugar and Society in China: Peasants, Technology, and the World Market* (Cambridge, MA: Harvard University Press, 1998), 54.

11. Ping-ti Ho, *Studies on the Population of China, 1368–1953* (Cambridge, MA: Harvard University Press, 1959), 283; Frederic Wakeman Jr., *Strangers at the Gate: Social Disorder in South China, 1839–1861* (Berkeley and Los Angeles: University of California Press, 1966), 180.

12. By "farmer," I mean a person who owns his or her own farm; by "peasant" or "peasant laborers," I mean people who had very little land and relied on working for others for income.

13. G. William Skinner, "Chinese Peasants and the Closed Community: An Open and Shut Case," *Comparative Studies in Society and History* 13 (3) (1971): 270–281.

14. Wong, "The Family Genealogy."

15. Mazumda, *Sugar and Society in China,* 230–233.

16. James Hayes, "Written Materials in the Village World," in David Johnson, Andrew J. Nathan, and Evelyn S. Rawski, eds., *Popular Culture in Late Imperial China* (Berkeley and Los Angeles: University of California Press, 1982), 87

17. Ping-ti Ho, *The Ladder of Success in Imperial China: Aspects of Social Mobility, 1368–1911* (New York: Columbia University Press, 1962), 314.

18. See photograph.

19. This information is from recollections by several old friends, contained in Tennyson's *Special Booklet.*

20. Ronald Takaki, *A History of Asian Americans: Strangers from a Different Shore* (1989; repr., New York: Little, Brown and Co., 1998), 33.

21. Han-sheng Chen,, *The Present Agrarian Problem in China* (Shanghai: China Institute of Pacific Relations, 1933), 7. Also Maurice Freedman, *Lineage Organization in Southeastern China* (London: University of London, Athlone Press, 1958), 17.

22. Weiqiang Mei and Guoxiong Zhang, eds., *Wuyi huaqiao huaren shi* [*A History of Overseas Chinese in the Five Districts*] (Guangzhou, China: Guandong gaodeng jiaoyu chubanshe, 2001), 29; Frederic Wakeman Jr., *The Fall of Imperial China* (New York: The Free Press, 1975), 14.

23. For a detailed discussion of market towns in Guangdong, see Robert B. Marks, *Rural Revolution in South China: Peasants and the Making of History in Haifeng Country, 1570–1930* (Madison: University of Wisconsin Press, 1984), 54–64.

24. One Chinese *li* is about 0.3107 mile. Records of the INS, Los Angeles District Segregated Chinese Case Files, 1893–1935: Files 4935/6 (Box108) at NARALN.

25. G. William Skinner, "Marketing and Social Structure in China, Part 1," *Journal of Asian Studies* 1 (1964): 34.

26. Wanxiu Yang and Zhuo'an Zhong, *Guangzhou jianshi* [*A Concise History of Guangzhou*] (Guangzhou: Guangdong renmin chubanshe, 1996), 170–172; Mei and Zhang, ed., *Wuyi huaqiao huaren shi.*

27. Hansheng Chen, *Landlord and Peasant in China* (New York: International Publishers, 1936), 37.

28. Dajun Qu, *Guangdong Xinyu* [*New Things in Guangdong*] (1700; reprint Beijing: Zhonghua shuju, 1997), 464.

29. Chen, *Present Agrarian Problem,* 41.

30. Records of the INS, Los Angeles District Segregated Chinese Case Files, 1893–1935: Files 4935/6 (Box108) at NARALN.

31. Shimiza Taiji, *Shina no kazoku to sonraku nookushitsu* [*The Special Characteristics of Chinese Households and Villages*] (Tokyo: 1927), 67–68.

32. T. Grimm, "Academies and the Urban System in Kwangtung" in G. William Skinner, ed., *The City in Imperial China* (Stanford: Stanford University Press, 1977); Hsiao King-chuan, *Rural China: Imperial Control in the Nineteenth Century* (Seattle: University of Washington Press, 1960); and Liu Pei Chi (Boji) *Guangdong shuyuan zhiduo* [*System of Guangdong Academies*] (Taibei: Taiwan Books, 1958).

33. Wakeman, *Social Disorder,* 181; Liu, *Guangdong shuyuan zhiduo,* 46–78.

34. Mazumda, *Sugar and Society in China,* 246.

35. For in-depth discussions on the civil service examination, see Ho, *Ladder of Success in Imperial China,* and Benjamin A. Elman, *A Cultural History of Civil Examinations in Late Imperial China* (Berkeley and Los Angeles: University of California Press, 2000).

36. Sam to Tennyson and Constance on 3 January 1928.

37. Sam Chang's second brother was never able to come to America, and died of illness in China; therefore he did not have an English name.

38. Tadashi Fukutake, *Asian Rural Society: China, India, Japan* (Seattle: University of Washington Press, 1967), 86.

39. Shiga Shuzo, "Family Property and the Law of Inheritance in Traditional China," in David Buxbaum, ed., *Chinese Family Law and Social Change* (Seattle: University of Washington Press, 1978).

40. Sam to Tennyson and Constance on 3 January 1928.

41. Ho, *Ladder of Success in Imperial China,* 164 and 302.

42. *Daqing Luli Huitong Xinzuan* [*The Law of the Qing Dynasty*] (Taibei, 1964), 4:2795.

43. Sam to Tennyson and Constance on 3 January 1928.

44. Sam to Tennyson on 4 December 1928.

45. Ibid.

CHAPTER 2   *Yitang as a Merchant Immigrant*

1. Records of the INS, Los Angeles District Segregated Chinese Case Files, 1893–1935: Files 4935/6 (Box108), at NARALN.

2. Ibid.

3. Arthur Chung interview.

4. "The Family Genealogy," written by Lillian Wong.

5. Sam Chang interview.

6. John G. Kerr, *A Guide to the City and Suburbs of Canton* (Hong Kong and Shanghai: Kelly and Walsh, 1904).

7. Wan Xiuyang and Zhuo'an Zhong, *Guangdong jianshi* [*A Brief History of Guangdong*] (Guangzhou, China: Guangdong renmin chubanshe, 1996), 333.

8. In the flyer for Yitang Chung's seventieth birthday celebration, he was praised for sending all his children to good schools.
9. For new schools in Guangdong during this period, see Edward Rhoads, *China's Republican Revolution: the Case of Kwangtung, 1895–1913* (Cambridge, MA: Harvard University Press, 1975), 72–76.
10. The above information is from the flyer for Yitang Chung's seventieth birthday celebration.
11. Dorothy Perkins, "Coming to San Francisco by Steamship," in *The Chinese American Experience: Papers from the Second National Conference on Chinese American Studies (1980),* Genny Lim, ed. (San Francisco: The Chinese Historical Society of America, 1980), 26–33.
12. The information is based on a brief telephone interview with Estelle Wang on 11 July 1992.
13. Records of the INS, Los Angeles District Segregated Chinese Case Files, 1893–1935: Files 4935/6 (Box108), at NARALN.
14. Nellie Chung (Chang) interview of 1975.
15. Stanford Lyman, *The Asian in the West* (Reno and Las Vegas: Western Studies Center, Desert Research Institute, University of Nevada System, 1970), 69.
16. Records of the INS, Los Angeles District Segregated Chinese Case Files, 1893–1935: File 1370 (Box 34), at NARALN. This file includes a list of partners, in both Chinese and English, prepared by the company, and transcripts of several testimonies by Yitang Chang and his white partners.
17. Ibid.
18. For the terms *Nine Family* and *Three Family,* see chapter 1.
19. Sam to Tennyson and Constance on 3 January 1928.
20. Ibid.
21. Sam to his cousins on 20 August 1928.
22. Sam to Tennyson and Constance on 3 January 1928.
23. Baker, *Chinese Family and Kinship*, 150.
24. Baker, *Chinese Family and Kinship*, 149; Wakeman, *Strangers at the Gate*, 112.
25. Records of the INS, Los Angeles District Segregated Chinese Case Files, 1893–1935: Files 4935/6 (Box108), at NARALN.
26. Nellie Chung interview.
27. William Mason, "The Chinese in Los Angeles," *Museum Alliance Quarterly* 6 (2) (fall 1967): 20–28; Lucie Cheng and Suellen Cheng, "Chinese Women of Los Angeles, A Social Historical Survey," in *Linking Our Lives: Chinese American Women of Los Angeles*, California: Asian American Studies Center, University of California, Los Angeles and Chinese Historical Society of Southern California, 1984.
28. Nellie Chung interview.
29. Ibid.
30. Ibid.
31. Ibid.
32. Cheng and Cheng, "Chinese Women of Los Angeles," 2–7.
33. Ibid, 2.
34. Nellie Chung interview.
35. Cheng and Cheng, "Chinese Women of Los Angeles," 8–9, 2.

36. Nellie Chung interview.
37. For Wu's activities in Los Angeles, also see Thomas W. Chinn, *Bridging the Pacific: San Francisco Chinatown and Its People* (San Francisco: Chinese Historical Society of America, San Francisco, 1989), 99.
38. See *1910 Census, Abstract and Supplement for California*, 590.
39. Ibid.
40. Records of the INS, Los Angeles District Segregated Chinese Case Files, 1893–1935: 29160/141 and 142 (Box 358), at NARALN.
41. Courtesy of the National Archives and Records Administration at Laguna Niguel, I have obtained a copy of the petition.
42. Records of the INS, Los Angeles District Segregated Chinese Case Files, 1893–1935: 29160/141 and 142 (Box 358), at NARALN.
43. Cheng and Cheng, "Chinese Women of Los Angeles," 8–9.
44. Records of the INS, Los Angeles District Segregated Chinese Case Files, 1893–1935: 4935/6 (Box 108), at NARALN.
45. Sam to his niece on 26 December 1925.
46. Hsu, *Dream of Gold, Dreaming of Home*, 88.
47. The original draft of this biography is still preserved in the collection of Sam Chang's family papers.
48. Wakeman, *Strangers at the Gate*, 113.

CHAPTER 3   *Herbal Medicine as a Transplanted Culture*

1. William M. Tisdale, "Chinese Physicians in California," in *Lippincott's Magazine* 63 (March 1899), 411.
2. According to Ralph Croizier, famous Chinese scholars of medicine practiced it out of purely benevolent motives. See Croizier, *Traditional Medicine in Modern China: Science, Nationalism, and the Tensions of Cultural Change* (Cambridge, MA: Harvard University Press, 1968), 14.
3. Thomas W. Chinn, H.M. Lai, and Philip Choy, eds., *A History of the Chinese in California: A Syllabus* (San Francisco, Chinese Historical Society of America, 1969), 78.
4. Paul Buell and Christopher Muench, "Chinese Medical Recipes from Frontier Seattle," in Douglas W. Lee, ed., *The Annals of the Chinese Historical Society of the Pacific Northwest* (Bellingham, WA, 1984), 102.
5. Ibid., 100–105.
6. "Chinese Directory," *The Oriental*, 8 February 1856: English section.
7. John Kuo Wei Tchen, ed., *Genthe's Photographs of San Francisco's Old Chinatown* (New York: Dover Publications, 1984), 58–59.
8. Liu Pei Chi (Poji), *Meiguo huaqiao shi* [*A History of the Chinese in the United States of America*] (Taibei: Commission of Overseas Chinese Affairs, 1976), 314.
9. Charles Hillinger, *Hillinger's California: Stories from All 58 Counties* (Santa Barbara, CA: Capra Press, 1997), 25–26.
10. Item 1025 in Him Mark Lai, ed., *A History Reclaimed: An Annotated Bibliography of Chinese Language Materials on the Chinese of America* (Los Ange-

les: Asian America Studies Center, University of California–Los Angeles, 1986), 108.

11. Liu, *Meiguo huaqiao shi*, 343.
12. Stewart Culin, "Chinese Drug Stores in America," *American Journal of Pharmacy* (December 1887), 596.
13. A. W. Loomis, "Medical Art in the Chinese Quarter," *Overland Monthly* 2 (June 1869), 496.
14. Jeffrey Barlow and Christine Richardson, *China Doctor of John Day* (Portland, OR: Thomas Binford Publisher, 1979); Buell and Muench, "Chinese Medical Recipes from Frontier Seattle," and Muench, "One Hundred Years of Medicine: The Ah-Fong Physicians of Idaho," in Henry Schwarz, ed., *Chinese Medicine on the Golden Mountain* (Seattle, 1984).
15. Liu, *Meiguo huaqiao shi*, 314.
16. Zhu, Jianping, *Zhongguo yixue shi yanjiu* [*A Study of Chinese Medical History*], (Beijing: Zhongyi guji chubanshe, 2003), 173–175.
17. John G. Kerr, *A Guide to the City and Suburbs of Canton* (Hong Kong and Shanghai: Kelly and Walsh, 1904).
18. Joan B. Trauner, "The Chinese as Medical Scapegoats in San Francisco, 1870–1905," *California History* 57 (1) (1978): 72.
19. For specific examples, see Trauner's article.
20. Sam to Tingxun and Yuhua on 30 April 1924.
21. Thomas W. Chin, 22. According to Sucheng Chan, San Francisco had 8 percent of the state's Chinese population in 1860. See Chan, *Asian Californians* (San Francisco: MTL/Boyd and Fraser, 1991), 30.
22. Trauner, "The Chinese as Medical Scapegoats," 73.
23. Ibid., 81.
24. Ibid., 84.
25. William G. Rothstein, "The Botanical Movements and Orthodox Medicine," in Norman Gevitz, ed., *Other Healers: Unorthodox Medicine in America* (Baltimore: Johns Hopkins University Press, 1988), 30.
26. Croizier, *Traditional Medicine in Modern China,* 13 and 19.
27. There were a limited number of scholarly writings on Chinese traditional medicine before the 1980s. These include Croizier, *Traditional Medicine in Modern China;* S. M. Hiller and J. A. Jewell, *Health Care and Traditional Medicine in China, 1800–1982* (London and Boston: Rutledge and Kegan Paul, 1983); Richard Hyatt, *Chinese Herbal Medicine: An Ancient Art and Modern Healing Science* (New York: Thorsons: 1984, 1978); and Paul D. Buell, Douglas W. Lee, Jeffery L. MacDonald, Christopher Muench, and Margaret Wilson, *Chinese Medicine on the Golden Mountain: An Interpretive Guide* (Seattle: Wing Luke Memorial Museum, 1984).
28. Buell and Muench, "Chinese Medical Recipes from Frontier Seattle," 101.
29. Tisdale, "Chinese Physicians in California," 412.
30. Ibid.
31. Barlow and Richardson, *China Doctor of John Day*, 64.
32. Fong Wan, *Herbal Lore,* 3d edition (Oakland, CA, 1933), 15.
33. Barlow and Richardson, *China Doctor of John Day,* 1–2, 67.

34. Rothstein, "Botanical Movements and Orthodox Medicine," 29–51.

35. Tan Fuyuan [Tom Foo Yuen], *The Science of Oriental Medicine: Its Principles and Methods* (Los Angeles: The Foo and Wing Herb Company/G. Rice and Sons, 1897). The book had a revised edition in 1902.

36. The Nellie Chung interview and the Arthur Chung interview done in 1979 are available at Chinese Historical Society of Southern California.

37. Much of the information cited here and afterwards is from the Nellie Chung interview.

38. Paul Chace has kindly offered me a photocopy of these advertisements.

39. Fong, *Herbal Lore,* 140.

40. For the popularity of medical publishing, see Li Jingwei and Li Zhidong, *Zhongguo gudai yixue shi* [*A History of Medicine in Ancient China*] (Shijia zhuang: Hebei kexue jishu chubanshe, 1990), chapter 10.

41. Lui, *Secrets of Chinese Physicians* (Los Angeles: B. N. Robertson, 1943), 104; *Herbal Lore,*140.

42. For information on Li and Tan, see Liu, 315, and Fuyuan (Foo Yuen), *Science of Oriental Medicine*, 93–100.

43. Tom Leung, *Chinese Herbal Medicine: Its Principles and Methods* (Los Angeles: T. Leung Herb Company, 1928), 8.

44. Garding Lui, *Inside Los Angeles Chinatown* (Los Angeles: 1948), 201.

45. International Chinese Business Directory Co., *International Chinese Business Directory of the World for the Year 1913* (San Francisco, California, 1913). See the Los Angeles Section.

46. William Mason, "The Chinese in Los Angeles," *Museum Alliance Quarterly* 6 (2) (1967): 16; David Chan, "The Five Chinatowns of Los Angeles," *Bridge* (2) (1973): 41–45.

47. Croizier, *Traditional Medicine in Modern China,* 33.

48. For the specific figures, see Stanford Lyman, *The Asian in the West* (Reno and Las Vegas: Western Studies Center, Desert Research Institute, University of Nevada System, 1970), 69.

49. Carey McWilliams, *Southern California: An Island of the Land* (Salt Lake City: Gibbs M. Smith, 1983), 258.

50. This is the impression of Estelle Wang and Joyce Koe when they read and made comments on my article. During my second visit to Lillian and Estelle, on 11 June 1992, Estelle told me she and Marie, Yitang's youngest daughter, recalled that once Nellie dressed up to visit McWilliams for a legal consultation.

51. Arthur Chung interview.

52. Nellie Chung interview.

53. Records of the INS, Los Angeles District Segregated Chinese Case Files, 1893–1935: Files 4935/6 (Box108), at NARALN.

54. According to Rose Hum Lee, the survival of Chinatown would depend on either a large Chinese resident population or a large mobile labor force. See Lee, "The Decline of Chinatown in the United States," *American Journal of Sociology,* no. 55 (1949): 422–432.

55. Mason, "The Chinese in Los Angeles," 20.

56. Records of the INS, Los Angeles District Segregated Chinese Case Files, 1893–1935: Files 4935/6 (Box108), at NARALN.
57. Arthur Chung interview and Nellie Chung interview.
58. Louise Leung Larson, *Sweet Bamboo: A Saga of a Chinese American Family* (Los Angeles: Chinese Historical Society of Southern California, 1989), 33 and 135.
59. Alexander McLeod, *Pigtails and Gold Dust: A Panorama of Chinese Life in Early California* (Caldwell, ID: The Caxton Printers, 1948), 141.
60. Tisdale, "Chinese Physicians in California," 412.
61. Raymond Lou, "The Chinese American Community of Los Angeles, 1870–1900: A Case of Resistance, Organization, and Participation" (Ph.D. diss., University of California, Irvine, 1982), 44 and 72.
62. Helen Zeese Papnikolas, *Toil and Rage in a New Land: The Greek Immigrants in Utah* (Salt Lake City: Utah Historical Society, 1974).
63. Fuyuan (Foo Yuen), *The Science of Oriental Medicine: Its Principles and Methods* (Los Angeles: G Rice and Sons, 1897). The book had a revised edition in 1902.
64. Leung, *Chinese Herbal Science.*
65. Fong, *Herbal Lore.*
66. Lui, *Secrets of Chinese Physicians.*
67. Nellie Chung interview.
68. Larson, *Sweet Bamboo*, 21.
69. Records of the INS, Los Angeles District Segregated Chinese Case Files, 1893–1935: Files 4935/6 (Box108), at NARALN.
70. See Chittenden Turner, *The Rise of Chiropractic* (Los Angeles: Powell Publishing, 1931); Walter I. Wardwell, "Chiropractors: Evolution to Acceptance," in Gevitz, ed., *Other Healers,* 157–191.
71. Lui, *Inside Los Angeles Chinatown*, 204.
72. Stewart Culin, "Chinese Drug Stores in America," *American Journal of Pharmacy* (December 1887).
73. She spoke Cantonese instead of Mandarin.
74. Nellie Chung interview.
75. Ibid.
76. Records of the INS, Los Angeles District Segregated Chinese Case Files, 1893–1935: Files 5530/546 (Box 249), at NARALN.
77. Records of the INS, Los Angeles District Segregated Chinese Case Files, 1893–1935: Files 8402/188 (Box 3), at NARALN.
78. Liu, 314; Larson, *Sweet Bamboo*, 20.
79. Foo Yuen (Fuyuan), *Science of Oriental Medicine*, 96.
80. Tan Fu-yuan, *The Science of Oriental Medicine,* 8.
81. Ibid., 11.
82. Tisdale, "Chinese Physicians in California," 416.
83. Fong, *Herbal Lore,* 35.
84. Larson, *Sweet Bamboo*, 35.
85. This is what Estelle Wang told me in a conversation.
86. Larson, *Sweet Bamboo,* 71.

87. Arthur Chung interview, 12.
88. The Los Angeles District Segregated Chinese Case Files: No. 26160/140 (Box 340), at NARALN.

Chapter 4   *Between Troubled Home and Racist America*

1. Records of the INS, Los Angeles District Segregated Chinese Case Files, 1893–1935: Files 5530/546 (Box 249) at National Archives and Records Administration at Laguna Niguel, California, at NARALN.
2. Sam to Tennyson on 25 December 1921.
3. David Wong, "Eulogy of Mr. Sam Chang." I have a copy of the eulogy.
4. The information is based on a phone interview with Estelle Wang on 11 July 1992.
5. Ping-ti Ho, *Studies on the Population of China, 1368–1953* (Cambridge, MA: Harvard University Press, 1959), 73.
6. Edward J. Rhoads, *China's Republican Revolution: The Case of Kwangtung, 1895–1913* (Cambridge, MA: Harvard University Press, 1975), 59; Wanxiu Yang and Zhuo'an Zhong, *Guangzhou jianshi* [*A Brief History of Guangzhou*], (Guangzhou, China: Guangdong renmin chubanshe, 1996), 341.
7. *Special Booklet*, 20.
8. Ibid., 6.
9. Yang and Zhong, *Guangzhou jianshi*, 342–343.
10. Records of the Immigration and Naturalization Service, San Francisco District, Arrival Investigative Case Files 1884–1944, Case Number 14390/35–2 (Box 927).
11. For the Wuchang Uprising, see Vidya Prakash Dutt, "The First Week of Revolution: The Wuchang Uprising," in Mary Clabaugh Wright, ed., *China in Revolution: The First Phase, 1900–1913* (New Haven and London: Yale University Press, 1968); Tao Ju-yin, *Beiyang junfa tongzhi shiqi shihua* [*A History of Northern Warlord Politics*] (Beijing: Shenghuo, dushu, xinzhi chubanshe, 1957), 54–57.
12. For Chen's activities in the Revolution, see Rhoads, *China's Republican Revolution*, 216–264.
13. Ibid., 228–230; Yang and Zhong, *Guangzhou jianshi*, 356–359.
14. Records of the INS, Los Angeles District Segregated Chinese Case Files, 26160/140 (Box 340), at NARALN.
15. Tao, *Beiyang junfa tongzhi* [*Northern Warlord Politics*], 168; Rhoads, *China's Republican Revolution*, 260–261.
16. Rhoads, *China's Republican Revolution*, 263.
17. *Special Booklet*, 6.
18. Ibid., 6.
19. Huang, a native of Hunan Province, was the chief of the army for the Republican government. Hu, a Cantonese, was the secretary general for the president's office.
20. On Chinese warlords, see Hsi-sheng Ch'i, *Warlord Politics in China: 1916–1928* (Stanford: Stanford University Press, 1976), and Arthur Waldron, "The Warlord:

Twentieth-Century Chinese Understanding of Violence, Militarism, and Imperialism," *American Historical Review* 96 (October1991): 1073–1100.

21. This information is based on Rhoads, *China's Republican Revolution*, 217–265.
22. Wong, "Eulogy of Mr. Sam Chang."
23. Yang and Zhong, *Guangzhou jianshi*, 355 and 358.
24. *Special Booklet*, 46.
25. Records of the Immigration and Naturalization Service, San Francisco District, Arrival Investigative Case Files 1884–1944, Case Number 14390/35–2 (Box 927).
26. Ch'i, *Warlord Politics in China*, 94.
27. Wong's eulogy of Sam Chang.
28. Ibid.
29. I have copies of these advertisements.
30. I have copies of these advertisements.
31. Helen Zeese Papnikolas, *Toil and Rage in a New Land: The Greek Immigrants in Utah* (Salt Lake City: Utah Historical Society, 1974).
32. Sam Chang interview.
33. Sam to Tennyson on 15 February 1923.
34. Sam to Tennyson on 27 April 1923.
35. Ibid.
36. Sam to Tennyson on 17 June 1923.
37. Ibid.
38. Sam to a cousin on 19 January 1927.
39. Tennyson (Tingxun) to parents on 25 May 1928.
40. Evelyn S. Rawski, *Education and Popular Literacy in Ch'ing China* (Ann Arbor: University of Michigan Press, 1979), 149 and 7.
41. Records of the INS, Los Angeles District Segregated Chinese Case Files: Files 9402/461 (Box 20), at NARALN.
42. Records of the INS, Los Angeles District Segregated Chinese Case Files, 1893–1935: Files 5530/546 (Box 249), at NARALN.
43. As previously noted, the Chang family members used "Chang" and "Chung" in spelling their name.
44. I have a copy of the eulogy.
45. Records of the INS, Los Angeles District Segregated Chinese Case Files, 1893–1935: Files 5530/546 (Box 249), at NARALN.
46. Ibid.
47. All the interview information is based on Records of the Immigration and Naturalization Service, San Francisco District, Arrival Investigative Case Files, 1884–1944, Case Number 14390/35–2 (Box 927).
48. *U.S. Statutes* 1883–85 (Washington, DC, 1885), 23, 116–118.
49. Sam to his twelfth uncle on 7 July 1925.
50. Sam to Ruyuan on 9 August 1925.
51. Unless otherwise footnoted, information in this section is mainly based on the Los Angeles District Segregated Chinese Case Files, Box 340, No. 26160/140 at NARALN.
52. The Chang family genealogy authored by Lillian Wong, daughter of Yitang,

mentioned Choy Bing as the tenth son of Chunli, born to him by his third wife Liang.

53. Sam to Weizong on 4 August 1922.
54. Ibid.
55. Sam to his cousins on 4 October 1927.
56. Sam to a female cousin on 5 January 1922.
57. Sam to Weizong on 9 March 1922.
58. Sam to Tennyson on 15 September 1922.

CHAPTER 5 *Asparagus Farming as a Family Business*

1. On Chinese asparagus farmers in Northern California, see George Chu, "Chinatown in the Delta: The Chinese in the Sacramento–San Joaquin Delta, 1870–1960" in *California Historical Society Quarterly* 49 (1) (March 1970), and Thomas W. Chinn, *Bridging the Pacific: San Francisco Chinatown and Its People* (San Francisco: Chinese Historical Society of America, 1989), 107. In his interview, Sam recalled how he observed other Chinese grow asparagus.
2. Sam to a friend on 23 February 1922.
3. Sam to Weizong on 4 August 1922.
4. Sam to Tennyson on 16 November 1924.
5. Sam Chang's farming notes.
6. Sam to Tennyson on 6 February 1926.
7. Sam to Tennyson and Constance on 3 January 1928.
8. Records of the INS, Los Angeles District Segregated Chinese Case Files, 1929–1934: Files 9402/387 (Box 19), at NARALN.
9. Sam Chang interview.
10. Carey McWilliams, *Southern California: An Island on the Land* (Salt Lake City: Peregrine Smith Books, 1983), 187–191.
11. Sam to Tennyson and Constance on 20 August 1928.
12. Sam to Tennyson on 4 December 1928.
13. Ibid.
14. Sam to Tennyson on 30 July 1928.
15. Sam to Tennyson on 3 January 1928.
16. Ibid.
17. Sam to an aunt on 29 January 1929.
18. Letter from Sam to a friend, 19 July 1932.
19. Sam to a relative, 24 June 1933.
20. Sam Chang interview.
21. Sam to Tennyson on 17 June 1923.
22. Sam to Tennyson on 2 April 1926.
23. Sam to Tennyson on 17 June 1923.
24. Sam to a relative, 24 June 1933.
25. Sam to his uncle on 3 November 1932.
26. Ibid.
27. Sam to Tennyson on 22 November 1923.
28. Ibid.

29. Sam to a nephew on 31 November 1931.
30. Sam to Tennyson, who was studying in Washington, D.C., on 12 September 1933.
31. Sam to Tennyson on 24 July 1939.
32. Sam to a friend, 24 December 1941.
33. Sam to Constance on 28 May 1943.
34. Sam to Tennyson on 11 December 1944.
35. Sam to Tennyson on 17 October 1947.
36. Sam Chang's farming notes.
37. Sam to a cousin, 24 September 1922.
38. Sam to Tennyson on 22 November 1923.
39. Sam to Tennyson and Constance on 23 August 1923.
40. Ibid.
41. For a description of the Sam Chang collection, see the bibliography section "Archives."
42. On Ah Quin, see Yong Chen, *Chinese San Francisco 1850–1943: A Trans-Pacific Community* (Stanford: Stanford University Press, 2000), 96–123; Susie Lan Cassel, "To Inscribe the Self Daily: The Discovery of the Ah Quin Diary," in Susie Lan Cassel, ed., *The Chinese in America: A History from Gold Mountain to the New Millennium* (Walnut Creek, CA: Altamira Press, 2002), 54–76; Murray K. Lee, "Ah Quin: One of San Diego's Founding Fathers" in Cassel, ed., *Chinese in America*, 308–328.
43. Fan served as the minister of education for three terms between 1912 and 1922, though each term was quite short as China's political situation was unstable. Fan was also president of two famous universities in China. Together with Cai Yuanpei, another celebrated educator, Fan recommended the establishment of a Chinese language school in the Los Angeles community. Following Fan and Cai's suggestions, the Chinese community in Los Angeles set up two schools in 1927. One was located in Chinatown and the other in the Ninth Street produce market area. See Liu, *Meiguo hua qiao shi*, 368.
44. Sam Chang's farming notes.
45. Sun Yatsen was a political leader, but Hu Shi, Chen Duxiu, and Cai Yuanpei influenced modern China with their literary ideas.
46. Sam Chang's farming notes.
47. Ibid.
48. Sam Chang interview.
49. Sam Chang's farming notes.
50. Ronald Takaki, *Strangers from a Different Shore: A History of Asian Americans* (Boston: Little, Brown and Co., 1989), 194–197; Yuji Ichioka, *The Issei: The World of the First Generation Japanese Immigrants, 1885–1924* (New York: The Free Press, 1988), 146–150.
51. For Chinese farmers' activities, see Raymond Lou, "The Chinese American Community of Los Angeles, 1870–1900: A Case of Resistance, Organization, and Participation" (Ph.D. diss., University of California, Irvine, 1982), 130; Patricia Lin, "Perspectives on the Chinese in Nineteenth-Century Orange County," *Journal of Orange County Studies,* no. 3/4 (fall 1989/spring 1990), 28–36; and Charles Choy Wong, "Chinese Grocers in Southern California," *Journal of Ethnic Studies* 8 (2) (1980): 63–64.

52. Sam Chang's farming notes.
53. According to Charles Choy Wong, before the city market was established, there had been the Union Wholesale Terminal Market at Sixth and Alameda Streets. When disputes erupted on the future development of the market, one group of merchants stayed and another group left to build, in 1909, the city market at Ninth and San Pedro Streets. Of the two markets, the city market was dominant. It was created through the cooperative efforts of Chinese, Caucasians, and Japanese. The Chinese were led by Louis Quan, who, by virtue of his solid English-speaking ability and business acuity, promoted a Chinese company of 373 stockholders and raised eighty-two thousand dollars, or 41 percent of the city market shares. See Wong, "Chinese Grocers," 65; see also Elsie and George Yee, "Chinese and the Los Angeles Produce Market," in Susie Ling, ed., *Bridging the Centuries: History of Chinese Americans in Southern California* (Los Angeles: Chinese Historical Society of Southern California, 2001), 44–52.
54. Sam Chang interview.
55. The novel was translated in 1901. See R. David Arkush and Leo O. Lee, ed. and trans., *Land Without Ghosts: Chinese Impressions of America from the Mid-Nineteenth Century to the Present* (Berkeley and Los Angeles: University of California Press, 1989), 77.
56. John K. Fairbank and Edwin O. Reischauer, *China: Tradition and Transformation,* rev. ed. (Boston: Houghton Mifflin, 1989), 401.
57. William Mason, "The Chinese in Los Angeles," *Museum Alliance Quarterly* 6 (2) (fall 1967): 20–28.
58. For example, see Isamu Nodera, "A Survey of the Vocational Activities of the Japanese in the City of Los Angeles" (M.A. thesis, University of Southern California, 1936), 101.
59. Link Mathewson, "Chinese Farmers of Yesteryear Honored," *Los Angeles Times,* Part 5, 6 November 1985.

CHAPTER 6   *Education as a Family Agenda*

1. Ichisada Miyazaki, *China's Examination Hell: The Civil Service Examinations of Imperial China,* Conrad Schirokauger, trans. (New Haven, CT: Yale University Press, 1963).
2. Evelyn S. Rawski, *Education and Popular Literacy in Ch'ing China* (Ann Arbor: University of Michigan Press, 1979), 163.
3. Daniel Harrison Kulp, *Country Life in South China: The Sociology of Familism* (New York, 1925), 230.
4. Sam to Tennyson on 25 December 1921.
5. Sam to Tennyson on 24 July 1923.
6. Sam to Tennyson on 25 December 1921.
7. Sam to Tennyson on 13 December 1922.
8. Sam to Constance on 21 December 1922.
9. Yang Wan Xiu and Zhuo'an Zhong, *Guangzhou jianshi* [*A Brief History of Guangzhou*] (Guangzhou, China: Guangdong renmin chubanshe, 1996), 276.
10. I have a copy of Constance's notebook.

11. Sam to Tennyson on 15 February 1922.
12. Constance to Tennyson (dates unknown)
13. Hai Rei and Zeng Guofan were well-known prime ministers in feudal China, Sun Yatsen a revolutionary leader of the Republic of China.
14. Sam to Tennyson on 3 January 1925.
15. Dated 1 August 1924, this letter was copied in one of Constance's notebooks.
16. Constance to Tennyson on 12 November 1925.
17. The letter has no date but seems to have been written around 1925 to a female relative in China.
18. Sam to Tennyson on 24 May 1922.
19. Sam to Tennyson. The letter has no date but seems to have been written circa 1925.
20. Ibid.
21. Sam to Tennyson on 25 December 1921.
22. Sam to Tennyson on 22 July 1922.
23. Sam to Tennyson on 27 April 1923.
24. Lee, *The Chinese in the United States*, 99.
25. Sam to Tennyson on 20 July 1922.
26. *Guangdong jianshi*, 276.
27. Rose Hum Lee, *The Chinese in the United States of America* (Hong Kong: Hong Kong University Press, 1960), 88.
28. Sam to Tennyson and Constance on 23 August 1923.
29. Sam to Tennyson on 22 November 1923.
30. Sam to Tennyson on 12 May 1924.
31. Sam to Tennyson on 22 November 1923.
32. Sam to Tennyson on 15 September 1922.
33. Ibid.
34. Sam to Tennyson on 12 May 1924.
35. Sam to Tennyson on 16 November 1924.
36. On Nankai School, see Fairbanks, *China*, 393; and Chi Meng's *Chinese American Understanding: A Sixty-Year Search* (New York: China Institute in America, 1981), 77–100.
37. Sam to Tennyson on 3 January 1925.
38. Qian Zhongshu, Zheng Zhenduo, A-ying, and Mar Tailai, *Linshu de fanyi* [The Translation of Lin Shu] (Beijing, Shangwu chubanshe, 1981).
39. Tennyson to Sam on 25 February 1925.
40. Sam to Tennyson on 2 April 1926.
41. Tennyson to Sam on 12 October 1927.
42. Sam to Tennyson on 15 November 1927.
43. Jonathan D. Spence, *The Search for Modern China* (New York: W. W. Norton and Co., 1999), 238.
44. Tennyson to Sam on 26 February 1929.
45. Sam to Tennyson on 29 January 1929.
46. Sam to Constance on 31 January 1931.
47. Sam to Constance on 10 November 1931.
48. Sam to Constance on 3 April 1931.

49. Sam to Constance on 14 February 1932.
50. Sam to his uncle on 23 February 1932.
51. Sam to Tennyson on 20 February 1933.
52. Sam to Tennyson on 5 June 1933.
53. Sam to Elbert on 9 December 1933.
54. Shih-shan Tsai, *The Chinese Experience in America* (Bloomington and Indianapolis: Indiana University Press, 1986), 111
55. Sam to Tennyson on 22 October 1934.
56. Sam to Tennyson on 6 November 1934.
57. Sam to Constance on 13 November 1934.
58. Sam to Constance on 6 March 1935.
59. Sam to Tennyson on 19 September 1935.
60. Sam to Tennyson on 22 December 1937.
61. Sam to Tennyson on 22 August 1941.
62. Sam to Constance on 25 February 1940.
63. Sam to Tennyson on 31 February 1945.
64. Sam to Tennyson on 4 February 1946; Sam to a nephew on 22 February 1946; and Sam to Tennyson on 27 February 1946.
65. Tennyson to his parents on 7 April 1948.

CHAPTER 7   *China as a Cultural Home*

1. Sauling Wong, "The Language Situation of Chinese Americans," in Sandra Lee McKay and Sauling Cynthia Wong, eds., *Language Diversity: Problem or Resource* (New York: Newbury House Publishers, 1988), 213.
2. Ronald Takaki, *Strangers from the Different Shore: A History of Asian Americans* (Boston: Little, Brown and Co., 1989), 267.
3. For the contest essays, see Ging Hawk Club, *Chinese America: History and Perspectives* (1992), 149–175.
4. Sam to a few cousins, 1 December 1928.
5. Sam to Tennyson and Constance on 14 November 1928.
6. Sam to his uncle, 21 November 1928.
7. Sam to Tennyson and Constance on 12 January 1929.
8. Arthur W. Chung, *Of Rats, Sparrows, and Flies: A Lifetime in China* (Stockton, CA: Heritage West Books, 1995), 174.
9. Nellie Chung interview.
10. Records of the INS, San Pedro Office Segregated Chinese Case Files, 1894–1965: Files 14036/598 B (Box 125), at NARALN.
11. Records of the INS, Los Angeles District Segregated Chinese Case Files, 1893–1935: Files 29160/141 and142 (Box 358), at NARALN.
12. Records of the INS, Los Angeles District Segregated Chinese Case Files, 1893–1935: Files 8402/188 (Box 3), at NARALN.
13. Ibid.
14. Sam to Tennyson on 16 November 1924.
15. Ibid.
16. Elbert Chang's eulogy, by David Wong.

17. Sam to Tennyson and Constance on 6 October 1928.
18. Jessie Gregory Lutz, *China and the Christian Colleges: 1850–1950* (Ithaca, NY: Cornell University Press, 1971), 505.
19. J. A. Jewell, "The Development of Chinese Health Care, 1911–49," in S. M. Hiller and J. A. Jewell, eds., *Health Care and Traditional Medicine in China, 1800–1982* (London: Routlege and Kegan Paul, 1983), 44.
20. Sam to Yitang on 10 December 1928.
21. Sam to Elbert (Ximing) on 4 February 1930.
22. Ibid.
23. Chung, *A Lifetime in China*, 13–22.
24. Sam to Elbert on 9 December 1933.
25. Arthur Chung interview.
26. Ibid.
27. Sam to Tennyson on 13 February 1937. In a telephone conversation, Joyce told the author that it was her mother who read her the story.
28. Sam to Tennyson on 13 December 1926.
29. Ibid.
30. I have a copy of that photo.
31. This is a letter from Arthur Chung to me.
32. Arthur Chung interview.
33. Sam to Tennyson and Constance on 3 January 1928.
34. Sam to Constance on 31 January 1931.
35. Sam to Tennyson on 3 January 1925.
36. Sam to Tennyson on 1 June 1926.
37. Arthur Chung interview.
38. Sam to Tennyson and Constance on 3 January 1928.
39. Arthur Chung interview.
40. Chung, *A Lifetime in China,* 22–23.
41. Records of the Immigration and Naturalization Service, San Francisco District, Arrival Investigative Case Files, 1884–1944, Case Number 22753/11–9 (Box 1902).
42. Constance to Sam on 10 July 1927.
43. Constance to Cen on 23 August 1927.
44. Constance to Cen on 14 October 1927.
45. Tennyson to his parents, 15 May 1928.
46. Constance to her parents, 27 May 1928.
47. Constance to Sam on 10 July 1927.
48. Constance to her mother, 10 March 1928.
49. Constance to her parents, 29 January 1930.
50. Sam to Constance on 6 January 1930.
51. Constance to Sam on 3 October 1928.
52. Sam to Rui-huan and Yu-pei on 7 January 1931.
53. Sam to Constance on 24 October 1929.
54. Sam to Elbert on 7 February 1931.
55. Ibid.
56. Sam to Constance on 8 November 1932.

57. Sam to Constance on 16 June 1931.
58. Sam to Constance on 24 October 1929.
59. Sam to Constance on February 12, 1929.
60. Sam to Constance on 24 October 1929.
61. Tan Sizhe ed., *Jiangmen wuyi haiwai mingren zhuan* [*Famous Overseas Chinese from Jiangmen*], vol. 5 (Guangzhou: Guangdong renmin chubanshe, 1996), 8–15.
62. Sam to Elbert on 25 December 1932.
63. Sam to Constance on 6 November 1935.
64. Sam to Constance on 29 January 1937.
65. Sam to Tennyson on 26 August 1937.
66. Renqiu Yu, *To Save China, To Save Ourselves: The Chinese Hand Laundry Alliance of New York* (Philadelphia: Temple University Press, 1992), 97.
67. Sam to Constance on 20 June 1939.
68. Sam to Constance, 27 April 1943.
69. Yu, *Chinese Hand Laundry Alliance*, 183.
70. Sam Chang wrote those remarks when he composed a poem for Wensheng Tang. I have a copy of this poem.
71. Records of the INS, Los Angeles District Segregated Chinese Case Files, 1893–1935: Files 8402/188 (Box 3), at NARALN.
72. Records of the INS, Los Angeles District Segregated Chinese Case Files, 1893–1935: Files 8402/188 (Box 3), at NARALN. Chang Ting Way was actually a son of Sam's second brother. This "Mr. Nardini" had first interviewed the Chang family in 1923 and had interviewed family members several dozens of times since.
73. Sam to Estelle on 10 October 1934.
74. Sam to his uncle, 17 June 1931
75. Sam Chang interview.
76. Arthur Chung interview.
77. Carey McWilliams, *Brothers Under the Skin* (Boston: Little, Brown and Co., 1942), 144–145.
78. Arthur Chung interview.
79. Records of the INS, Los Angeles District Segregated Chinese Case Files, 1893–1935, 29160/141, at NARALN.
80. Nellie Chung interview.
81. Arthur W. Chung, *A Lifetime in China*, 38.
82. Lutz, *China and the Christian Colleges*, 342–347.
83. Chung, *A Lifetime in China*, 85–91.
84. Records of the INS, Los Angeles District Segregated Chinese Case Files, 1893–1935, 14036/3107, at NARALN.
85. Chung, *A Lifetime in China*, 114–140.
86. This information is based on the Arthur Chung interview.

GLOSSARY

Entries are arranged by the *pinyi* spellings. If two words form one vocabulary, such as "Beijing," this vocabulary is arranged in a letter-by-letter manner with no word or syllable breaks. Two vocabularies, like "Cuncheng shushi," will have a break in between. Cantonese spelling or translation is provided in brackets when necessary.

Beijing	北京
Beizha cun	北闸 村
bo, zhong, shu, ji	伯仲叔季
Cai Tingkai	蔡廷锴
Cai Yuanpei	蔡元培
Cen Zhiyuan	岑治元
Chen Duxiu	陈独秀
Chen Hansheng	陈翰笙
Chen Jinghua (Chen King Wah)	陈景华
Chongqing	重庆
Chung Sat Yat Po	中西日报
citang	祠堂
Cuncheng Shushi	存诚书室
Dabu	大埠
Dan	石
dianshi	殿试
Enping	恩平
Fan Yuanlian	范源廉
fangbian yiyuan	方便医院

feng shui	风水
fugongsheng	副贡生
fu kao	复考
gong sheng	贡生
Guan	关（姓）
Guangxi	广西
Guan Tingqu	关澄弼
Guangdong	广东
Hai Rei	海瑞
hongpishu (red paper book)	红皮书
Hubei	湖北
Hu Hanmin	胡汉民
Hu Shi	胡适
Huaiyuan	怀园
Huang Xing	黄兴
huiguan	会馆
huishi	会试
Hushan	虎山
jia	家
Jiang Jieshi (Chiang Kai-shek)	蒋介石
jinshan ke	金山客
Jinshan shibao	金山时报
jinshi	进士
juren	举人
Kaiping	开平
keijia (Hakka, or guest people)	客家
Langxia xiang	廊厦乡
laojia	老家
Lei Jieqiong	雷洁琼
Li	李（姓）
Liang	梁（姓）
Liang Ruhuai	梁汝怀
Liang Siyi	梁思懿
lingongsheng	廪贡生
Long Jiguang	龙济光
majiang	麻将

Mao Zedong (Mao Tze-dung)	毛泽东
Meizhou huaqiao ribao	美洲华侨日报
mu	亩
Nanfeng (South Wind) and).	南风
Nanhai	南海
Nankai	南开
Nie	聂（姓）
Niushan cun	牛山村
Panyu	番禺
Paoxi xiang	袍溪乡
Qian Zhongshu	钱钟书
Qichang Yu (Yee Yee Hay or Yee Kay Hung)	于其章
Qing Dynasty	清朝
Qingdao	青岛
Qinghua	清华
Qu Dajun	屈大均
Qu Yuchao	区裕朝
Rouhuai School	柔怀学校
Sanyi (Sam Yup)	三邑
Shandong	山东
Shanghai	上海
Shanxi	山西
Shaonian shibao	少年时报
shuguan	书馆
Shunde	顺德
shushi	书室
shuwu	书屋
shuyuan	书院
Shuzheng School	淑正学校
sishu	私塾
sishu wujing	四书五经
Siyi (Szeyup)	四邑
Song Dynasty	宋代
Sun Yatsen	孙中山
Taishan	台山

Tang Dynasty	唐代
Tang Mingzhao	唐明照
Tangren	唐人
Tang Weisheng	唐闻生
Tianjin	天津
Tongsheng Bao	童声报
Tongzhi School	同治学校
Wang Yangming	王阳明
Wu	吴（姓）
Wu Chengen	吴承恩
Wu Panzhao (Ng Poon Chew)	伍盼照
Wuchang	武昌
wufu (five mourning grades in a lineage)	五服
Wuniushan	五牛山
xian kao	县考
xiang shi	乡试
xiaoti	孝悌
Xin Qingnian (New Youth)	新青年
Xinhui	新会
Xinshali	新沙里
xiucai	秀才
Xiyou ji	西游记
Xuantong (Empower)	宣统皇帝
xuetang	学堂
Yangqiao	杨桥
Yanjing (Yenching) University	燕京
Yen Xiu	严修
Yuan	袁（姓）
Yuan Shikai	袁世凯
Yunnan	云南
Zan Shou Tang（Dun Sow Hong Company)	赞寿堂
Zeng Guofan	曾国藩
Zhang	张（姓）
Zhang Anmin	张安民
Zhang Biaobing	张彪炳
Zhang Boling	张伯苓
Zhang Boxun	张伯勋

Zhang Caichen (Cheung Tsoi Shan)	张采臣
Zhang Chunli	张椿里
Zhang Dapei	张达培
Zhang Libing	张理炳
Zhang Pengbing (Cheung Pang Bing)	张彭炳
Zhang Qiaoshang	张巧裳
Zhang Qiaoxin	张巧新
Zhang Qiaozhuang	张巧壮
Zhang Ruyuan	张汝元
Zhang Siyi	张思逸
Zhang Tianpei	张天培
Zhang Tingdong	张廷栋
Zhang Tingqu	张廷驱
Zhang Tingwei	张廷尉
Zhang Tingxun	张廷勋
Zhang Weixi	张炜樨
Zhang Weixun	张炜逊
Zhang Weiying	张炜英
Zhang Weizong	张炜宗
Zhang Xixian	张希仙
Zhang Yitang (Cheung Yick Hong)	张翊唐
Zhang Yuchu	张玉楚
Zhang Yucui	张玉翠
Zhang Yuhua	张玉华
Zhang Yujian	张玉坚
Zhang Yujie	张玉洁
Zhang Yumin	张郁文
Zhang Yupei	张玉佩
Zhang Yuyao	张玉瑶
Zhang Yuyu	张玉瑜
Zhang Yuzai	张玉栽
Zhang Yupei	张俞培
Zhang Zhandong	张占东
Zhang Zhongping	张仲平
Zhang Zhaopei	张兆培
Zhao	赵（姓）
Zhejiang	浙江
Zheng Banqiao	郑板桥
Zhenguang School	真光学校
Zhili	直隶

Zhongshan xian	中山县
Zhonghua Huiguan (Chinese Consolidated Benevolent Association)	中华会馆
Zhou Enlai	周恩来
zhou kao	州考
Zhujing sanjiaozhou (Pearl River Delta)	珠江三角洲
Zuozhuan	左传

SELECTED BIBLIOGRAPHY

Archives

CHINESE HISTORICAL SOCIETY OF SOUTHERN CALIFORNIA, LOS ANGELES. SAM CHANG FAMILY PAPERS

Sam Chang's letters to his children, siblings, cousins, and nephews from 25 December 1921 to 15 December 1947 (about nine hundred letters, which had been copied into eighteen student notebooks.)

Sam Chang's letters to clan members and friends, as well as his farming notes, essays, poems, and recollections of Chinese and American life and culture (about twelve hundred letters and other writings, copied down in twenty-nine student notebooks.)

Letters to Sam Chang from his children, relatives, and friends (about three hundred letters.)

Dozens of pamphlets, placards, posters, and commercial flyers.

Booklet for Sam Chang's and his wife's eightieth birthday celebration, compiled by Sam's son Tennyson Chang (referred to as "Special Booklet" in the notes to this volume).

Other family documents, including a family genealogy composed by Yitang's daughter Lillian Wong, and the announcement that Sam Chang wrote for Yitang's seventieth birthday celebration.

INTERVIEWS

Chang, Sam. Interview with David Wong, Laura Lai, and Him Mark Lai, 4 April 1975.

Chung (Chang), Arthur. Interview with Beverly Chan, summarized by Suellen Cheng, 23 and 25 October 1979.

Chung, Nellie. Interview with the Chinese Historical Society of Southern California, 1979.

NATIONAL ARCHIVES AND RECORDS ADMINISTRATION, PACIFIC SIERRA REGION AT SAN BRUNO, CALIFORNIA

Records of the Immigration and Naturalization Service, San Francisco District, Arrival Investigative Case Files, 1884–1944.

NATIONAL ARCHIVES AND RECORDS ADMINISTRATION, PACIFIC SOUTHWEST RE-
GION AT LAGUNA NIGUEL, CALIFORNIA

Records of U.S. District Court, Central District of California Naturalization Petitions.

Records of the INS, Los Angeles District Segregated Chinese Case Files, 1893–1935;
Records of the INS, Los Angeles District Segregated Chinese Case Files, 1929–
1934.

Records of the INS, San Pedro Office Segregated Chinese Case Files, 1894–1965.

Books and Articles

Baily, Samuel, and Franco Ramella, eds. *One Family, Two Worlds: An Italian Family's Correspondence across the Atlantic, 1901–1922.* New Brunswick, NJ: Rutgers University Press, 1988.

Baker, Hugh D. R. *Chinese Family and Kinship.* London: The Macmillan Press, 1979.

Barlow, Jeffrey, and Christine Richardson. *China Doctor of John Day.* Portland, OR: Thomas Binford Publisher, 1979.

Barth, Gunther. *Bitter Strength: A History of the Chinese in the United States, 1850–1870.* Cambridge, MA: Harvard University Press, 1964.

Barton, Arnold, ed. *Letters from the Promised Land: Swedes in America, 1840–1912.* Minneapolis: University of Minnesota Press, 1975.

Beesley, David. "From Chinese to Chinese American: Chinese Women and Families in a Sierra Nevada Town." *California History* 67 (September 1988): 168–179.

Blegen, Theodore, ed. *Land of Their Choice: The Immigrants Write Home.* Minneapolis: University of Minnesota Press, 1955.

Bodnar, John. *The Transplanted: A History of Immigrants in Urban America.* Bloomington: Indiana University Press, 1985.

Booth, Martin. *Opium: A History.* New York: St Martin's Press, 1998.

Buell, Paul, and Christopher Muench. "Chinese Medical Recipes from Frontier Seattle." In *Annals of the Chinese Historical Society of the Pacific Northwest,* ed. Douglas W. Lee, 100–105. Seattle: Wing Luke Memorial Museum, 1984.

Carr, Caleb. *The Devil Soldier.* New York: Random House, 1992.

Cassel, Susie Lan, ed. *The Chinese in America: A History from Gold Mountain to the New Millennium.* Walnut Creek, CA: Altamira Press, 2002.

Chan, David. "The Five Chinatowns of Los Angeles." *Bridge* 2 (1973): 41–45.

Chan, Sucheng. *Asian Americans: An Interpretive History.* Boston: Twayne Publishers, 1991.

―――. "European and Asian Immigration into the United States." In *Immigration Reconsidered: History, Sociology, and Politics,* ed. Virginia Yan-McLaughlin, 37–75. Oxford: Oxford University Press, 1990.

―――. *This Bitter Sweet Soil: The Chinese in California Agriculture, 1860–1910.* Berkeley and Los Angeles: University of California Press, 1986.

Chen, Han-sheng. *Landlord and Peasant in China.* New York: International Publishers, 1936.

―――. *The Present Agrarian Problem in China.* Shanghai: China Institute of Pacific Relations, 1933.

Chen, Hsian-Shui. *Chinatown No More: Taiwanese Immigrants in Contemporary New York*. Ithaca, NY: Cornell University Press, 1992.

Chen, Jack. *The Chinese of America*. San Francisco: Harper and Row, 1980.

Chen, Ta. *Chinese Migrations, with Special Reference to Labor Conditions*. Washington, D.C., 1923.

Chen, Yong. *Chinese San Francisco, 1850–1943: A Trans-Pacific Community*. Stanford: Stanford University Press, 2000.

———. "In Their Own Words: The Significance of Chinese-Language Sources for Studying Chinese American History." *Journal of Asian American Studies* 5 (3) (October 2002): 243–268.

Cheng, Lucie, and Edna Bonacich, eds. *Labor Immigration under Capitalism: Asian Workers in the United States before World War Two*. Berkeley and Los Angeles: University of California Press, 1984.

Cheng, Lucie, and Suellen Cheng. "Chinese Women of Los Angeles, A Social Historical Survey." In *Linking Our Lives: Chinese American Women of Los Angeles*, ed. Asian American Studies Center, University of California, Los Angeles, and Chinese Historical Society of Southern California, 1–26. Los Angeles: Chinese Historical Society of Southern California, 1984.

Ch'i, Hsi-sheng. *Warlord Politics in China: 1916–1928*. Stanford: Stanford University Press, 1976.

Chin, Ko-lin. *Chinatown Gangs: Extortion, Enterprise, and Ethnicity*. New York: Oxford University Press, 1996.

Chinn, Thomas W. *Bridging the Pacific: San Francisco Chinatown and Its People*. San Francisco: Chinese Historical Society of America, San Francisco, 1989.

Chinn, Thomas W., H. M. Lai, and Philip Choy, eds. *A History of the Chinese in California: A Syllabus*. San Francisco: Chinese Historical Society of America, 1969.

Chu, George. "Chinatown in the Delta: The Chinese in the Sacramento–San Joaquin Delta, 1870–1960." *California Historical Society Quarterly* 49 (March 1970): 21–37.

Chung, Arthur W. *Of Rats, Sparrows, and Flies: A Lifetime in China*. Stockton, CA: Heritage West Books, 1995.

Conway, Alan, ed. *The Welsh in America: Letters from the Immigrants*. Minneapolis: University of Minnesota Press, 1961.

Coolidge, Mary. *Chinese Immigration*. New York: Henry Holt, 1909.

Cressy, David. *Coming Over: Migration and Communication between England and New England in the Seventeenth Century*. Cambridge: Cambridge University Press, 1987.

Croizier, Ralph. *Traditional Medicine in Modern China: Science, Nationalism, and the Tensions of Cultural Change*. Cambridge, MA: Harvard University Press, 1968.

Culin, Stewart. "Chinese Drug Stores in America." *American Journal of Pharmacy* (December 1887): 593–598.

Daniels, Roger. *Asian America: Chinese and Japanese in the United States since 1850*. Seattle: University of Washington Press, 1988.

———. *Coming to America: A History of Immigration and Ethnicity in American Life*. New York: Harper Perennial, 1991.

Erickson, Charlotte, ed. *Invisible Immigrants: The Adaptation of English and Scottish Immigrants in Nineteenth-Century America.* Coral Gables, FL: University of Miami Press, 1972.

Fairbank, John K. *China: A New History.* Cambridge, MA: Harvard University Press, 1992.

———, ed. *The Missionary Enterprise in China and America.* Cambridge, MA: Harvard University Press, 1974.

Fairbank, John K., and Edwin O. Reischauer. *China: Tradition and Transformation.* Rev. ed. Boston: Houghton Mifflin, 1989.

Faure, David. *The Rural Economy of Pre-Liberation China: Trade Expansion and Peasant Livelihood in Jiangsu and Guangdong, 1870–1937.* Hong Kong: Oxford University Press, 1989.

Fong, Wan. *Herb Lore.* 3d edition. Oakland, CA, 1933.

Freedman, Maurice. *Lineage Organization in Southeastern China.* London: University of London, The Athlone Press, 1958.

Friday, Chris. *Organizing Asian American Labor: The Pacific Coast Canned-Salmon Industry, 1870–1942.* Philadelphia: Temple University Press, 1974.

Gallicchio, Marc S. *The African American Encounter with Japan and China: Black Internationalism in Asia, 1895–1945.* Chapel Hill: University of North Carolina Press, 2000.

Gardella, Robert. *Harvesting Mountain: Fujian and the China Tea Trade, 1757–1937.* Berkeley and Los Angeles: University of California Press, 1994.

Gevitz, Norman. ed. *Other Healers: Unorthodox Medicine in America.* Baltimore: Johns Hopkins University Press, 1988.

Glen, Evelyn Nakano. "Split Household, Small Producer, and Dual Wage Earner: An Analysis of Chinese-American Family Strategies." *Journal of Marriage and the Family* (February 1983): 35–46.

Glen, Evelyn Nakano, and Stacey G. H. Yap. "Chinese American Families." In *Minority Families in the United States: A Multicultural Perspective,* ed. Ronald L. Taylor, 115–145. Englewood Cliffs, NJ: Prentice-Hall, 1994.

Glick, Charles E. *Sojourners and Settlers: Chinese Migrants in Hawaii.* Honolulu: University Press of Hawaii, 1980.

Gordon, June A. "Asian American Resistance to Selecting Teaching as a Career: The Power of Community and Tradition." *Teachers College Record* 102 (1) (February 2000): 173–175.

Gulick, Edward V. *Peter Parter and the Opening of China.* Cambridge, MA: Harvard University Press, 1973.

Gyory, Andrew. *Closing the Gate: Race, Politics, and the Chinese Exclusion Act.* Chapel Hill: University of North Carolina Press, 1998.

Hillier, Sheila M. *Health Care and Traditional Medicine in China, 1800–1982.* Boston: Routledge and Kegan Paul, 1983.

Hillinger, Charles. *Hillinger's California: Stories from All 58 Counties.* Santa Barbara: Capra Press, 1997.

Hillinger, Charles, and Morrison Wong. "The Extraordinary Educational Attainment of Asian Americans: A Search for Historical Evidence and Explanations." *Social Forces* 65 (1986): 1–27.

Hing, Bill Ong. *Making and Remaking Asian America through Immigration Policy, 1850–1990.* Stanford: Stanford University Press, 1993.

Ho, Ping-ti. *The Ladder of Success in Imperial China.* New York: Columbia University Press, 1962.

———. *Studies on the Population of China, 1368–1953.* Cambridge, MA: Harvard University Press, 1959.

Honig, Emily. *Sisters and Strangers: Women in the Shanghai Cotton Mills, 1911–1949.* Stanford: Stanford University Press, 1986.

Hsu, Madeline. *Dreaming of Gold, Dreaming of Home: Transnationalism and Migration between the United States and South China, 1882–1942.* Stanford: Stanford University Press, 2000.

Huang, Philip C. *The Peasant Family and Rural Development in the Yangzi Delta, 1350–1988.* Stanford: Stanford University Press, 1990.

Hyatt, Richard. *Chinese Herbal Medicine: An Ancient Art and Modern Healing Science.* New York: Schocken Books, 1978.

Ichioka, Yuji. *The Issei: The World of the First Generation Japanese Immigrants, 1885–1924.* New York: The Free Press, 1988.

International Chinese Business Directory Co. *International Chinese Business Directory of the World for the Year 1913.* San Francisco, 1913

Ishii-Kuntz, Masako. "Diversity within Asian American Families." In *Handbook of Family Diversity*, ed. David H. Demon, Katherine R. Allen, and Mark A. Fine, 274–292. New York: Oxford University, 2000.

Irick, Robert L. *Ch'ing Policy towards the Coolie Trade, 1847–1878.* Taibei: Chinese Material Center, 1982.

Kamphoefner, Walter, Wolfgang Helbich, and Ulrike Sommer, eds. *News from the Land of Freedom: German Immigrants Write Home.* Ithaca, NY: Cornell University Press, 1991.

Keohn, Peter H., and Xiao-huang Yin, eds. *The Expanding Roles of Chinese Americans in U.S.-China Relationship: Transnational Networks and Trans-Pacific Interactions.* New York: M. E. Sharp, 2002.

Kerr, John G. *A Guide to the City and Suburbs of Canton.* Hong Kong and Shanghai: Kelly and Walsh, 1904.

Kindead, Gwen. *Chinatown: A Portrait of a Closed Society.* New York: HarperCollins, 1992.

Kulp, Daniel Harrison. *Country Life in South China: The Sociology of Familism.* New York, 1925.

Kung, S. W. *Chinese in American Life: Some Aspects of Their History, Status, Problems, and Contributions.* Seattle: University of Washington Press, 1962.

Kuo, Joyce. "Excluded, Segregated, and Forgotten: A Historical View of the Discrimination of Chinese Americans in Public Schools." *Asian Law Journal* 5 (1) (May 1998): 181–212.

Kwong, Peter. *Chinatown, New York: Labor and Politics, 1930–1950.* New York: Monthly Review Press, 1979.

———. *Forbidden Workers: Illegal Chinese Immigrants and American Labor.* New York: The New Press, 1997.

———. *The New Chinatown*, 2nd edition. New York: Hill and Wang, 1996.

Laguerre, Michel S. *The Global Ethnopolis: Chinatown, Japantown, and Manilatown in American Society.* New York: St. Martin's Press, 2000.

Lai, Him Mark, and Philip P. Choy. *Cong huaqiao dao huaren: ershi shiji meiguo huaren shehui fazhanshi* [*From Overseas Chinese to Chinese Americans: A Social History of Twentieth-Century Chinese Americans*]. Hong Kong: Sanlian shudian, 1992.

———. *A History Reclaimed: An Annotated Bibliography of Chinese-Language Materials on the Chinese of America.* Los Angeles: Asian America Studies Center, UCLA, 1986.

———. *Outlines: History of the Chinese in America.* San Francisco: Chinese American Studies Planning Group, 1972.

Larson, Louise Leung. *Sweet Bamboo: A Saga of a Chinese American Family.* Los Angeles: Chinese Historical Society of Southern California, 1989.

Lee, Leo O., ed. and trans. *Land without Ghosts: Chinese Impressions of America from the Mid-Nineteenth Century to the Present.* Berkeley and Los Angeles: University of California Press, 1989.

Lee, Robert. *Orientals: Asian Americans in Popular Culture.* Philadelphia: Temple University Press, 1999.

Lee, Rose Hum. *The Chinese in the United States of America.* Hong Kong: Hong Kong University Press, 1960.

———. "The Decline of Chinatown in the United States." *American Journal of Sociology,* no. 55 (1949): 422–432.

Lei, Jieqiong (Kit King Louis). "Problems of Second-Generation Chinese." *Sociology and Social Research* 16 (May–June 1932): 250–258.

———. "A Study of American-Born, American-Reared Chinese in Los Angeles." Master's thesis, University of Southern California, 1931.

Leung, Tom. *Chinese Herbal Science: Its Principles and Methods.* Los Angeles: T. Leung Herb Company, 1928.

Li, Chunhui. *Meizhou Huaqiao huaren shi* [*A History of the Chinese in America*]. Beijing: Dongfang Press, 1990.

Ling, Huping. "Family and Marriage of Late-Nineteenth- and Early-Twentieth-Century Chinese Immigrant Women" *Journal of American Ethnic History* 19 (2) (winter 2000): 43–63.

———. *Surviving on the Gold Mountain: A History of Chinese American Women and Their Lives.* Albany: State University of New York Press, 1998.

Liu, Haiming. "Historical Connections between the Chinese Trans-Pacific Family and U.S.-China Relations." In *The Expanding Roles of Chinese Americans in U.S.-China Relationship: Transnational Networks and Trans-Pacific Interactions,* ed. Peter H. Keohn and Xiao-huang Yin, 3–19. New York: M. E. Sharp, 2002.

———. "The Resilience of Ethnic Culture: Chinese Herbalists in the American Medical Profession." *Journal of Asian American Studies* 1 (2) (June 1998): 173–191.

———. "The Social Origin of the Early Chinese Immigrants: A Revisionist Perspective." In *From Gold Mountain to the New Millennium: Chinese American Studies to the Twenty-First Century,* ed. Susie Lan Cassel, 21–36. Walnut Creek, CA: Alta Mira Press, 2002.

———. "Transnational Historiography: Chinese American Studies Reconsidered." *Journal of the History of Ideas* 65 (1) (spring 2004): 135–153.

Liu, John M. "A Centennial Retrospective of the Asian American Legacy in Orange County." *Journal of Ethnic Studies* 8 (2) (summer 1980): 37–45.

Liu, Pei Chi (Boji). *Guangdong Shuyuan Zhidu* [*System of Guangdong Academies*]. Taibei: Taiwan Books, 1958.

———. *Meiguo huaqiao shi* [*A History of Overseas Chinese in America*]. Taibei: Xingzhenyuau qiaowu weiyuanhui, 1976.

Loomis, A. W. "Medical Art in the Chinese Quarter." *Overland Monthly* 2 (June 1869): 496–506.

Lou, Raymond. "The Chinese American Community of Los Angeles, 1870–1900: A Case of Resistance, Organization, and Participation." Ph.D. diss., University of California, Irvine, 1982.

Lui, Garding. *Inside Los Angeles: Chinatown, Los Angeles*. 1948.

———. *Secrets of Chinese Physicians*. Los Angeles: B. N. Robertson, 1943.

Lutz, Jessie Gregory. *China and the Christian Colleges: 1850–1950*. Ithaca, NY: Cornell University Press, 1971.

Lydon, Sandy, *Chinese Gold: The Chinese in the Monterey Bay Region*. Capitola, CA: Capitola Book Company, 1985.

Lyman, Stanford M. *Chinese Americans*. New York: Random House, 1974.

———. *The Asian in the West*. Reno and Las Vegas: Western Studies Center, Desert Research Institute, University of Nevada System, 1970.

Ma, L. Eve Armentrout. *Hometown Chinatown: History of Oakland's Chinese Community*. New York: Garland Publishers, 2000.

Mann, Susan. "The Male Bond in Chinese History and Culture." *American Historical Review* 105 (5) (December 2000): 1600–1614.

Mark, Mei Lin, and Ginger Chih. *A Place Called Chinese America*. Dubuque, Iowa: Kendall/Hunt, 1982.

Marks, Robert B. *Rural Revolution in South China: Peasants and the Making of History in Haifeng Country, 1570–1930*. Madison: University of Wisconsin Press, 1984.

Mason, Sarah R. "Liang May Seen and the Early Chinese Community in Minneapolis." *Minnesota History* (spring 1995): 223–233.

Mason, William. "The Chinese in Los Angeles." *Museum Alliance Quarterly* 6 (2) (fall 1967): 20–28.

Mazumdar, Sucheta. *Sugar and Society in China: Peasant, Technology, and the World Market*. Cambridge, MA: Harvard University Asia Center, 1998.

McClain, Charles J., ed. *Chinese Immigrants and American Law*. Garland, 1994.

———. *In Search of Equality: The Chinese Struggle against Discrimination in the Nineteenth Century*. Berkeley and Los Angeles: University of California Press, 1996.

McClellan, Robert. *The Heathen Chinee: A Study of American Attitudes toward China, 1890–1905*. Columbus: Ohio State University Press, 1971.

McDannold, Thomas A. *California's Chinese Heritage: A Legacy of Places*. Stockton, CA: Heritage West Books, 2000.

McKee, Delber L. *Chinese Exclusion versus the Open Door Policy, 1900–1906:*

Clashes over China Policy in the Roosevelt Era. Detroit: Wayne State University Press, 1977.

McKeown, Adam. "The Sojourner as Astronaut: Paul Siu in Global Perspective." In *Re/Collecting Early Asian America: Essays in Cultural History*, ed. Josephine Lee, Imogene L. Lim, and Yuko Matsukawa, 128–142. Philadelphia: Temple University Press, 2002.

———. "Transnational Chinese Families and Chinese Exclusion, 1875–1974," *Journal of American Ethnic History* 18 (winter 1999): 73–110.

McWilliams, Carey. *Brothers Under the Skin*. Boston: Little, Brown and Co., 1942.

———. *Southern California: An Island of the Land*. Salt Lake City: Gibbs M. Smith, 1983.

Mei, June. "Socioeconomic Origins of Emigration: Guangdong to California, 1850–1882." In *Labor Immigration under Capitalism*, ed. Cheng and Bonacich, 219–245.

Mei, Weiqiang, and Zhang Guowei. *Wuyi huaqiao huaren hhi* [*A History of Overseas Chinese in the Five Districts*]. Guangzhou: Guangdong gaodeng jiaoyu chubanshe, 2001.

Meng, Chi. *Chinese-American Understanding: A Sixty-Year Search*. New York: China Institute in America, 1981.

Miller, Stuart Creighton. *The Unwelcome Immigrant: The American Image of the Chinese, 1785–1882*. Berkeley and Los Angeles: University of California Press, 1969.

Miscevic, Dusanka Dusana, and Peter Kwong. *Chinese Americans: The Immigrant Experience*. Southport, CT: Hugh Lauter Levin Associates, 2000.

Miyazaki, Ichisada. *China's Examination Hell: The Civil Service Examinations of Imperial China*. Conrad Schirokauger, trans. New Haven, CT: Yale University Press, 1963.

Morawska, Ewa. "The Sociology and Historiography of Immigration." In *Immigration Reconsidered*, ed. Yans-McLaughlin, 187–238.

Ng, Franklin. "The Sojourner, Return Migration, and Immigration History." In *Chinese America, History and Perspective, 53–71*. San Francisco: Chinese Historical Society of America, 1987.

Papnikolas, Helen Zeese. *Toil and Rage in a New Land: The Greek Immigrants in Utah*. Salt Lake City: Utah Historical Society, 1974.

Park, Robert Ezra, and Herbert A. Miller. *Old World Traits Transplanted*. New York: Harper, 1921.

———. *Race and Culture*. Glencoe, IL: Free Press, 1950.

Pascoe, Peggy. *Relations of Rescue: The Search for Female Moral Authority in the American West, 1874–1939*. New York, 1990.

Perkins, Dorothy, "Coming to San Francisco by Steamship." In *The Chinese American Experience: Papers from the Second National Conference on Chinese American Studies (1980)*, ed. Genny Lim, 26–33. San Francisco: Chinese Historical Society of America and the Chinese Culture Foundation of San Francisco, 1984.

Pfeiffer, George Anthony. *If They Don't Bring Their Women Here: Chinese Female Immigration before the Exclusion*. Urbana and Chicago: University of Illinois Press, 1999.

Pomerantz, Linda. "The Chinese Bourgeoisie and the Anti-Chinese Movement in the United States, 1850–1906." *Amerasia Journal* 11 (1) (1984): 1–34.

Portes, Alejandro, and Ruben G. Gumbaut. *Immigrant America: A Portrait.* Berkeley and Los Angeles: University of California Press, 1990.

Purcell, Victor. *The Chinese in Southeast Asia.* London: Oxford University Press, 1965.

Qu, Dajun. *Guangdong Xinyu [New Things in Guangdong].* Beijing: Zhonghua shuju, 1997 (reprint of the 1700 edition).

Rawski, Evelyn S. "Economic and Social Foundations of Late Imperial Culture." In *Popular Culture in Late Imperial China,* ed. David Johnson, Andrew Nathan, and Evlyn S. Rawski, 3–33. Berkeley and Los Angeles: University of California Press, 1985.

———. *Education and Popular Literacy in Ch'ing China.* Ann Arbor: University of Michigan Press, 1979.

Rhoads, Edward J. *China's Republican Revolution: The Case of Kwangtung, 1895–1913.* Cambridge, MA: Harvard University Press, 1975.

Rothstein, William G. "The Botanical Movements and Orthodox Medicine." In *Other Healers: Unorthodox Medicine in America,* ed. Norman Gevitz. Baltimore: Johns Hopkins University Press, 1988.

Rouse, Roger. "Mexican Migration and the Social Space of Postmodernism." *Diaspora* 1 (1) (spring 1991): 8–23.

Saloutos, Theodore. *They Remember America: The Story of the Repatriated Creek Americans.* Berkeley and Los Angeles: University of California Press, 1958.

Sandmeyer, Elmer Clarence. *The Anti-Chinese Movement in California.* Reprint. Urbana and Chicago: University of Illinois Press, 1991.

Saxton, Alexander. *The Indispensable Enemy: Labor and the Anti-Chinese Movement in California.* Berkeley and Los Angeles: University of California Press, 1971.

Schwarz, Henry, ed. *Chinese Medicine on the Golden Mountain.* Seattle, 1984.

Schwindinger, Robert J. "Investigating Chinese Immigrant Ships and Sailors." *The Chinese American Experience: Papers from the Second National Conference on Chinese American Studies,* ed. Genny Lim, 16–25. San Francisco: The Chinese Historical Society of America and the Chinese Culture Foundation of San Francisco, 1980.

———. "North from Panama, West to the Orient: The Pacific Mail Steamship Company, as Photographed by Carleton E. Watkins." *California History* 57 (1) (spring 1978): 46–57.

See, Lisa. *On Gold Mountain: The One-Hundred-Year Odyssey of My Chinese-American Family.* New York: Vintage Books, 1995.

Skinner, G. William. "Chinese Peasants and the Closed Community: An Open and Shut Case." *Comparative Studies in Society and History* 13 (3) (1971): 270–281.

———. "Marketing and Social Structure in China, Part 1." *Journal of Asian Studies* (1964): 34 ff.

Spence, Jonathan D. *The Search for Modern China.* New York: W. W. Norton, 1999.

Stockard, Janice E. *Daughter of the Canton Delta: Marriage Pattern and Economic Strategies in South China, 1860–1930.* Stanford: Stanford University Press, 1989.

Sun, Yumei. "From Isolation to Participation: *Chung Sai Yat Po (China West Daily)* and San Francisco's Chinatown, 1900–1920." Ph.D. diss., University of Maryland, College Park, 2000.

Takaki, Ronald. *Strangers from the Different Shore: A History of Asian Americans.* Boston: Little, Brown and Co., 1989.

Tan, Fu-yuan (Tom Foo Yuen). *The Science of Oriental Medicine: A Concise Discussion of Its Principles and Methods, Biographical Sketches of Its Leading Practitioners, Its Treatment of Various Prevalent Diseases, Useful Information on Matters. . . .* Los Angeles: Foo and Wing Herb Company/G. Rice and Sons, 1897 (revised edition 1902.).

Tao, Ju-yin. *Beiyang junfa tongzhi shiqi shihua [A History of Warlord Politics in North China].* Vol. 1. Beijing: Shenghuo, dushu, xinzhi chubanshe, 1957.

Tchen, John Kuo Wei. *Genthe's Photographs of San Francisco's Chinatown: Photographs by Arnold Genthe, Selection and Text by John Kuo Wei Tchen.* New York: Dover Publications, 1984.

———. *New York before Chinatown: Orientalism and the Shaping of American Culture, 1776–1882.* Baltimore: Johns Hopkins University Press, 1999.

Thomas, William I., and Florian Znaniecki. *The Polish Peasant in Europe and America.* Boston: Knopf, 1927.

Tisdale, William M. "Chinese Physicians in California." *Lippincott's Magazine* 63 (March 1899), 411–416.

Tom, K. "Functions of the Chinese Language Schools." *Sociology and Social Research* 25 (1941): 557–561.

Tong, Benson. *The Chinese Americans.* Westport, CT: Greenwood Press, 2000.

Trauner, Joan B. "The Chinese as Medical Scapegoats in San Francisco, 1870–1906." *California History* 57 (1978): 70–87.

Tsai, Shih-shan. *China and Overseas Chinese in the United States, 1868–1911.* Fayetteville: University of Arkansas Press, 1983.

———. *The Chinese Experience in America.* Bloomington and Indianapolis: Indiana University Press, 1986.

Turner, Chittenden. *The Rise of Chiropractic.* Los Angeles: Powell Publishing, 1931.

Wakeman, Frederick Jr. *Strangers at the Gate: Social Disorder in South China, 1839–1861.* Berkeley and Los Angeles: University of California Press, 1966.

Waldron, Arthur. "The Warlord: Twentieth-Century Chinese Understanding of Violence, Militarism, and Imperialism." *American Historical Review* 96 (4) (October 1991): 1073–1100.

Wang, Laura. "Vallejo's Chinese Community, 1860–1960." *Chinese America, History and Perspective* (1988): 153–168.

Wardwell, Walter I. "Chiropractors: Evolution to Acceptance." In *Other Healers,* ed. Gevitz, 157–191.

Weiss, Melford S. *Valley City: A Chinese Community in America.* San Francisco: R and E Research Associates, 1971.

West, Philip. *Yenching University and Sino-Western Relations, 1916–1952.* Cambridge, MA: Harvard University Press, 1976.

Wong, Charles Choy. "The Continuity of Chinese Grocers in Southern California." *Journal of Ethnic Studies* 8 (2) (summer 1980): 63–82.

Wong, Sauling [Cynthia]. "The Language Situation of Chinese Americans." In *Lan-*

guage Diversity: Problem or Resource, ed. Sandra Lee McKay and Sauling Cynthia Wong. New York: Newbury House Publishers, 1988.

Woon, Yuen-Fong. *The Excluded Wife*. Montreal: McGill-Queens University Press, 1999.

Wtulich, Josephine, ed. *Writing Home: Immigrants in Brazil and the United States, 1890–1891*. New York: Columbia University Press, 1986.

Wyman, Mark. *Round-Trip to America: The Immigrants Return to Europe, 1880–1930*. Ithaca, NY: Cornell University Press, 1993.

Yang, Philip Q. "The 'Sojourner Hypothesis' Revisited." *Diaspora* 9 (2) (2000): 235–258.

Yang, Wanxiu, and Zhuo'an Zhong. *Guangzhou jianshi* [*A Brief History of Guangzhou*]. Guangzhou, China: Guangdong renmin chubanshe, 1996.

Yans-McLaughlin, Virginia. *Family and Community: Italian Immigrants in Buffalo, 1880–1930*. Ithaca, NY: Cornell University Press, 1971.

———, ed. *Immigration Reconsidered: History, Sociology, and Politics*. Oxford and New York: Oxford University Press, 1990.

Yin, Xiao-huang. *Chinese American Literature since the 1850s*. Urbana and Chicago: University of Illinois Press, 2000.

Yu, Renqiu. *To Save China, To Save Ourselves: The Chinese Hand Laundry Alliance of New York*. Philadelphia: Temple University Press, 1992.

Yung, Judy. *Unbound Feet: A Social History of Chinese Women in San Francisco*. Berkeley and Los Angeles: University of California Press, 1995.

———. *Unbound Voices: A Documentary History of Chinese Women in San Francisco*. Berkeley and Los Angeles: University of California Press, 1999.

Zhou, Min. *Chinatown: The Socioeconomic Potential of an Urban Enclave*. Philadelphia: Temple University Press, 1992.

Zhao, Xiaojian. *Remaking Chinese America: Immigration Family, and Community, 1940–1965*. New Brunswick, NJ: Rutgers University Press, 2002.

Zo, Kil Young. *Chinese Emigration into the United States*. New York: Arno Press, 1978.

INDEX

Abiko Kyutaro, 121–122
acupuncture, 50
agricultural market, 13, 20, 122–125, 226n53
agriculture. *See* agricultural market; asparagus farming; asparagus farming, by Chang family
Ah-Fong, 53
Alien Land Act of 1913, 61, 104, 117, 200
Amador County, herbal store in, 47
American-born Chinese: bilingualism and, 164; discrimination/racism toward, 7, 163, 181; exposure to Chinese culture, 64, 72, 90, 178, 180, 201–202; immigration law and, 5, 41, 203–204; land ownership and, 104; reverse migration by, 5, 7–8, 199. *See also* Chang, Tennyson; Chung, Arthur; Chung, Lillian; Chung, Marian; Tang, Nancy; Yee, Nellie
American Journal of Pharmacy, 47
American Medical Association, 61, 68
ancestor respect/worship, 15–19, 168
ancestral hall, 14, 21–22, 42–43, 44
Angel Island Immigration Station, 37, 82, 89, 156
Asian Magazine, 208
asparagus farming, 78, 101–102; Chinese dominance in, 120–122
asparagus farming, by Chang family: first farm, 100–103; during Great Depression, 112–114; labor pool

diversity in, 107–108; labor relations in, 110–112; notes by Sam about, 118–120; relatives as laborers in, 108–110; and Sam's perceptions of Chinese farm life, 115–118; second farm, 103–106; wages in, 107–108, 109–110; during World War II, 114–115

Baker, Hugh, 14, 36
Barlow, Jeffrey, 51
Beijing Foreign Language Institute, 198
Beijing (Peking) Union Medical College, 4, 8, 146, 171, 172, 173, 176, 180, 205, 207
Beijing University, 141, 142–143, 145, 146, 147, 161–162
bilingualism, 140, 164
Board of Medical Examiners, 67
botanical healing, 50, 51, 61
British-American Tobacco Company, 173
Buck, Pearl, 208
Buell, Paul, 46–47, 50

Cai Tingkai, 159–160
Cai Yuanpei, 71, 119, 129, 130, 154, 179, 225n43
Cantonese: as Chinese diplomats, 30; in Chinese government, 73, 75, 76, 77; feud with Hakka, 20, 36; social networks and, 148
Cantonese language, 60, 85, 125, 169, 182, 205

ABOUT THE AUTHOR

Haiming Liu is an associate professor of Asian American studies in the Ethnic and Women's Studies Department, California Polytechnic State University, Pomona, California. He received his undergraduate and master's degrees in American Literature from Beijing Foreign Studies University in China, and a Ph.D. from the University of California, Irvine.